AUTHORS

OF THE

MEDIEVAL AND

RENAISSANCE

ERAS

1100 TO 1660

heal

AUTHORS
OF THE
MEDIEVAL AND
RENAISSANCE
ERAS
1100 TO 1660

EDITED BY ADAM AUGUSTYN, ASSISTANT MANAGER,
CORE REFERENCE GROUP

Britannica®
Educational Publishing

IN ASSOCIATION WITH

ROSEN
EDUCATIONAL SERVICES

Published in 2014 by Britannica Educational Publishing (a trademark of Encyclopædia Britannica, Inc.) in association with Rosen Educational Services, LLC

29 East 21st Street, New York, NY 10010.

Distributed exclusively by Rosen Educational Services.
For a listing of additional Britannica Educational Publishing titles, call toll free (800) 237-9932.

First Edition

Britannica Educational Publishing
J.E. Luebering: Director, Core Reference Group
Adam Augustyn: Assistant Manager, Core Reference Group
Marilyn L. Barton: Senior Coordinator, Production Control
Steven Bosco: Director, Editorial Technologies
Lisa S. Braucher: Senior Producer and Data Editor
Yvette Charboneau: Senior Copy Editor
Kathy Nakamura: Manager, Media Acquisition

Rosen Educational Services
Hope Lourie Killcoyne: Executive Editor
Nelson Sá: Art Director
Cindy Reiman: Photography Manager
Brian Garvey: Designer, Cover Design
Introduction by Joseph Kampff

Library of Congress Cataloging-in-Publication Data

Authors of the Medieval and Renaissance eras, 1100 to 1660/edited by Adam Augustyn.—
First edition
    pages cm—(The Britannica guide to authors)
"In association with Britannica Educational Publishing, Rosen Educational Services."
Includes bibliographical references and index.
ISBN 978-1-61530-998-6 (library binding)
1. Authorship—History—To 1500. 2. Authorship—History—17th century. 3. Authors, Medieval. 4. Creation (Literary, artistic, etc.)—History—To 1500. 5. Creation (Literary, artistic, etc.)—History—17th century. I. Augustyn, Adam, 1979– editor of compilation. II. Encyclopaedia Britannica, Inc.
PN144.A98 2014
820.9'001—dc23

2012042133

Manufactured in the United States of America

On the cover, p. iii: Geoffrey Chaucer—solider, diplomat, justice of the peace, and member of Parliament—is remembered today not for those many accomplishments, but rather for being one of England's most noteworthy poets. Although his language, Middle English, is difficult reading for some, the playfulness and humor of his characters in his signature work, *The Canterbury Tales*, nevertheless still speaks to modern readers. *Stock Montage/ Archive Photos/Getty Images*

CONTENTS

99

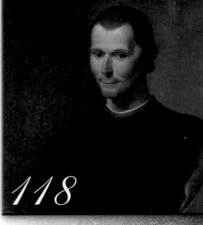

118

151

INTRODUCTION

The term *medieval* is used to refer to people, places, events, and the general cultural characteristics of the Middle Ages, the approximately thousand-year historical period between the collapse of the Western Roman Empire in the 5th century and the beginning of the Renaissance in Europe between 1200 to 1400 CE. Closely associated with the "Dark Ages"—an expression that has fallen out of favor with modern historians—the concept of a "middle age" was deployed initially by Renaissance scholars as a way to talk disparagingly about the long period that separated them from the era of classical antiquity they admired. The pejorative connotation of *medieval* lingers with us today. Contemporary discourse preserves an ostensibly sharp distinction between the medieval and the Renaissance eras that we have inherited from the Renaissance itself. Today we know, however, that if the Renaissance era signifies a "flowering of arts and literature," the seeds were at least to some extent sown during the Middle Ages.

Contrary to popular conceptions of the Middle Ages as a stagnant, if not regressive, period in European history, the medieval era was a time of intense growth and transformation in the continent. Long-lasting institutions such as Christian monasticism, papal monarchy, and the modern university have their origins in the Middle Ages. The universities of Oxford and Cambridge were both founded during this period. And for better or worse, enduring religious identities were also shaped during the Middle Ages. As Christianity became the predominant religion of Europe, Jews were identified as distinct from Christians for the first time. Artists of the period represented Jews differently, they were required to wear identifying clothing, and marginalizing social forces compelled them to take up

Dante Alighieri, the greatest of Italian poets, is considered with William Shakespeare and Johann Wolfgang von Goethe to be one of the universal masters in Western literature. Dante's masterpiece, La divina commedia (The Divine Comedy), continues to be widely read and celebrated more than 650 years after his death. Universal Images Group/Getty Images

occupations (such as money-lending) that differed from those of Christians. Europe also began to construct its own identity against its anxiety about Islamic expansion—even as Europe profited enormously from commercial, intellectual, and cultural exchange with Muslims. Indeed, it was during the Middle Ages that Europe itself began to coalesce into a discrete geographic and cultural entity. Thus, the artificial distinctions between the Middle Ages and the Renaissance are much less stable than previously imagined. Rather, the two periods form a continuum along which one may chart the ascendency of Europe to prominence in the early modern period.

Authors of the Medieval and Renaissance Eras: 1100 to 1660 presents the possibility for effectively mapping the cultural and political developments of Europe during this time through detailed biographical, contextual, bibliographical, and critical information on authors of the period. One finds in the life and writing of Dante Alighieri (1265–1321) an innovative literary engagement with Christianity. Giovanni Boccaccio (1313–1375), an important forerunner to the Renaissance, worked to elevate vernacular literature to the exalted level of the classics. In *Don Quixote* by Miguel de Cervantes (1547–1616), one finds the forerunner of the modern novel. Furthermore, some historians and philosophers regard the Italian political philosopher Niccolò Machiavelli (1469–1527) as one of the founding thinkers of modernity. William Shakespeare (1564–1616) and John Milton (1608–1674) are undoubtedly the most important English authors of the period, and their influence continues to extend far beyond England to all parts of the globe. And despite the possible implied Euro-centrism of the concepts "medieval" and "Renaissance," the scope of this guide is not limited to Europe. Rather, it also encompasses a diverse range of authors from outside of Europe, such as the Persian mystic and poet Rūmī (1207–1273) and Anne Bradstreet (c. 1612–1672)—sometimes called "the Tenth Muse"—one of America's earliest poets.

Dante Alighieri was born in Florence, Italy, in 1265, a time of significant change for the city as it grew both politically and intellectually. The time and place were fertile ground for the young poet, who claims to have mastered the art of writing verse by the time he was eighteen years old. Dante was also a philosopher, and his intellectual acuity soon gave him an entry point into the political life of Florence. In addition to his poetic works, Dante wrote the important political *Il convivio* (*The Banquet*), in which he argued that the Pope does not have authority over government. Dante identified intensely with his native city, and he suffered a major crisis when a shift in Florentine political power resulted in his exile from the city in 1301—at first for two years, then in perpetuity. He died in Ravenna in 1321.

Upon its completion just before Dante's death in 1321, *The Divine Comedy* was titled simply *La Commedia*. The work—undoubtedly Dante's magnum opus—soon met with widespread acclaim. Dante's *Commedia* was the subject of numerous critical commentaries within the first hundred years of its appearance and was the basis of his current literary reputation as one of the most important authors to have ever lived. As Dante's posthumous reputation grew, he acquired the honorary title *divino poeta* (divine poet), and, by extension, his *Commedia* took on the adjective, becoming *The Divine Comedy* in a 1555 edition of the text.

Although the 14th century Italian poet Giovanni Boccaccio is best known for his masterpiece *The Decameron*—an ostensibly traditional medieval allegory—he was also an important founding figure for Renaissance humanism. Renaissance humanism represented a profoundly secular turn in philosophy, politics, and literature that stressed the centrality of humanity. The nascent humanism in Boccaccio's work appears in the first line of the author's forward to *The Decameron*, which begins "It is inherently human to show pity to those who are afflicted." Beneath the surface of *The Decameron*'s one hundred love stories, Boccaccio's work departs from other medieval allegories—which rely heavily for their substance on religious doctrine—by persistently reinterpreting human experience through the lens of human perception and reason. By following Dante in composing his works in Italian, Boccaccio's prose set the standard for later writers of the Italian Renaissance.

Born in Spain in 1547, Miguel de Cervantes' influence extends far beyond Spanish literature. Although he experimented in a wide variety of literary genres, Cervantes' most influential work is his picaresque novel *Don Quixote*. Initially published in two parts (the first in 1605 and the second in 1615), the novel was extraordinarily popular from the outset. *Don Quixote* received its first translation into English in 1612, relatively soon after it appeared in print. The novel relates the misadventures of (the self-styled) Don Quixote—an aging knight whose outmoded worldview closely resembles the ideals espoused in popular chivalric romances—and his squire, Sancho Panza. Together, Don Quixote and Sancho Panza represent the prototype for a literary duo that has been replicated not only in countless literary texts, but also in many television shows and films. Cervantes' enormous contribution to world literature cannot be overstated.

Often reviled as much as he is revered, the Florentine political philosopher Niccolò Machiavelli nevertheless stands as one of the most influential thinkers of the early modern period. Indifferent to the utopian political narratives that prevailed at the time, Machiavelli expounded a political philosophy that sought to engage practically with the world as it really was. Following the secularizing trend set by Dante, Machiavelli wrote *The Prince* in the Italian vernacular instead of Latin. In this pithy, accessible treatise on the responsibilities of princes, Machiavelli urges new princes to forgo the common logic that says the best way to rule is by emulating the practices of an ideal leader. Rather, he advises that new princes allow necessity to dictate their actions. Thus, many critics came to regard him as an amoral cynic, an advocate for evil. The adjective *Machiavellian*—"marked by cunning, duplicity, or bad faith"—comes from this impression of *The Prince*. Despite this common mischaracterization of its author, *The Prince* is often cited as one of the seminary works of modern political philosophy.

Although the exact date of William Shakespeare's birth is unknown, there is evidence that he was baptized in Warwickshire, England on April 26, 1564. Extremely popular in his own time, Shakespeare remains the world's most celebrated dramatist, as well as one of the most renowned poets of all time. Since his death in 1616, Shakespeare's works have been translated into countless languages and his plays have been staged and adapted for film, television, and radio with a frequency that far exceeds the works of any other playwright. Although, with the exception of his longer, narrative poems *The Rape of Lucrece* and *Venus and Adonis*, Shakespeare composed most of his poetry in the sonnet form. His theatrical works encompass a number of genres, such as romantic comedies, history plays, and tragedies. His most well-known romantic comedies include the immensely popular *A Midsummer Night's Dream*, *The Merchant of Venice*, and *Twelfth Night*. But his greatest achievements are the tragedies *Hamlet*, *Othello*, *King Lear*, and *Macbeth*.

The English poet John Milton is arguably second only to Shakespeare in his country's stellar literary history.

Born in London in 1608 to an upper-middle-class Puritan family, Milton established his reputation as a poet of the highest caliber by 1640 with his early poems *Comus* and *Lycidas*. In 1639, Milton became active in political and religious matters, and wrote a series of pamphlets on a variety of important social topics, including the abolition of the Church of England and of the Royalist government, over the remainder of his life. Although he achieved notoriety early in life, Milton's masterpiece, *Paradise Lost*, did not appear in print until 1667. Dictated late in life to his wife—Milton was blind by this time—*Paradise Lost* adapts classical epic form to retell the biblical story of Adam and Eve's temptation into sin by Satan. It is the greatest epic poem ever composed in the English language.

And great works of literature were being created far beyond the quills and parchment of Europe. Born in 1207 in what is now Afghanistan, Rūmī was a celebrated 13th-century Persian poet and a Sufi mystic. Sufism is the mystical dimension of Islam in which Muslims attain divine knowledge and love through personal experience of God. It would be impossible to dissociate Rūmī's mysticism from his poetry. He composed ecstatically, often to the accompaniment of music. In fact, Rūmī wrote many of his verses to be sung at Sufi gatherings, and the dances he performed to complement his poems inspired the formation of the whirling dervishes. Rūmī's *Masnavī-yi Ma'navī* ("Spiritual Couplets"), a collection of long, didactic poems rich in mystical imagery, is widely regarded as one of the most influential works of Islamic literature. Long celebrated in Iran and Turkey as one of the greatest poets, Rūmī's popularity has grown steadily, and today his works enjoy a large readership throughout the world, particularly in the United States and Western Europe.

A window into America's Puritan heritage can be found in the life and works of Anne Bradstreet. Born in Northampton, England, circa 1612, Bradstreet (née Dudley) left England with her parents and husband to help settle the Puritan colony at Massachusetts Bay in America. Bradstreet's father, Thomas Dudley, was one of the most prominent political figures in the Massachusetts Bay Colony. In fact, much of the severity of New England Puritanism can be traced to his policies. In her later poems, which she often addressed to her family, Bradstreet worked through her own spiritual development as she came to terms with the Puritan creed. Although her poetry was well received at the time of its initial publication (without her knowledge) in England in 1650—in a collection titled *The Tenth Muse Lately Sprung Up in America*—and in America in 1678, Bradstreet was not usually considered an important poet until her works were reevaluated by twentieth-century critics.

The medieval and Renaissance eras comprise a dynamic period in world history during which many of the cultural, linguistic, political, national, and religious identities we recognize today began to stabilize. These identities were in significant ways shaped by authors. Many authors of the period have proven profoundly resilient: Their works not only withstand the passage of time, but often find new or renewed admiration in the twenty-first century. In its scope and detail, this guide serves as a point of entry into the lives, worlds, and works of medieval and Renaissance-era authors throughout the world. In many ways, it presents a key to understanding modern life.

Ibn Gabirol

(b. *c.* 1022, Málaga, caliphate of Córdoba—d. *c.* 1058/70,
Valencia, kingdom of Valencia)

Solomon ben Yehuda Ibn Gabirol was one of the outstanding figures of the Hebrew school of religious and secular poetry during the Jewish Golden Age in Moorish Spain. He was also an important Neoplatonic philosopher.

Early Life and Career

Born in Málaga about 1022, Ibn Gabirol received his higher education in Saragossa, where he joined the learned circle of other Cordoban refugees established there around famed scholars and the influential courtier Yekutiel ibn Ḥasan. Protected by this patron, whom Ibn Gabirol immortalized in poems of loving praise, the 16-year-old poet became famous for his religious hymns in masterly Hebrew. The customary language of Andalusian literature had been Arabic, and Hebrew had only recently been revived as a means of expression for Jewish poets. At 16 he could rightly boast of being world famous:

> ...My song is a crown for kings and mitres on the heads
> of governors.
> My body walks upon the earth, while my spirit ascends
> to the clouds.
> Behold me: at sixteen my heart like that of a man of
> eighty is wise.

He made, however, the mistake of lampooning Samuel ha-Nagid, a rising Jewish statesman and vizier in the

Berber kingdom of Granada, who was also a talented poet, Talmudist, strategist, and model writer of letters. After making poetical amends, Ibn Gabirol seems to have been admitted to the favour of this vizier, whose main court encomiast he subsequently became.

This series of events happened while the poet was involved (on the Saragossan side) in the disproportionate strife between the grammarians of Saragossa and those of Granada concerning Hebrew linguistics. Being an emancipated Cordoban, he offended the orthodox with heresies such as recommending childlessness, denunciation of the "world," Neoplatonism, and an almost insane self-aggrandizement (coupled with the use of animal epithets for his opponents). He apparently had to flee from Saragossa; the circumstances leading to his departure are described in his "Song of Strife":

> *Sitting among everybody crooked and foolish his [the poet's] heart only was wise.*
> *The one slakes you with adder's poison, the other, flattering, tries to confuse your head.*
> *One, setting you a trap in his design will address you: "Please, my lord."*
> *A people whose fathers I would despise to be dogs for my sheep...*

His "Song of Strife" and other poems show that his being a Jewish poet did not protect him against the hatred of his co-religionists in Saragossa, who called him a Greek because of his secular leanings.

Against all warnings by his patron Yekutiel, Ibn Gabirol concentrated on Neoplatonic philosophy, after having composed a non-offensive collection of proverbs in Arabic, *Mukhtār al-jawāhir* ("Choice of Pearls"), and a more original, though dated, ethical treatise (based on contemporary theories of the human temperaments), also in Arabic, *Kitāb iṣlāḥ al-akhlāq* ("The Improvement of the Moral Qualities"). The latter contains chapters on pride, meekness, modesty, and impudence, which are linked with the sense of sight; and on love, hate, compassion, and cruelty, linked with hearing and other senses.

In need of a new patron after the execution of Yekutiel in 1039 by those who had murdered his king and taken over power, Ibn Gabirol secured a position as a court poet with Samuel ha-Nagid, who, becoming the leading statesman of Granada, was in need of the poet's prestige. Ibn Gabirol composed widely resounding poems with a messianic tinge for Samuel and for Jehoseph (Yūsuf), his son and later successor in the vizierate of Granada. All other biographical data about Ibn Gabirol except his place of death, Valencia, must be extrapolated from his poetry.

Poetry

The Jewish subculture of Moorish Andalusia (southern Spain) was engendered by the cultural "pressure" of the Arab peers. Ibn Gabirol's dual education, typical for the Jewish intelligentsia in the larger cities, must have encompassed both the entire Hebrew literary heritage—the Bible, Talmud, and other rabbinic writings and, in particular, Hebrew linguistics—and the Arabic, including the Qur'ān, Arabic secular and religious poetry and poetics, and the philosophical, philological, and possibly medical literature.

His poetry, like that of the entire contemporary Hebrew school, is modelled after the Arabic. Metrics, rhyme systems, and most of the highly developed imagery follow the Arabic school, but the biblical language adds a particular tinge. Many of Ibn Gabirol's poems show the influence of the knightly Arab bard al-Mutanabbī and the pessimistic Abū al-'Alā' al-Ma'arrā.

His secular topics included exaggerated, Arab-inspired self-praise, justified by the fame of the child prodigy; love poems (renouncing yet keenly articulate); praise of his noble and learned protectors, together with scathingly satirical reproach of others; dirges (the most moving of which are linked with the execution of the innocent Yekutiel); wine songs (sometimes libertine); spring and rain poems; flower portraits; the agonizingly realistic description of a skin ailment; and a long didactic poem on Hebrew grammar. Ibn Gabirol's long poetic description of a castle led to the discovery of the origins of the first Alhambra palace, built by the aforementioned Jehoseph. Of a very rich production, about 200 secular poems and even more religious ones were preserved, though no collection of his poems survived. Many manuscript fragments of the former came to light only recently, preserved in synagogue attics by his co-religionists' respect for the Hebrew letter. Many of his religious poems were included in Jewish prayer books throughout the world.

His religious poems, in particular the poignant short prayers composed for the individual, presuppose the high degree of literacy typical of Moorish Spain, and they, too, show Arabic incentive. His famed rhymed prose poem "Keter malkhut" ("The Crown of the Kingdom"), a meditation stating the measurements of the spheres of the universe, jolts the reader into the abject feeling of his smallness but, subsequently, builds him up by a proclamation of the divine grace.

The following morning meditation exemplifies Ibn Gabirol's religious poetry:

> *See me at dawn, my Rock; my Shelter, when my plight*
> *I state before Thy face likewise again at night,*
> *Outpouring anguished thought—that Thou behold'st*
> *my heart*

and what it contemplates I realise in fright.
Low though the value be of mind's and lip's tribute
to Thee (accomplishes aught my spirit with its might?).
Most cherish'st Thou the hymn we sing before Thee. Thus,
while Thou support'st my breath, I praise Thee in Thine
height.
Amen.

Philosophy

His *Fountain of Life,* in five treatises, is preserved in toto only in the Latin translation, *Fons vitae,* with the author's name appearing as Avicebron or Avencebrol; it was re-identified as Ibn Gabirol's work by Salomon Munk in 1846. It had little influence upon Jewish philosophy other than on León Hebreo (Judah Abrabanel) and Benedict de Spinoza, but it inspired the Kabbalists, the adherents of Jewish esoteric mysticism. Its influence upon Christian Scholasticism was marked, although it was attacked by St. Thomas Aquinas for equating concepts with realities. Grounded in Plotinus and other Neoplatonic writers yet also in Aristotelian logic and metaphysics, Ibn Gabirol developed a system in which he introduced the conception of a divine will, like the Logos (or divine "word") of Philo. It is an essential unity of creativity of and with God, mutually related like sun and sunlight, which mediates actively between the transcendent deity and the cosmos that God created out of nothingness (to be understood as the potentiality for creation). Matter emanates directly from the deity as a prime matter that supports all substances and even the "intelligent" substances, the sphere-moving powers and angels. This concept was accepted by the Franciscan school of Scholastics but rejected by the Dominicans, including St. Thomas, for whom form (and only one, not many) and not matter is the creative principle. Since matter, according to

Aristotle and Plotinus, "yearns for formation" and, thus, moving toward the nearness of God, causes the rotation of the spheres, the finest matter of the highest spheres is propelled by the strongest "yearning," which issues from God and returns to him and is active in man (akin to the last line of Dante's *Divine Comedy*: "The love which moves the sun and the other stars").

Yet, the dry treatise does not betray the passionate quest of the Neoplatonist author. A philosophical poem, beginning "That man's love," reveals the human intent. Therein, a disciple asks the poet-philosopher what importance the world could have for the deity (to be understood in Aristotelian terms as a deity that only contemplates its own perfection). The poet answers that all of existence is permeated, though to different degrees, by the yearning of matter toward formation, and he declares that this yearning may give God the "glory" that the heavens proclaim, as the Bible teaches.

OMAR KHAYYAM

(b. May 18, 1048, Neyshābūr [also spelled Nīshāpūr], Khorāsān [now Iran]—d. December 4, 1131, Neyshābūr)

The Persian mathematician, astronomer, and poet Ghiyāth al-Dīn Abū al-Fatḥ 'Umar ibn Ibrāhīm al-Nīsābūrī al-Khayyāmī was renowned in his own country and time for his scientific achievements but is chiefly known to English-speaking readers through the translation of a collection of his *robāʿīyāt* ("quatrains") in *The Rubáiyát of Omar Khayyám* (1859), by the English writer Edward FitzGerald.

His name Khayyam ("Tentmaker") may have been derived from his father's trade. He received a good education in the sciences and philosophy in his native Neyshābūr before traveling to Samarkand (now in Uzbekistan), where he completed the algebra treatise, *Risā lah fi'l-barāhīn 'alā masā'il al-jabr wa'l-muqābalah* ("Treatise on Demonstration of Problems of Algebra"), on which his mathematical reputation principally rests. In this treatise he gave a systematic discussion of the solution of cubic equations by means of intersecting conic sections. Perhaps it was in the context of this work that he discovered how to extend Abu al-Wafā's results on the extraction of cube and fourth roots to the extraction of nth roots of numbers for arbitrary whole numbers n.

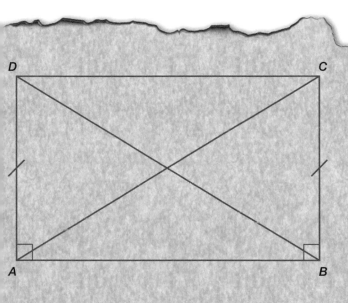

$\triangle ABD$ is congruent to $\triangle BAC$ (because they have two sides and the included angle that are equal, respectively). Hence, $AC = BD$, so $\triangle ADC$ is congruent to $\triangle BCD$ (the two triangles having three equal sides). Therefore, $\angle ADC = \angle BCD$.

Omar Khayyam constructed the quadrilateral shown in the figure in an effort to prove that Euclid's fifth postulate, concerning parallel lines, is superfluous. He began by constructing line segments AD and BC of equal length perpendicular to the line segment AB. Omar recognized that if he could prove that the internal angles at the top of the quadrilateral, formed by connecting C and D, are right angles, then he would have proved that DC is parallel to AB. Although Omar showed that the internal angles at the top are equal (as shown by the proof demonstrated in the figure), he could not prove that they are right angles. Encyclopædia Britannica, Inc.

He made such a name for himself that the Seljuq sultan Malik-Shāh invited him to Eṣfahān to undertake the astronomical observations necessary for the reform of the calendar. To accomplish this task an observatory was built there, and a new calendar was produced, known as the Jalālī calendar. Based on making 8 of every 33 years leap years, it was more accurate than the present Gregorian calendar, and it was adopted in 1075 by Malik-Shāh. In Eṣfahān he also produced fundamental critiques of Euclid's theory of parallels as well as his theory of proportion. In connection with the former his ideas eventually made their way to Europe, where they influenced the English mathematician John Wallis (1616–1703); in connection with the latter he argued for the important idea of enlarging the notion of number to include ratios of magnitudes (and hence such irrational numbers as 2 and ϖ).

His years in Eṣfahān were very productive ones, but after the death of his patron in 1092 the sultan's widow turned against him, and soon thereafter Omar went on a pilgrimage to Mecca. He then returned to Neyshābūr where he taught and served the court as an astrologer. Philosophy, jurisprudence, history, mathematics, medicine, and astronomy are among the subjects mastered by this brilliant man.

Omar's fame in the West rests upon the collection of *robāʿīyāt*, or "quatrains," attributed to him. (A quatrain is a piece of verse complete in four lines, usually rhyming *aaaa* or *aaba*; it is close in style and spirit to the epigram.) Omar's poems had attracted comparatively little attention until they inspired FitzGerald to write his celebrated *The Rubáiyát of Omar Khayyám*, containing such now-famous phrases as "A Jug of Wine, a Loaf of Bread—and Thou," "Take the Cash, and let the Credit go," and "The Flower that once has blown forever dies." These quatrains have been translated into almost every major language and are largely responsible for colouring European ideas about Persian poetry. Some scholars have doubted that Omar wrote poetry. His contemporaries took no notice of his verse, and not until two centuries after his death did a few quatrains appear under his name. Even then, the verses were mostly used as quotations against particular views ostensibly held by Omar, leading some scholars to suspect that they may have been invented and attributed to Omar because of his scholarly reputation.

Each of Omar's quatrains forms a complete poem in itself. It was FitzGerald who conceived the idea of combining a series of these *robā'īyāt* into a continuous elegy that had an intellectual unity and consistency. FitzGerald's ingenious and felicitous paraphrasing gave his translations a memorable verve and succinctness. They are, however, extremely free translations, and more recently several more faithful renderings of the quatrains have been published.

The verses translated by FitzGerald and others reveal a man of deep thought, troubled by the questions of the nature of reality and the eternal, the impermanence and uncertainty of life, and man's relationship to God. The writer doubts the existence of divine providence and the afterlife, derides religious certainty, and feels keenly man's frailty and ignorance. Finding no acceptable answers to his perplexities, he chooses to put his faith instead in a joyful appreciation of the fleeting and sensuous beauties of the material world. The idyllic nature of the modest pleasures he celebrates, however, cannot dispel his honest and straightforward brooding over fundamental metaphysical questions.

Al-Ḥarīrī

(b. 1054, near Al-Baṣrah, Iraq—d. 1122, Al-Baṣrah)

A scholar of Arabic language and literature and a government official, Abū Muḥammad al-Qāsim ibn ʿAlī al-Ḥarīrī is primarily known for the refined style and wit of his collection of tales, the *Maqāmāt*, published in English as *The Assemblies of al-Harîrî* (1867, 1898).

Al-Ḥarīrī's works include a long poem on grammar

(*Mulḥat al-iʿrāb fī al-naḥw*), for which he also wrote a commentary, and a book on errors of expression in Arabic (*Durrat al-ghawwāṣ fī awhām al-khawaṣṣ*). The *Maqāmāt* recounts in the words of the narrator, al-Ḥārith ibn Hammām, his repeated encounters with AbūZayd al-Sarūjī, an unabashed confidence artist and wanderer possessing all the eloquence, grammatical knowledge, and poetic ability of al-Ḥarīrī himself. Time and

Discussion near a village, from the 43rd maqāmah *of the* Maqāmāt *("Assemblies") of al-Harīrī, miniature painted by Yaḥyā ibn Maḥmūd al-Wāsiṭī, 1237; in the* Bibliothèque Nationale, Paris. **Courtesy of the Bibliothèque Nationale, Paris**

again, al-Ḥārith finds AbūZayd at the centre of a throng of people in a new city. Abū Zayd brings tears to his listeners' eyes with the vivid description of his pretended hardships and dazzles them with his poetry and then suddenly disappears with their presents. Al-Ḥarīrī's *Maqāmāt* seems to unite his experiences as an information officer with his authoritative knowledge of Arabic grammar, style, and verse. These tales are filled not only with humour and adventure but with linguistic and poetic feats as well. This *maqāmah* ("assembly") style was not al-Ḥarīrī's invention. He openly acknowledged his debt to its creator, al-Hamadhānī, but, unlike al-Hamadhānī, he composed his tales in writing and presented them in his own "authorized" version. Al-Ḥarīrī's *Maqāmāt* was a popular subject for book illustrators during the 18th century and was the basis for lively depictions of scenes of everyday life.

PETER ABELARD

(b. 1079, Le Pallet, near Nantes, Brittany [now in France]—d. April 21, 1142, Priory of Saint-Marcel, near Chalon-sur-Saône, Burgundy [now in France])

Peter Abelard (also spelled Abailard) was a French theologian and philosopher best known for his solution of the problem of universals and for his original use of dialectics. He is also known for his poetry and for his celebrated love affair with Héloïse.

Early Life

The outline of Abelard's career is well known, largely because he described so much of it in his famous *Historia*

Peter Abelard, with Héloïse, miniature portrait by Jean de Meun, 14th century; in the Musee Conde, Chantilly, France. Courtesy of the Musée Condé, Chantilly; photograph, Giraudon/Art Resource, New York

calamitatum ("History of My Troubles"). He was born the son of a knight in Brittany south of the Loire River. He sacrificed his inheritance and the prospect of a military career in order to study philosophy, particularly logic, in France. He provoked bitter quarrels with two of his masters, Roscelin of Compiègne and Guillaume de Champeaux, who represented opposite poles of philosophy in regard to the question of the existence of universals. (A universal is a quality or property that each individual member of a class of things must possess if the same general word is to apply to all the things in that class. Redness, for example, is a universal possessed by all red objects.) Roscelin was a nominalist who asserted that universals are nothing more than mere words; Guillaume in Paris upheld a form of Platonic realism according to which universals exist. Abelard in his own logical writings brilliantly elaborated an independent philosophy of language. While showing how words could be used significantly, he stressed that language itself is not able to demonstrate the truth of things (*res*) that lie in the domain of physics.

Abelard was a peripatetic both in the manner in which he wandered from school to school at Paris, Melun, Corbeil, and elsewhere and as one of the exponents of

Aristotelian logic who were called the Peripatetics. In 1113 or 1114 he went north to Laon to study theology under Anselm of Laon, the leading biblical scholar of the day. He quickly developed a strong contempt for Anselm's teaching, which he found vacuous, and returned to Paris. There he taught openly but was also given as a private pupil the young Héloïse, niece of one of the clergy of the cathedral of Paris, Canon Fulbert. Abelard and Héloïse fell in love and had a son whom they called Astrolabe. They then married secretly. To escape her uncle's wrath Héloïse withdrew into the convent of Argenteuil outside Paris. Abelard suffered castration at Fulbert's instigation. In shame he embraced the monastic life at the royal abbey of Saint-Denis near Paris and made the unwilling Héloïse become a nun at Argenteuil.

Career as a Monk

At Saint-Denis Abelard extended his reading in theology and tirelessly criticized the way of life followed by his fellow monks. His reading of the Bible and of the Fathers of the Church led him to make a collection of quotations that seemed to represent inconsistencies of teaching by the Christian church. He arranged his findings in a compilation entitled *Sic et non* ("Yes and No"); and for it he wrote a preface in which, as a logician and as a keen student of language, he formulated basic rules with which students might reconcile apparent contradictions of meaning and distinguish the various senses in which words had been used over the course of many centuries. He also wrote the first version of his book called *Theologia*, which was formally condemned as heretical and burned by a council held at Soissons in 1121. Abelard's dialectical analysis of the mystery of God and the Trinity was held to be erroneous, and he himself was placed for a while in the abbey of Saint-Médard under house arrest. When he returned to Saint-Denis he applied his dialectical methods to the subject of the abbey's patron saint; he argued that St. Denis of Paris, the martyred apostle of Gaul, was not identical with Denis of Athens (also known as Dionysius the Areopagite), the convert of St. Paul. The monastic community of Saint-Denis regarded this criticism of their traditional claims as derogatory to the kingdom; and, in order to avoid being brought for trial before the king of France, Abelard fled from the abbey and sought asylum in the territory of Count Theobald of Champagne. There he sought the solitude of a hermit's life but was pursued by students who pressed him to resume his teaching in philosophy. His combination of the teaching of secular arts with his profession as a monk was heavily criticized by other men of religion, and Abelard contemplated flight outside Christendom altogether. In 1125, however, he accepted election as abbot of the remote Breton monastery of Saint-Gildas-de-Rhuys. There, too, his relations with the community deteriorated, and, after attempts had been made upon his life, he returned to France.

Héloïse had meanwhile become the head of a new foundation of nuns called the Paraclete. Abelard became the abbot of the new community and provided it with a rule and with a justification of the nun's way of life; in this he emphasized the virtue of literary study. He also provided books of hymns he had composed, and in the early 1130s he and Héloïse composed a collection of their own love letters and religious correspondence.

Final Years

About 1135 Abelard went to the Mont-Sainte-Geneviève outside Paris to teach, and he wrote in a blaze of energy and of celebrity. He produced further drafts of his *Theologia* in which he analyzed the sources of belief in the Trinity and praised the pagan philosophers of classical antiquity for their virtues and for their discovery by the use of reason of many fundamental aspects of Christian revelation. He also wrote a book called *Ethica* or *Scito te ipsum* ("Know Thyself"), a short masterpiece in which he analyzed the notion of sin and reached the drastic conclusion that human actions do not make a man better or worse in the sight of God, for deeds are in themselves neither good nor bad. What counts with God is a man's intention; sin is not something done (it is not *res*); it is uniquely the consent of a human mind to what it knows to be wrong. Abelard also wrote *Dialogus inter philosophum, Judaeum et Christianum* ("Dialogue Between a Philosopher, a Jew, and a Christian") and a commentary on St. Paul's letter to the Romans, the *Expositio in Epistolam ad Romanos*, in which he outlined an explanation of the purpose of Christ's life, which was to inspire men to love him by example alone.

On the Mont-Sainte-Geneviève Abelard drew crowds of pupils, many of them men of future fame, such as the English humanist John of Salisbury. He also, however, aroused deep hostility in many by his criticism of other masters and by his apparent revisions of the traditional teachings of Christian theology. Within Paris the influential abbey of Saint-Victor was studiously critical of his doctrines, while elsewhere William of Saint-Thierry, a former admirer of Abelard, recruited the support of Bernard of Clairvaux, perhaps the most influential figure in Western Christendom at that time. At a council held at Sens in 1140, Abelard underwent a resounding condemnation, which was soon confirmed by Pope Innocent II. He withdrew to the great monastery of Cluny in Burgundy. There, under the skillful mediation of the abbot, Peter the Venerable, he made peace with Bernard of Clairvaux and retired from teaching. Now both sick and old, he lived the life of a Cluniac monk. After his death, his body was first sent to the Paraclete; it now lies alongside that of Héloïse in the cemetery of Père-Lachaise in Paris. Epitaphs composed in his honour suggest that Abelard impressed some of his contemporaries as one of the greatest thinkers and teachers of all time.

LI QINGZHAO

(b. 1084, Jinan, Shandong province, China—d. after 1155, Jinhua, Zhejiang province)

Li Qingzhao (Li Ch'ing-chao) was China's greatest woman poet, whose work, though it survives only in fragments, continues to be as highly regarded today as it was in her own day.

Li Qingzhao was born into a literary family and produced well-regarded poetry while still a teenager. In 1101 she married Zhao Mingcheng, a noted antiquarian, but their marriage was cut short in 1129 by his death during their escape from the Juchen dynasty's takeover of Kaifeng, the capital of the Song dynasty. Continuing alone, she arrived at Hangzhou by 1132. Two years later she fled to Jinhua, where she died, probably after 1155.

Li Qingzhao produced seven volumes of essays and six volumes of poetry, but most of her work is lost except for some poetry fragments. She wrote *ci* poetry, a song form. Her mastery of the metrical rules of the form was such that she produced one of the earliest known scholarly studies of *ci*. Her poetry is noted for its striking diction as well as for her focus on relating her personal experiences, giving her work more emotional intensity than that of her peers. Her poetic oeuvre reflects the dramas of her lifetime, with the earlier works marked by a carefree vitality and the pieces that she wrote after her husband's death and her exile reflecting a sombre, grief-stricken tone.

ANONYMOUS: LA CHANSON DE ROLAND

The Old French epic poem *La Chanson de Roland* (*The Song of Roland*) is probably the earliest (*c.* 1100) chanson de geste ("song of deeds;" poems that form the core of the Charlemagne legends) and is considered the masterpiece of the genre. The poem's probable author was a Norman poet, Turold, whose name is introduced in its last line.

The poem takes the historical Battle of Roncesvalles (Roncevaux) in 778 as its subject. Though this encounter was actually an insignificant skirmish between Charlemagne's army and Basque forces, the poem transforms Roncesvalles into a battle against Saracens and magnifies it to the heroic stature of the Greek defense of Thermopylae against the Persians in the 5th century BCE.

The poem opens as Charlemagne, having conquered all of Spain except Saragossa, receives overtures from the Saracen king and sends the knight Ganelon, Roland's stepfather, to negotiate peace terms. Angry because Roland proposed him for the dangerous task, Ganelon plots with the Saracens to achieve his stepson's destruction and, on his return, ensures that Roland will command the rear guard of the army when it withdraws from Spain. As the army crosses the Pyrenees, the rear guard is surrounded at the pass of Roncesvalles by an overwhelming Saracen force. Trapped against crushing odds, the headstrong hero Roland is the paragon of the unyielding warrior victorious in defeat.

The composition of the poem is firm and coherent, the style direct, sober, and, on occasion, stark. Placed in

The death of Roland at Roncesvalles, from a 14th-century Great Chronicles of France manuscript. DEA Picture Library/De Agostini/Getty Images

the foreground is the personality clash between the recklessly courageous Roland and his more prudent friend Oliver (Olivier), which is also a conflict between divergent conceptions of feudal loyalty. Roland, whose judgment is clouded by his personal preoccupation with renown, rejects Oliver's advice to blow his horn and summon help from Charlemagne. On Roland's refusal, the hopeless battle is joined, and the flower of Frankish knighthood is reduced to a handful of men. The horn is finally sounded, too late to save Oliver, Turpin, or Roland, who has been struck in error by the blinded Oliver, but in time for Charlemagne to avenge his heroic vassals. Returning to France, the emperor breaks the news to Aude, Roland's betrothed and the sister of Oliver, who falls dead at his feet. The poem ends with the trial and execution of Ganelon.

Lu You

(b. 1125, Shanyin [now Shaoxing], Zhejiang province, China—
d. 1210, Shanyin)

One of the most important and prolific Chinese writers of the Southern Song dynasty was Lu You (Lu Yu), noted for his collection of nearly 10,000 poems as well as numerous prose pieces.

Primarily a poet, Lu gained renown for his simple, direct expression and for his attention to realistic detail, features that set him apart from the elevated and allusive style characteristic of the prevailing Jiangxi school of poetry. As a conservative in matters of form, however, he wrote a number of poems in the *gushi* ("old poetry") mode and excelled at the *lüshi* ("regulated poetry") form, the sharply defined tonal and grammatical patterns of which had been perfected by the great masters of the Tang dynasty.

Lu has been most admired for the ardour of his patriotic poems, in which he protested the Jin invasion of Song in 1126, the year after his birth, and chided the Southern Song court for its passive attitude toward driving out the invaders and reconquering its lost northern territories. Because of his hawkish views, expressed at a time when the displaced court was controlled by a peace faction, Lu failed to advance in his career as an imperial official. Four times demoted for his outspoken opinions, Lu finally resigned his civil-service commission and retired to his country estate.

During retirement Lu devoted most of his poetry to the appreciation and praise of rural life. Like the poet Tao Qian, whom he took as his model, Lu depicted the rural countryside in homely detail, evoking its moods and scenes through fresh and precise imagery.

Anvarī

(b. *c.* 1126, Abivard, Turkistan [now in Turkmenistan]—d. *c.* 1189, Balkh, Khorāsān [now in Afghanistan])

Anvarī (a pseudonym of Awḥad al-Dīn ʿAlī ibn Vāḥid al-Dīn Muḥammad Khāvarānī) was a poet considered one of the greatest panegyrists of Persian literature. He wrote with great technical skill, erudition, and a strong satirical wit.

Anvarī was not only well versed in Persian and Arabic literature but was skilled in such other fields as geometry, astronomy, and astrology. His work is replete with extremely erudite and obscure allusions, making his poems difficult to understand without some accompanying commentary.

Anvarī was a prolific writer who especially excelled in the art of the *qaṣīdah* (ode) and *ghazal* (lyric). His odes display great formal virtuosity, while his comparatively simple lyrics are noted for their tenderness and charm. In his divan, or collected poems, there are 632 pages of *qaṣīdah*s and *ghazal*s, *robāʿī*s (quatrains), *qiṭah*s (shorter poems), and *maṣnavī*s (couplets). Of his life relatively little is known. Rather early in his career he certainly served as court poet of Sultan Sanjar of the great Seljuq dynasty (11th to 13th century). Later he composed biting and satirical works sharply criticizing all aspects of the social order. His longest poem is a lament on the devastation wrought in Khorāsān (largely in northeastern Persia [now Iran]) in 1153 by invading Oğuz tribesmen.

Anvarī did not think poetry the loftiest skill and scorned the life of a court poet. But he noted resentfully and sarcastically that patronage was the only means to acquire adequate wealth. Thus he remained a court poet until later in life, when circumstances forced him to follow the more independent and probably much-preferred course of the scholar, and he ended his life in quiet seclusion.

Nezāmī

(b. *c.* 1141, Ganja, Seljuq empire [now Ganca, Azerbaijan]—
d. 1209, Ganja)

Elyās Yūsof Nezāmī Ganjavī was the greatest romantic epic poet in Persian literature. Nezāmī (also spelled Nizāmī) brought a colloquial and realistic style to the Persian epic.

Little is known of Nezāmī's life. Orphaned at a young age, he spent his entire life in Ganja, leaving only once to meet the ruling prince. Although he enjoyed the patronage of a number of rulers and princes, he was distinguished by his simple life and straightforward character.

Only a handful of his *qasīdah*s ("odes") and *ghazal*s ("lyrics") have survived; his reputation rests on his great *Khamseh* ("The Quintuplet"), a pentalogy of poems written in *masnavī* verse form (rhymed couplets) and totaling 30,000 couplets. Drawing inspiration from the Persian epic poets Ferdowsī and Sanā'ī, he proved himself the first great dramatic poet of Persian literature. The first poem in the pentology is the didactic poem *Makhzan al-asrār* (*The Treasury of Mysteries*), the second the romantic epic *Khosrow o-Shīrīn* ("Khosrow and Shīrīn"). The third is his

Illustration depicting the story of Layla and Majnun, from Nezāmī's Khamseh *collection of poems.* Werner Forman/Hulton Fine Art Collection/Getty Images

rendition of a well-known story in Islamic folklore, *Leyli o-Mejnūn* (*The Story of Leyla and Majnun*). The fourth poem, *Haft paykar* (*The Seven Beauties*), is considered his masterwork. The final poem in the pentalogy is the *Sikandar* or *Eskandar-nāmeh* ("Book of Alexander the Great"; Eng. trans. of part I, *The Sikander Nama*), a philosophical portrait of Alexander.

Nezāmī is admired in Persian-speaking lands for his originality and clarity of style, though his love of language for its own sake and of philosophical and scientific learning makes his work difficult for the average reader.

GOTTFRIED VON STRASSBURG

(d. *c.* 1210)

O ne of the greatest medieval German poets, Gottfried von Strassburg is the author of the courtly epic *Tristan und Isolde*, the classic version of this famous love story.

The date of his birth is unknown and that of his death an educated guess; in fact, the only information about him consists of references to him in the work of other poets as well as inferences from his own work. The breadth of learning displayed in *Tristan und Isolde* reveals that he must have enjoyed the fullest education offered by the cathedral and monastery schools of the Middle Ages. Together with the authoritative tone of his writing, this background indicates that, although not himself of noble birth, he spent his life in the society of the wellborn. *Tristan* was probably written about 1210. Gottfried is thus a literary contemporary of Hartmann von Aue, Walther von der Vogelweide, and Wolfram von Eschenbach.

The Celtic legend of Tristan and Iseult (German: Isolde) reached Germany through French sources. The first German version is that of Eilhart von Oberg (*c.* 1170), but Gottfried, although he probably knew Eilhart's poem, based his own work on the Anglo-Norman version of Thomas of Brittany (1160–70).

Gottfried's moral purpose, as he states it in the prologue, is to present to courtiers an ideal of love. The core of this ideal, which derives from the romantic cult of woman in medieval courtly society, is that love (*minne*) ennobles through the suffering with which it is inseparably linked. This ideal Gottfried enshrines in a story in which actions are motivated and justified not by a standard ethic but by the conventions of courtly love. Thus, the love potion, instead of being the direct cause of the tragedy as in primitive versions of the Tristan story, is sophisticatedly treated as a mere outward symbol of the nature of the lovers' passion—tragic because adulterous but justified by the "courts of love" because of its spontaneity, its exclusiveness, and its completeness.

Although unfinished, Gottfried's is the finest of the medieval versions of the Tristan legend and one of the most perfect creations of the medieval courtly spirit, distinguished alike by the refinement and elevated tone of its content and by the elaborate skill of its poetic technique. It was the inspiration for Richard Wagner's opera *Tristan und Isolde* (1859).

FARĪD AL-DĪN 'AṬṬĀR

(b. 1142?, Nīshāpūr, Iran—d. *c.* 1220, Mecca, Arabia
[now in Saudi Arabia])

The Persian Muslim poet Farīd al-Dīn Muḥammad ibn Ibrāhīm 'Aṭṭār was one of the greatest Sufi (mystical) writers and thinkers, composing at least 45,000 distichs (couplets) and many brilliant prose works.

As a young man Farīd al-Dīn traveled widely, visiting Egypt, Syria, Arabia, India, and Central Asia. He finally settled in his native town, Nīshāpūr, in northeastern Iran, where he spent many years collecting the verses and sayings of famous Sufis. His name, 'Aṭṭār, which literally means a perfumer or apothecary, may indicate that he, his father, or his grandfather practiced that trade. There is much controversy among scholars concerning the exact details of his life and death as well as the authenticity of many of the literary works attributed to him.

The greatest of his works is the well-known *Manṭeq al-ṭayr* (*The Conference of the Birds*). This is an allegorical poem describing the quest of the birds (i.e., Sufis) for the mythical Sīmorgh, or Phoenix, whom they wish to make their king (i.e., God). In the final scene the birds that have survived the journey approach the throne contemplating their reflections in the mirrorlike countenance of the Sīmorgh, only to realize that they and the Sīmorgh are one.

Other important works of this prolific poet include the *Elāhī-nāma* (*The Ilahī-nāma or Book of God*) and the *Moṣībat-nāma* ("Book of Affliction"), both of which are mystical allegories similar in structure and form to *Manṭeq al-ṭayr*; the *Dīvān* ("Collected Poems"); and the famous prose work *Tadhkerat al-Awlīyāʾ*, an invaluable source of information on the early Sufis (abridged Eng. trans., *Muslim Saints and Mystics*). From the point of view of ideas, literary themes, and style, ʿAṭṭār's influence was strongly felt not only in Persian literature but also in other Islamic literatures.

ᴋᴀᴍᴏ Cʜōᴍᴇɪ

(b. 1155, Japan—d. July 24, 1216, Kyōto)

Kamo Chōmei was a poet and critic of Japanese vernacular poetry, one of the major figures in the history of Japanese poetics. He is best known as a classic example of the man of sensibility turned recluse and as the author of *Hōjō-ki* (1212; *The Ten Foot Square Hut*), a description of his life in seclusion.

The son of a Shintō priest of Kyōto, Chōmei was given a thorough artistic training. Despite his comparatively humble origin, his poetic gifts brought him grudging recognition from the court and, eventually, a court-appointed office. Shortly after his position was established, Chōmei took Buddhist orders (1204) and turned his back on the world. He lived first for four or five years in the hills of Ōhara and then built his tiny hermit's hut in the Hino foothills southeast of the capital and completed his *Hōjō-ki*. The work is a series of brief accounts of the disasters that had befallen Kyōto during Chōmei's lifetime, followed by a contrasting description of the natural beauty and peace of his hermit's life. The whole is dominated by a characteristic Buddhist view of the vanity of human endeavour and the impermanence of material things. The *Hōjō-ki* bears a more than coincidental resemblance to the *Chitei-ki* ("Account of My Cottage by the Pond") of Yoshishige Yasutane (934?–997), a work in Chinese prose dating from 981.

Chōmei, in fact, kept in touch with the court and the poetic world after his retirement. In 1205, to his great delight, 10 of his poems were included in the first draft of the *Shin kokinshū*, the eighth imperial anthology of court poetry. About 1208 or 1209 he began work on his *Mumyō shō* ("Nameless Notes"), an extremely valuable collection of critical comments, anecdotes, and poetic lore. In 1214 or 1215 he is believed to have completed his *Hosshin shū* ("Examples of Religious Vocation"). His other works include a selection of his own poems (probably compiled in 1181) and the *Ise-ki* ("Record of a Journey to Ise"), no longer extant. Chōmei's poetry is representative of the best of an age that produced many poets of the first rank. His poetry was unusual in its extreme difficulty but possessed great tonal depth and resonance.

SHOTA RUSTAVELI

(b. 1160 — d. after *c.* 1220)

T he Georgian poet Shota Rustaveli is the author of *Vepkhvistqaosani* (*The Knight in the Panther's Skin*, or *The Lord of the Panther-Skin*), the Georgian national epic.

Very little is known of Rustaveli, and what is known is uncertain. A portrait in Jerusalem inscribed with the word *Shota* may not necessarily be of him, although legendary sources assert variously that he was a patron of the Georgian church in Jerusalem and that he was a pilgrim

Shota Rustaveli, bas-relief. ppi/Shutterstock.com

there. All speculation about his life—e.g., that he was brought up by a monk and that he was a feudal lord or a royal treasurer—is devoid of documentation. Some theories (e.g., that the name Rustaveli was the pseudonym of a captive Persian princess) are completely groundless. Evidence derived from his work suggests that he was highly educated (although he knew more Persian than Greek), religiously tolerant, and familiar with the court and that he was an adoring subject of the Georgian queen Tamara.

On stylistic and thematic grounds, several early 13th-century poems, particularly in praise of Tamara, are attributed to him. His masterpiece, *The Knight in the Panther's Skin*—in which he names himself as the author—was likely composed about 1220. It tells how Queen Tinatin, who is very like Tamara, orders her beloved general Avtandil to help a knight, Tariel, found weeping and wearing a black panther's skin, to retrieve his beloved Nestan-Darejan from captivity and his kingdom from usurpers. After many adventures, natural and supernatural, love and chivalry triumph, and both couples marry and reign.

The poem has elements strongly reminiscent of Persian poetry: Ferdowsī's 11th-century epic *Shāh-nāmeh* has a character, Rostom, clad in panther skin, while Fakhr al-Din Gorgānī's 11th-century romance *Vīs o-Rāmīn* ("Vīs and Rāmīn") has a similar level of passion. While never explicitly Georgian, in the sense that there are no recognizable Georgian place-names or specific historical figures, *The Knight in the Panther's Skin* is an idiosyncratic blend of Platonism, Christianity, and worldly wisdom. Its inventive metaphors, wildly imaginative plotting, and over-the-top passion alternate with sober philosophy and paradoxical aphorisms; "Just as a long race and great gallop prove a horse...so speaking and drawing out long poems proves the poet" is the credo set out in its prologue.

To a reader familiar with English literature, *The Knight in the Panther's Skin* most resembles Edmund Spenser's 16th-century poem *The Faerie Queene*. For a Georgian, Rustaveli's poem is a compendium of sayings, phrases, and images that represents the climax of Georgia's cultural golden age and stands as a reference for everything written after it. It exemplifies and prescribes the Georgian ethos of manliness, friendship, and love and a distinctly Georgian eclecticism in which Hellenic, pagan Caucasian, and Christian values coexist.

The poem has been translated several times into English and other major languages in both verse and prose, but the virtuosity of Rustaveli's rhyme, rhythm, and imagery is very difficult to replicate.

FUJIWARA SADAIE

(b. 1162, Japan—d. September 26, 1241, Kyōto)

Fujiwara Sadaie (also known as Teika or Fujiwara Teika) was one of the greatest poets of his age and Japan's most influential poetic theorist and critic until modern times.

Fujiwara was the son and poetic heir of the gifted and influential Shunzei (or Toshinari, 1114–1204), compiler of the seventh Imperial anthology of Japanese poetry, *Senzaishū* (*c.* 1188; "Collection of a Thousand Years"). Teika hoped not only to consolidate Shunzei's poetic gains and add to them in his own right but also to raise his family in political importance. He did not advance politically, however, until he was in his 50s.

As a literary figure, Teika was a supremely accomplished and original poet. His ideal of *yōen* ("ethereal beauty") was a unique contribution to a poetic tradition that accepted innovation slowly. In his poems of ethereal beauty, Teika employed traditional language in startling new ways, showing that the prescriptive ideal of "old diction, new treatment" inherited from Shunzei might accommodate innovation and experimentation as well as ensure the preservation of the language and styles of the classical past.

Teika's poems attracted the favourable notice of the young and poetically talented former emperor Go-Toba (1180–1239), who appointed him one of the compilers of the eighth Imperial anthology *Shin kokinshū* (c. 1205, "New Collection of Ancient and Modern Times"). In 1232 Teika was appointed sole compiler of the ninth anthology, *Shin chokusenshū* (1235; "New Imperial Collection"), thereby becoming the first person ever to participate in the compilation of two such anthologies.

During his 40s, Teika underwent a profound inner conflict that greatly hindered his creativity and modified his poetic ideals. The chief poetic ideal of his later years was *ushin* ("conviction of feeling"), an ideal advocating poetry in more direct, simple styles than the technically complex poetry of *yōen*. Teika's achievements in these later styles were impressive, but in his late years he was mainly occupied as a critic, editor, and scholar.

The best known of Teika's treatises and anthologies, regarded as scripture by generations of court poets, are: *Eiga taigai* (1216; "Essentials of Poetic Composition"); *Shūka no daitai* ("A Basic Canon of Superior Poems"); *Hyakunin isshū* (c. 1235 "Single Poems by One Hundred Poets"); *Kindai shūka* (1209; "Superior Poems of Our Time"); and *Maigetsushō* (1219; "Monthly Notes").

CHRÉTIEN DE TROYES

(fl. 1165–80)

The French poet Chrétien de Troyes is known as the author of five Arthurian romances: *Erec*; *Cligès*; *Lancelot, ou Le Chevalier à la charrette*; *Yvain, ou Le Chevalier au lion*; and *Perceval, ou Le Conte du Graal*. The non-Arthurian tale *Guillaume d'Angleterre*, based on the legend of St. Eustace, may also have been written by Chrétien.

Little is known of Chrétien's life. He apparently frequented the court of Marie, comtesse de Champagne, and he may have visited England. His tales, written in the vernacular, followed the appearance in France of Wace's *Roman de Brut* (1155), a translation of Geoffrey of Monmouth's *Historia regum Britanniae*, which introduced Britain and the Arthurian legend to continental Europe. Chrétien's romances were imitated almost immediately by other French poets and were translated and adapted frequently during the next few centuries as the romance continued to develop as a narrative form. *Erec*, for example, supplied some of the material for the 14th-century poem Sir Gawayne and the Grene Knight.

Chrétien's romances combine separate adventures into a well-knit story. *Erec* is the tale of the submissive wife who proves her love for her husband by disobeying his commands; *Cligès*, that of the victim of a marriage made under constraint who feigns death and wakens to a new and happy life with her lover; *Lancelot*, an exaggerated but perhaps parodic treatment of the lover who is servile to the god of love and to his imperious mistress Guinevere, wife of his overlord Arthur; *Yvain*, a brilliant extravaganza, combining the theme of a widow's too hasty marriage to her husband's slayer with that of the new husband's fall from grace and final restoration to favour. *Perceval*, which Chrétien left unfinished, unites the religious theme of the Holy Grail with fantastic adventure.

Chrétien was the initiator of the sophisticated courtly romance. Deeply versed in contemporary rhetoric, he treated love casuistically and in a humorously detached fashion, bringing folklore themes and love situations together in an Arthurian world of adventure. Interest in his works, at first concentrated on their folklore sources, was diverted during the 20th century to their structure and narrative technique.

WALTHER VON DER VOGELWEIDE

(b. *c.* 1170 — d. *c.* 1230, Würzburg? [Germany])

The greatest German lyric poet of the Middle Ages, Walther von der Vogelweide wrote poetry that emphasizes the virtues of a balanced life, in the social as in the personal sphere, and reflects his disapproval of those individuals, actions, and beliefs that disturbed this harmony. He was no respecter of persons: whoever came between him and his ideals, even the pope himself, received the full force of his anger.

The place of Walther's birth has never been satisfactorily identified, though the title *hêr*, which he is given by other poets, indicates that he was of knightly birth. It is clear from his poetry that he received a formal education at a monastery school. He learned the techniques of his art at the Viennese court of Leopold V, duke of Austria, but, when one of the latter's successors, Leopold VI, took up residence in Vienna, Walther failed to win his favour (for reasons perhaps connected with his rivalry with Reinmar von Hagenau, the most sophisticated of the earlier minnesingers, who was resident at the Viennese court). Instead, he gained the patronage of the Hohenstaufen Philip of Swabia, by writing in support of the Hohenstaufen cause against the Welf faction during their struggle for the kingship following the emperor Henry VI's death in 1197. Pope

Walther von der Vogelweide. DEA Picture Library/De Agostini/ Getty Images

Innocent III came out on behalf of the Welfs, and from this time dates the antipapal feeling that runs through much of Walther's political poetry.

Disappointed with Philip's treatment of him, however, Walther then served several masters until, in 1212, he once more entered the political arena—this time in support of the Welf emperor Otto IV against Innocent III. Again he was not treated with the generosity he expected, and, in the same year, when Frederick II reclaimed the throne for the house of Hohenstaufen, Walther turned to welcome the new ruler, who was crowned in 1215. From him he received a small fief (feudal estate), symbol of the security he had so long desired. Two 14th-century records suggest that it was in the see of Würzburg, and it is likely that he spent the rest of his life there.

Rather more than half of the 200 or so of Walther's poems that are extant are political, moral, or religious; the rest are love poems. In his religious poems he preached the need for man actively to meet the claims of his Creator by, for instance, going on pilgrimage or on Crusade; in his moral-didactic poems he praises such human virtues as faithfulness, sincerity, charity, and self-discipline—virtues that were not especially prominent in his own life. As a love poet, he developed a fresh and original treatment of the situations of courtly love and, ultimately, in such poems as the popular "Unter der Linden," achieved a free, uninhibited style in which the poses of court society gave way before the natural affections of village folk.

WOLFRAM VON ESCHENBACH

(b. *c.* 1170 — d. *c.* 1220)

Wolfram von Eschenbach was a German poet whose epic *Parzival*, distinguished alike by its moral elevation and its imaginative power, is one of the most profound literary works of the Middle Ages.

An impoverished Bavarian knight, Wolfram apparently served a succession of Franconian lords: Abensberg, Wildenberg, and Wertheim are among the places he names in his work. He also knew the court of the landgrave (German count) Hermann I of Thuringia, where he met the great medieval lyric poet Walther von der Vogelweide. Though a self-styled illiterate, Wolfram shows an extensive acquaintance with French and German literature, and it is probable that he knew how to read, if not how to write.

Wolfram's surviving literary works, all bearing the stamp of his unusually original personality, consist of eight lyric poems, chiefly *Tagelieder* ("Dawn Songs," describing the parting of lovers at morning); the epic *Parzival*; the unfinished epic *Willehalm*, telling the history of the Crusader Guillaume d'Orange; and short fragments of a further epic, the so-called *Titurel*, which elaborates the tragic love story of Sigune from book 3 of *Parzival*.

Parzival, probably written between 1200 and 1210, is a poem of 25,000 lines in 16 books. Likely based on an unfinished romance of Chrétien de Troyes, *Perceval, ou Le Conte du Graal*, it introduced the theme of the Holy Grail into German literature. Its beginning and end are new material, probably of Wolfram's own invention, although he attributes it to an unidentified and probably fictitious Provençal poet, Guiot. The story of the ignorant and naive Parzival, who sets out on his adventures without even knowing his own name, employs the classic fairy-tale motif of "the guileless fool" who, through innocence and artlessness, reaches a goal denied to wiser men. Wolfram uses Parzival's dramatic progress from folk-tale dunce to wise and responsible keeper of the Grail to present a subtle allegory of man's spiritual education and development. The complexity of Wolfram's theme is matched by his eccentric style, which is characterized by rhetorical flourishes, ambiguous syntax, and the free use of dialect.

Wolfram's influence on later poets was profound, and he is a member, with Hartmann von Aue and Gottfried von Strassburg, of the great triumvirate of Middle High German epic poets. Parzival also figures as the hero of Richard Wagner's last opera, *Parsifal* (1882).

SNORRI STURLUSON

(b. 1179, Hvammur, Iceland—d. September 22, 1241, Reykjaholt)

The Icelandic poet, historian, and chieftain Snorri Sturluson is the author of the *Prose Edda* and the *Heimskringla*.

Snorri, a descendant of the great poet and hero of the *Egils saga*, Egill Skallagrímsson, was brought up at Oddi from the age of three in the home of Jón Loptsson, the most influential chieftain in Iceland. From him Snorri acquired both a deep knowledge of Icelandic tradition and a European breadth of outlook.

In 1199 Snorri married an heiress and began to acquire lands and power. In 1206 he settled at Reykjaholt, where most of his works were written between 1223 and 1235. During 1215–18 and 1222–32 he was "lawspeaker," or president, of the Icelandic high court. In 1218 he was invited to Norway by King Haakon IV.

Snorri became involved in politics while visiting the Norwegians. He convinced Haakon that he could become king of Iceland, and he became Haakon's vassal. Snorri returned to Iceland in 1220, but in the ensuing years his relations with Haakon deteriorated, and, in 1241, by Haakon's order, Snorri was assassinated.

Snorri's writings are remarkable both for their scope and for their formal assurance. The *Prose Edda* is a handbook on poetics. In this work Snorri arranges and recounts the legends of Norse mythology in an entertaining way. He then explains the ornate diction of the ancient skaldic poets and explains the great variety of poetic metres used in skaldic and Eddic verse. Snorri also wrote a biography of St. Oláf of Norway, which he included in his *Heimskringla*, a history of the Norwegian kings from their legendary descent from the warrior-wizard god Odin down to Magnus Erlingsson (1184). A three-volume English translation by Samuel Laing (1844) has been frequently reprinted. Snorri based the *Heimskringla* on earlier histories, but he gathered much fresh material of his own. He particularly valued poems transmitted orally from the time of the original historical events they described, and he selected those poetic traditions that seemed to be both authoritative and reflective of contemporary politics and human nature. His genius lay in his power to present all that he perceived critically as a historian with the immediacy of drama.

The qualities of intelligence, warmth, and scholarly industry in Snorri's writings contrast sharply with the weak, shifty character that emerges in the account of his life by his nephew in the *Sturlunga saga*.

SAXO GRAMMATICUS

(fl. 12th century–early 13th century)

The historian Saxo Grammaticus is best known for his *Gesta Danorum* ("Story of the Danes"), the first important work on the history of Denmark and the first Danish contribution to world literature.

Little is known of Saxo's life except that he was a Zealander belonging to a family of warriors and was probably a clerk in the service of Absalon, archbishop of Lund from 1178 to 1201. Saxo is first mentioned in Svend Aggesen's *Historia Regum Danicae compendiosa* (1185; "Short History of the Danish Kings") as writing the history of Svend Estridsen (d. 1076).

The *Gesta Danorum* was written at the suggestion of Archbishop Absalon: its 16 volumes begin with the legendary King Dan and end with the conquest of Pomerania by Canute IV in 1185. The work is written in a brilliant, ornate Latin. It was his Latin eloquence that early in the 14th century caused Saxo to be called "Grammaticus." The first nine books of the *Gesta Danorum* give an account of about 60 legendary Danish kings. For this part Saxo depended on ancient lays (ballads), romantic sagas, and the accounts of Icelanders. His legend of *Amleth* is thought to be the source of William Shakespeare's *Hamlet*; his Toke, the archer, the prototype of William Tell. Saxo incorporated also myths of national gods whom tradition claimed as Danish kings, as well as myths of foreign heroes. Three heroic poems are especially noteworthy, translated by Saxo into Latin hexameters. These oldest-known Danish poems are *Bjarkemaalet*, a battle hymn designed to arouse warlike feelings; *Ingjaldskvadet*, a poem stressing the corruptive danger of luxury upon the old Viking spirit; and *Hagbard and Signe*, a tragedy of love and family feuds. The last seven books contain Saxo's account of the historical period, but he achieves independent authority only when writing of events close to his own time. His work is noteworthy for its sense of patriotic purpose based on a belief in the unifying influence of the monarchy. By presenting a 2,000-year-long panorama of Danish history, he aimed to show his country's antiquity and traditions. Saxo's work became a source of inspiration to many of the 19th-century Danish Romantic poets.

RŪMĪ

(b. *c.* September 30, 1207, Balkh [now in Afghanistan]—
d. December 17, 1273)

The greatest Sufi mystic and poet in the Persian language, Jalāl al-Dīn Rūmī (also known by the honorific Mawlānā) is famous for his lyrics and for his didactic epic *Maṣnavī-yi Ma'navī* ("Spiritual Couplets"), which widely influenced mystical thought and literature throughout the Muslim world. After his death, his disciples were organized as the Mawlawīyah order.

Jalāl al-Dīn's father, Bahā' al-Dīn Walad, was a noted mystical theologian, author, and teacher. Because of either a dispute with the ruler or the threat of the approaching Mongols, Bahā' al-Dīn and his family left their native town in about 1218. According to a legend, in Nīshāpūr, Iran, the family met Farīd al-Dīn 'Aṭṭār, a Persian mystical poet, who blessed young Jalāl al-Dīn. After a pilgrimage to Mecca and journeys through the Middle East, Bahā' al-Dīn and his family reached Anatolia (Rūm, hence the surname Rūmī), a region that enjoyed peace and prosperity under the rule of the Turkish Seljuq dynasty. After a short stay at Laranda (Karaman), where Jalāl al-Dīn's mother died and his first son was born, they were called to the capital, Konya, in 1228. Here, Bahā' al-Dīn Walad taught at one of the numerous madrasahs (religious schools); after his death in 1231 he was succeeded in this capacity by his son.

A year later, Burhān al-Dīn Muḥaqqiq, one of Bahā' al-Dīn's former disciples, arrived in Konya and acquainted

Jalāl al-Dīn more deeply with some mystical theories that had developed in Iran. Burhān al-Dīn, who contributed considerably to Jalāl al-Dīn's spiritual formation, left Konya about 1240. Jalāl al-Dīn is said to have undertaken one or two journeys to Syria (unless his contacts with Syrian Sufi circles were already established before his family reached Anatolia); there he may have met Ibn al-ʿArabī, the leading Islamic theosophist whose interpreter and stepson, Ṣadr al-Dīn al-Qunawī, was Jalāl al-Dīnn's colleague and friend in Konya.

The decisive moment in Rūmī's life occurred on November 30, 1244, when in the streets of Konya he met the wandering dervish (holy man) Shams al-Dīn (Sun of Religion) of Tabrīz, whom he may have first encountered in Syria. Shams al-Dīn cannot be connected with any of the traditional mystical fraternities; his overwhelming personality, however, revealed to Jalāl al-Dīn the mysteries of divine majesty and beauty. For months the two mystics lived closely together, and Rūmī neglected his disciples and family so that his scandalized entourage forced Shams to leave the town in February 1246. Jalāl al-Dīn was heartbroken; his eldest son, Sulṭān Walad, eventually brought Shams back from Syria. The family, however, could not tolerate the close relation of Jalāl al-Dīn with his beloved, and one night in 1247 Shams disappeared forever. In the 20th century it was established that Shams was indeed murdered, not without the knowledge of Rūmī's sons, who hurriedly buried him close to a well that is still extant in Konya.

This experience of love, longing, and loss turned Rūmī into a poet. His poems—*ghazals* (about 30,000 verses) and a large number of *robāʿiyāt* ("quatrains")—reflect the different stages of his love, until, as his son writes, "he found Shams in himself, radiant like the moon." The complete identification of lover and beloved is expressed by his inserting the name of Shams instead of his own pen name at the end of most of his lyrical poems. The *Dīvān-e Shams* ("The Collected Poetry of Shams") is a true translation of his experiences into poetry; its language, however, never becomes lost in lofty spiritual heights or nebulous speculation. The fresh language, propelled by its strong rhythms, sometimes assumes forms close to popular verses. There would seem to be cause for the belief, expressed by chroniclers, that much of this poetry was composed in a state of ecstasy, induced by the music of the flute or the drum, the hammering of the goldsmiths, or the sound of the water mill in Meram, where Rūmī used to go with his disciples to enjoy nature. He found in nature the reflection of the radiant beauty of the Sun of Religion and felt flowers and birds partaking in his love. He often accompanied his verses by a whirling dance, and many of his poems were composed to be sung in Sufi musical gatherings.

A few years after Shams al-Dīn's death, Rūmī experienced a similar rapture in his acquaintance with an illiterate goldsmith, Ṣalāḥ al-Dīn Zarkūb. It is said that one day, hearing the sound of a hammer in front of Ṣalāḥ al-Dīn's shop in the bazaar of Konya, Rūmī began his dance. The shop owner had long been one of Rūmī's closest and most loyal disciples, and his daughter became the wife of Rūmī's eldest son. This love again inspired Rūmī to write poetry. After Ṣalāḥ al-Dīn's death, Ḥusām al-Dīn Chelebi became his spiritual love and deputy. Rūmī's main work, the *Maṣnavī-yi Maʿnavī*, was composed under his influence. Ḥusām al-Dīn had asked him to follow the model of the poets ʿAṭṭār and Sanāʾi, who had laid down mystical teachings in long poems, interspersed with anecdotes, fables, stories, proverbs, and allegories. Their works were widely read by the mystics and by Rūmī's disciples. Rūmī followed Ḥusām al-Dīn's advice and composed nearly 26,000 couplets of the *Maṣnavī* during the following years. It is said that he would recite his verses even in the bath or on the roads, accompanied by Ḥusām al-Dīn, who wrote them down. The *Maṡnavī*, which shows all the different aspects of Sufism in the 13th century, often carries the reader away with loose associations of thought, so that one understands what subjects the master had in mind at a particular stage of his life. The work reflects the experience of divine love; both Ṣālāḥ al-Dīn and Ḥusām al-Dīn were, for Rūmī, renewed manifestations of Shams al-Dīn, the all-embracing light. He called Ḥusām al-Dīn,

Tomb of Jalāl al-Dīn Rūmī, Konya, Turkey. Fred J. Maroon/Photo Researchers

therefore, Ḍiyā' al-Ḥaqq ("Light of the Truth"); *ḍiyā'* is the Arabic term for sunlight.

Rūmī lived for a short while after completing the *Maṣnavī*. He always remained a respected member of Konya society, and his company was sought by the leading officials as well as by Christian monks. His burial procession, according to one of Rūmī's contemporaries, was attended by a vast crowd of people of many faiths and nationalities. His mausoleum, the Green Dome, is today a museum in Konya; it is still a place of pilgrimage, primarily for Turkish Muslims.

Ḥusām al-Dīn was Rūmī's successor and was in turn succeeded by Sulṭān Walad, who organized the loose fraternity of Rūmī's disciples into the Mawlawīyah, known in the West as the Whirling Dervishes because of the mystical dance that constitutes their principal ritual. Sulṭān Walad's poetical accounts of his father's life are the most important source of knowledge of Rūmī 's spiritual development.

Besides his poetry, Rūmī left a small collection of occasional talks as they were noted down by his friends; in the collection, known as *Fīhi mā fīhi* ("There Is in It What Is in It"), the main ideas of his poetry recur. There also exist sermons and a collection of letters (*Maktūbāt*) directed to different persons. It is impossible to systematize his ideas, which at times contradict each other, and changes in the use of symbols often puzzle the reader. His poetry is a most human expression of mystical experiences, in which readers can find their own favourite ideas and feelings — from enthusiastic flights into the heavens to matter-of-fact descriptions of daily life.

Rūmī's use of Persian and Arabic in his poetry, in addition to some Turkish and less Greek, has resulted in his being claimed variously for Turkish literature and Persian literature, a reflection of the strength of his influence in

Iran and Turkey. The influence of his writings in the Indian subcontinent is also substantial. By the end of the 20th century, his popularity had become a global phenomenon, with his poetry achieving a wide circulation in western Europe and the United States.

SA'DĪ

(b. *c.* 1213, Shīrāz, Iran—d. December 9, 1291, Shīrāz)

The Persian poet Sa'dī (byname of Musharrif al-Dīn ibn Muṣlih al-Dīn) is one of the greatest figures in classical Persian literature.

He lost his father, Muṣliḥ al-Dīn, in early childhood; later he was sent to study in Baghdad at the renowned Neẓāmīyeh College, where he acquired the traditional learning of Islam. The unsettled conditions following the Mongol invasion of Persia led him to wander abroad through Anatolia, Syria, Egypt, and Iraq. He refers in his work to travels in India and Central Asia, but these journeys cannot be confirmed. He claimed that he was held captive by the Franks and put to work in the trenches of the fortress of Tripoli (now in Lebanon); however, this story, like many of his other "autobiographical" anecdotes, is considered highly suspect. When he returned to his native Shīrāz, he was middle-aged; he seems to have spent the rest of his life in Shīrāz.

Sa'dī took his nom de plume from the name of a local *atabeg* (prince), Sa'd ibn Zangī. Sa'dī's best-known works are the *Būstān* (1257; *The Orchard*) and the *Gulistān* (1258; *The Rose Garden*). The *Būstān* is entirely in verse (epic metre) and consists of stories aptly illustrating the standard virtues recommended to Muslims (justice, liberality, modesty, contentment) as well as of reflections on the behaviour of dervishes and their ecstatic practices. The *Gulistān* is mainly in prose and contains stories and personal anecdotes. The text is interspersed with a variety of short poems, containing aphorisms, advice, and humorous reflections. The morals preached in the *Gulistān* border on expediency—e.g., a well-intended lie is admitted to be preferable to a seditious truth. Sa'dī demonstrates a profound awareness of the absurdity of human existence. The fate of those who depend on the changeable moods of kings is contrasted with the freedom of the dervishes.

For Western students the *Būstān* and *Gulistān* have a special attraction; but Sa'dī is also remembered as a great panegyrist and lyricist and as the author of a number of masterly general odes portraying human experience and also of particular odes such as the lament on the fall of Baghdad after the Mongol invasion in 1258. His lyrics are to be found in *Ghazalīyāt* ("Lyrics") and his odes in *Qaṣā'id* ("Odes"). Six prose treatises on various subjects are attributed to him; he is also known for a number of works in Arabic. The peculiar blend of human kindness and cynicism, humour, and resignation displayed in Sa'dī's works, together with a tendency to avoid the hard dilemma, make him, to many, the most widely admired writer in the world of Iranian culture.

JEAN, SIRE DE JOINVILLE

(b. *c.* 1224, Joinville, Champagne—d. December 24, 1317, Joinville)

Jean, sire de Joinville is the author of the famous *Histoire de Saint-Louis*, a chronicle in French prose, providing a supreme account of the Seventh Crusade (1248–54).

A member of the lesser nobility of Champagne, Joinville first attended the court of Louis IX at Saumur (1241), probably as a squire. The young Joinville took the crusader's cross at the same time as the king (1244) and set out with him (August 1248) on his expedition to Egypt, from where the crusaders planned to attack Syria. Captured with the entire army, Louis and Joinville were ransomed, and Joinville became friends with Louis during the king's subsequent stay at Acre. They returned to France in 1254. While in Syria, Joinville wrote the first draft of a minor work, his *Credo*, a rather naive statement of belief that was probably revised later. Made seneschal of Champagne on his return, he became an expert in court procedures and seems to have divided his time between the royal court and his fief of Joinville. He refused to accompany the king on his fatal crusade to Tunis (1270), having previously told him that it was folly. Joinville lived to testify for the canonization of the king (1282) and to see it enacted (1298); he controlled his domain until his death at 93.

Preliminary drafts of Joinville's major work, the *Histoire de Saint-Louis* (*The History of St. Louis*, or *The Life of St. Louis*), may have been begun as early as the 1270s, but the final form was commissioned by Jeanne of Champagne and Navarre, wife of King Philip IV the Fair. It was not completed at the time of her death (1305) and so was presented in 1309 to her son Louis X. The *Histoire* is a personal account, which, in the course of setting forth the exploits of his idol, King Louis IX, reveals Joinville himself as a deeply moving man: simple, honest, straightforward, affectionate. He makes no attempt to conceal his occasional cowardice, his lack of piety, his tactlessness, or his long-windedness. Although the short narratives of Louis's early life and of his later reign, death, and canonization are valuable because of the author's proximity to them, the heart of the book lies in its lengthy central section, the account of the Crusade. Besides telling the financial hardships, the dangers of sea voyages, and the ravages of disease, he vividly describes the confusion and lack of discipline in the crusading army. A blunt adviser, Joinville paints his king's sublime unworldliness against his own frank humanity. In addition, the book describes Muslim customs.

The original manuscript of the work disappeared from all records shortly after its composition. The *Histoire* was first printed and modernized from an inferior manuscript in 1547.

JACOB VAN MAERLANT

(b. 1225, Vrije van Brugge [Damme?]—d. 1291, Damme)

Jacob van Maerlant was a pioneer of the didactic poetry that flourished in the Netherlands in the 14th century.

The details of Maerlant's life are disputed, but he was probably sexton at Maerlant, near Brielle on Voorne, in 1255–65?, and was employed by Albrecht van Voorne; Nicholas Cats, lord of North Beveland; and Floris V, count of Holland. About 1266 he became clerk to the court at Damme. He had an intimate knowledge of both Latin and French. His early works were versions of medieval romances—*Alexanders Geesten*, based on Gautier de Châtillon's Latin *Alexandreis*; the *Historie van den Grale Merlyn* (c. 1260), freely translated from Robert de Borron's early contributions to the Arthurian cycle; *Torec* (c. 1262); and, most important, the *Historie van Troyen* (c. 1264), from the *Roman de Troie* ascribed to Benoît de Sainte Maure.

When Maerlant began to write with the aim of providing instruction, he turned entirely to Latin sources, writing a scientific compilation, *Der Naturen Bloeme* (1266–69?), after Thomas of Cantimpré's *De natura rerum*; a life of St. Francis (before 1273), based on Bonaventura; the *Rijmbijbel* (1271), after Petrus Comestor's *Historia Scolastica*; and, finally, his most important work, *Spieghel Historiael*, an adaptation with additions of his own of Vincent de Beauvais's *Speculum Historiale*, begun about 1282 and completed after his death by Philippe Utenbroeke and Lodewijk van Velthem. These moralizing rhymed encyclopaedic works were written to satisfy the rising class of commoners who wished for instructive reading in their own language.

His own considerable gifts as a religious poet are also fully shown in *Wapene Martijn*, a dialogue poem on the decadence of the period and moral problems, and in his fervent *Disputacie van Onser Vrouwen ende vanden Heilighen Cruce* and *Van den Lande van Oversee*, which scourges the laxity of the church and calls for a new crusade.

GUIDO CAVALCANTI

(b. *c.* 1255, Florence [Italy]—d. August 27/28, 1300, Florence)

The Italian poet Guido Cavalcanti was a major figure among the Florentine poets who wrote in the *dolce stil nuovo* ("sweet new style") and who is considered, next to Dante, the most striking poet and personality in 13th-century Italian literature.

Born into an influential Florentine family of the Guelf (papal) party, Cavalcanti studied under the philosopher and scholar Brunetto Latini, who earlier had been the teacher of Dante. Cavalcanti married the daughter of the rival Ghibelline (imperial) party leader Farinata degli Uberti but joined the White Guelf faction when, in 1300, that party split into Blacks and Whites. That same year, Dante, who had dedicated several poems to Cavalcanti and called him his "first friend," apparently was involved in banishing Cavalcanti from Florence. In exile in Sarzana, Cavalcanti contracted malaria and was permitted to return to Florence, where he died.

Cavalcanti's strong, temperamental, and brilliant personality and the poems that mirror it were admired by many contemporary poets and such important later ones as Dante Gabriel Rossetti and Ezra Pound. He left about 50 poems, many addressed to two women: Mandetta, whom he met in Toulouse in 1292, and Giovanna, whom he calls Primavera ("Springtime"). Cavalcanti's poems glow with the brilliance, grace, and directness of diction characteristic of the style at its best. Love is the poet's dominant theme, generally love that causes deep suffering.

Two of Cavalcanti's poems are canzoni, a type of lyric derived from Provençal poetry, of which the most famous is "Donna mi prega" ("A Lady Asks Me"), a beautiful and complex philosophical analysis of love, the subject of many later commentaries. Others are sonnets and ballate (ballads), the latter type usually considered his best. One of his best-known ballate was also one of his last, written when he went into exile: "Perch'io non spero di tornar giamai" ("Because I hope not ever to return"), a line that some hear echoed in T.S. Eliot's refrain from "Ash Wednesday," "Because I do not hope to turn again."

Cavalcanti's poetry was first collected in 1527 and later in *Le rime de Guido Cavalcanti* (1902). Many poems were translated by Dante Gabriel Rossetti in *The Early Italian Poets* (1861; later retitled *Dante and His Circle*) and by Ezra Pound in *The Sonnets and Ballate of Guido Cavalcanti* (1912).

DANTE

(b. *c.* May 21–June 20, 1265, Florence, Italy—
d. September 13/14, 1321, Ravenna)

The Italian poet, prose writer, literary theorist, moral philosopher, and political thinker Dante Alighieri is best known for the monumental epic poem *La commedia*, later named *La divina commedia* (*The Divine Comedy*).

Early Life and the Vita Nuova

Most of what is known about Dante's life he has told himself. He was born in Florence in 1265 under the sign of Gemini (between May 21 and June 20) and remained devoted to his native city all his life. Dante describes how he fought as a cavalryman against the Ghibellines, a banished Florentine party supporting the imperial cause. He also speaks of his great teacher Brunetto Latini and his gifted friend Guido Cavalcanti, of the poetic culture in which he made his first artistic ventures, his poetic indebtedness to Guido Guinizelli, the origins of his family in his great-great-grandfather, Cacciaguida, whom the reader meets in the central cantos of the *Paradiso* (and from whose wife the family name, Alighieri, derived), and, going back even further, of the pride that he felt in the fact that his distant ancestors were descendants of the Roman soldiers who settled along the banks of the Arno.

Dante was endowed with remarkable intellectual and aesthetic self-confidence. By the time he was 18, as he himself says in the *Vita nuova*, he had already taught himself the art of making verse (chapter III). He sent an early sonnet,

Dante Reading from the Divine Comedy, *painting by Domenico di Michelino, 1465; in the Cathedral of Santa Maria del Fiore, Florence.* David Lees/Time & Life Pictures/Getty Images

which was to become the first poem in the *Vita nuova*, to the most famous poets of his day. He received several responses, but the most important one came from Cavalcanti, and this was the beginning of their great friendship.

One of Dante's great spiritual guides, for whom Cavalcanti evidently did not have the same appreciation, was Beatrice, a figure in whom Dante created one of the most celebrated fictionalized women in all of literature. In keeping with the changing directions of Dante's thought and the vicissitudes of his career, she, too, underwent enormous changes in his hands—sanctified in the *Vita nuova*, demoted in the canzoni (poems) presented in the *Convivio*, only to be returned with more profound comprehension in *The Divine Comedy* as the woman credited with having led Dante away from the "vulgar herd."

La vita nuova (c. 1293; *The New Life*) is the first of two collections of verse that Dante made in his lifetime, the other being the *Convivio*. Each is a prosimetrum, that is, a work composed of verse and prose. In each case the prose is a device for binding together poems composed over about a 10-year period. The *Vita nuova* brought together Dante's poetic efforts from before 1283 to roughly 1292–93; the *Convivio*, a bulkier and more ambitious work, contains Dante's most important poetic compositions from just prior to 1294 to the time of *The Divine Comedy*.

Dante's Intellectual Development and Public Career

A second contemporary poetic figure behind Dante was Guido Guinizelli, the poet most responsible for altering the prevailing local, or "municipal," kind of poetry. What increased the appeal of his poetry was its intellectual, even philosophical, content. His poems were written in praise of the lady and of *gentilezza*, the virtue of kindness that she brought out in her admirer. It was Guinizelli's influence that was responsible for the poetic and spiritual turning point of the *Vita nuova*. As reported in chapters XVII to XXI, Dante experienced a change of heart, and rather than write poems of anguish, he determined to write poems in praise of his lady, especially the *canzone Donne ch'avete intelletto d'amore* ("Ladies Who Have Understanding of Love").

This interest in philosophical poetry led Dante into another great change in his life, which he describes in the *Convivio*. Looking for consolation following the death of Beatrice, Dante reports that he turned to philosophy, particularly to the writings of Boethius and Cicero. But what was intended as a temporary reprieve from sorrow became a lifelong avocation and one of the most crucial intellectual events in Dante's career. The *donna gentile* (kind woman) of the *Vita nuova* was transformed into Lady Philosophy, who soon occupied all of Dante's thoughts. He began attending the religious schools of Florence in order to hear disputations on philosophy, and within a period of only 30 months "the love of her [philosophy] banished and destroyed every other thought."

Another great change was Dante's more active political involvement in the affairs of the commune. In 1295 he became a member of the guild of physicians and apothecaries (to which philosophers could belong), which opened his way to public office. But he entered the public arena at a most perilous time in the city's politics. As it had been during the time of the Guelf and Ghibelline civil strife, in the 1290s Florence once again became a divided city. The ruling Guelf class of Florence became divided into a party of "Blacks" and a party of "Whites," to which Dante belonged. The Whites gained the upper hand and exiled the Blacks.

There is ample information concerning Dante's activities following 1295. In May 1300 he was part of an important embassy to San Gimignano, a neighbouring town, whose purpose it was to solidify the Guelf league of Tuscan cities against the mounting ambitions of the new and embattled pope Boniface VIII. When Dante was elected to the priorate in 1300, he presumably was already recognized as a spokesman for those in the commune determined to resist the Pontiff's policies. Dante thus experienced a complete turnabout in his attitudes concerning the extent of papal power. The hegemony of the Guelfs—the party supporting the Pope—had been restored in Florence in 1266 by an alliance forged between the forces of France and the papacy. By 1300, however, Dante had come to oppose the territorial ambitions of the Pope, and this in turn provided the intellectual motivation for another, even greater change: Dante, the Guelf moderate, would in time, through his firsthand experience of the ill effects of papal involvement in political matters, become one of the most fervently outspoken defenders of the position that the empire does not derive its political authority from the pope.

Events, moreover, propelled Dante into further opposition to papal policies. A new alliance was formed between the papacy, the French (the brother of King Philip IV, Charles of Valois, was acting in concert with Boniface), and the exiled Black Guelfs. When Charles of Valois wished permission to enter Florence, the city itself was thrown into political indecision. In order to ascertain the nature of the Pope's intentions, an embassy was sent to Rome to discuss these matters with him. Dante was one of the emissaries, but his quandary was expressed in the legendary phrase "If I go, who remains; if I remain, who goes?" Dante was outmaneuvered. The Pope dismissed the other two legates and detained Dante. In early November 1301 the forces of Charles of Valois were permitted entry to Florence. That very night the exiled Blacks surreptitiously reentered Florence and for six days terrorized the city. Dante learned of the deception at first in Rome and then more fully in Siena. In January 1302 he was called to appear before the new Florentine government and, failing to do so, was condemned, along with three other former priors, for crimes he had not committed. Again failing to appear, on March 10, 1302, Dante and

14 other Whites were condemned to be burned to death. Thus Dante suffered the most decisive crisis of his life. In *The Divine Comedy* he frequently and powerfully speaks of this rupture; indeed, he makes it the central dramatic act toward which a long string of prophecies points. But it is also Dante's purpose to show the means by which he triumphed over his personal disaster, thus making his poem into a true "divine comedy."

Exile, the Convivio, and the De Monarchia

Information about Dante's early years in exile is scanty; nevertheless, enough is known to provide a broad picture. It seems that Dante at first was active among the exiled White Guelfs in their attempts to seek a military return. These efforts proved fruitless. Evidently Dante grew disillusioned with the other Florentine outcasts, the Ghibellines, and was determined to prove his worthiness by means of his writings and thus secure his return. These are the circumstances that led him to compose *Il convivio* (*c.* 1304–07; *The Banquet*).

In the *Convivio* Dante's mature political and philosophical system is nearly complete. In this work Dante makes his first stirring defense of the imperial tradition and, more specifically, of the Roman Empire. He introduces the crucial concept of *horme*, that is, of an innate desire that prompts the soul to return to God. But it requires proper education through examples and doctrine. Otherwise it can become misdirected toward worldly aims and society torn apart by its destructive power. In the *Convivio* Dante establishes the link between his political thought and his understanding of human appetite: given the pope's craving for worldly power, at the time there existed no proper spiritual models to direct the appetite toward God; and given the weakness of the empire, there existed no law sufficient to exercise a physical restraint on the will. For Dante this explains the chaos into which Italy had been plunged, and it moved him, in hopes of remedying these conditions, to take up the epic task of *The Divine Comedy*.

However a political event occurred that at first raised tremendous hope but then plunged Dante into still greater disillusionment. In November 1308 Henry, the count of Luxembourg, was elected king of Germany, and in July 1309 the French pope, Clement V, who had succeeded Boniface, declared Henry to be king of the Romans and invited him to Rome, where in time he would be crowned Holy Roman emperor in St. Peter's Basilica. The possibility of once again having an emperor electrified Italy; and among the imperial proponents was Dante, who saw approaching the realization of an ideal that he had long held: the coming of an emperor pledged to restore peace while also declaring his spiritual subordination to religious authority. Within a short time after his arrival in Italy in 1310 Henry VII's great appeal began to fade. He lingered too long in the north, allowing his enemies to gather strength. Foremost among the opposition to this divinely ordained moment, as Dante regarded it, was the commune of Florence.

During these years Dante wrote important political epistles—evidence of the great esteem in which he was held throughout Italy, of his personal authority, as it were—in which he exalted Henry, urging him to be diligent, and condemned Florence. In subsequent action, however, which was to remind Dante of Boniface's duplicity, Clement himself turned against Henry. This action prompted one of Dante's greatest polemical treatises, his *De monarchia* (*c.* 1313; *On Monarchy*) in which he expands the political arguments of the *Convivio*. In the embittered atmosphere caused by Clement's deceit Dante turned his argumentative powers against papal insistence on its superiority over the political ruler, that is, against the argument that the empire derived its political authority from the pope.

The Divine Comedy

Dante's years of exile were years of difficult travels from one place to another. Throughout his exile Dante nevertheless was sustained by work on his great poem. *The Divine Comedy* was possibly begun prior to 1308 and completed just before his death in 1321, but the exact dates are uncertain.

The plot of *The Divine Comedy* is simple: a man, generally assumed to be Dante himself, is miraculously enabled to undertake an ultramundane journey, which leads him to visit the souls in Hell, Purgatory, and Paradise. He has two guides: Virgil, who leads him through the *Inferno* and *Purgatorio*, and Beatrice, who introduces him to *Paradiso*. Through these fictional encounters taking place from Good Friday evening in 1300 through Easter Sunday and slightly beyond, Dante learns of the exile that is awaiting him (which had, of course, already occurred at the time of the writing). This device allowed Dante not only to create a story out of his pending exile but also to explain the means by which he came to cope with his personal calamity and to offer suggestions for the resolution of Italy's troubles as well. Thus, the exile of an individual becomes a microcosm of the problems of a country, and it also becomes representative of the fall of man. Dante's story is thus historically specific as well as paradigmatic.

The basic structural component of *The Divine Comedy* is the canto. The poem consists of 100 cantos, which are grouped together into three sections, or canticles, *Inferno*, *Purgatorio*, and *Paradiso*. Technically there are 33 cantos in each canticle and one additional canto, contained in the *Inferno*, which serves as an introduction to the entire poem. For the most part the cantos range from about 136 to about 151 lines. The poem's rhyme scheme is the terza rima (*aba*, *bcb*, *cdc*, etc.) Thus, the divine number of three is present in every part of the work.

The *Inferno* represents a false start during which Dante, the character, must be disabused of harmful values that somehow prevent him from rising above his fallen world. Despite the regressive nature of the *Inferno*, Dante's meetings with the roster of the damned are among the most memorable moments of the poem: the Neutrals, the virtuous pagans, Francesca da Rimini, Filipo Argenti, Farinata degli Uberti, Piero delle Vigne, Brunetto Latini, the simoniacal popes, Ulysses, and Ugolino impose themselves upon the reader's imagination with tremendous force.

The visit to Hell is, as Virgil and later Beatrice explain, an extreme measure, a painful but necessary act before real recovery can begin. This explains why the *Inferno* is both aesthetically and theologically incomplete. For instance, readers frequently express disappointment at the lack of dramatic or emotional power in the final encounter with Satan in canto XXXIV. But because the journey through the *Inferno* primarily signifies a process of separation and thus is only the initial step in a fuller development, it must end with a distinct anticlimax. In a way this is inevitable because the final revelation of Satan can have nothing new to offer: the sad effects of his presence in human history have already become apparent throughout the *Inferno*.

In the *Purgatorio* the protagonist's painful process of spiritual rehabilitation commences; in fact, this part of the journey may be considered the poem's true moral starting point. Here the pilgrim Dante subdues his own personality in order that he may ascend. In fact, in contrast to the *Inferno*, where Dante is confronted with a system of models that needs to be discarded, in the *Purgatorio* few characters present themselves as models; all of the penitents are pilgrims along the road of life. Dante, rather than being an awed if alienated observer, is an active participant. If the *Inferno* is a canticle of enforced and involuntary alienation, in which Dante learns how harmful were his former allegiances, in the *Purgatorio* he comes to accept as most fitting the essential Christian image of life as a pilgrimage. As Beatrice in her magisterial return in the earthly paradise reminds Dante, he must learn to reject the deceptive promises of the temporal world.

Despite its harsh regime, the *Purgatorio* is the realm of spiritual dawn, where larger visions are entertained. Whereas in only one canto of the *Inferno* (VII), in which Fortuna is discussed, is there any suggestion of philosophy, in the *Purgatorio*, historical, political, and moral vistas are opened up. It is, moreover, the great canticle of poetry and the arts. Dante meant it literally when he proclaimed, after the dreary dimensions of Hell: "But here let poetry rise again from the dead." There is only one poet in Hell proper and not more than two in the *Paradiso*, but in the *Purgatorio* the reader encounters the musicians Casella and Belacqua and the poet Sordello and hears of the fortunes of the two Guidos, Guinizelli and Cavalcanti, the painters Cimabue and Giotto, and the miniaturists. Shortly after his encounters with the great artists comes the long-awaited reunion with Beatrice in the earthly paradise. Thus, from the classics Dante seems to have derived his moral and political understanding as well as his conception of the epic poem, that is, a framing story large enough to encompass the most important issues of his day, but it was from his native tradition that he acquired the philosophy of love that forms the Christian matter of his poem.

This means of course that Virgil, Dante's guide, must give way to other leaders, and in a canticle generally devoid of drama the rejection of Virgil becomes the single dramatic event. Dante's use of Virgil is one of the richest cultural appropriations in literature. To begin, in Dante's poem he is an exponent of classical reason. Virgil, moreover, is associated with Dante's homeland (his references are to contemporary Italian places), and his background is entirely imperial. (Born under Julius Caesar, he extolled Augustus Caesar.) He is presented as a poet, the theme of whose great epic sounds remarkably similar to that of Dante's poem: "I was a poet and sang of that just son of Anchises who came from Troy after proud Ilium was burned." So, too, Dante sings of the just son of a city, Florence, who was unjustly expelled, and forced to search, as Aeneas had done, for a better city, in his case the heavenly city.

Though an exponent of reason, Virgil has become an emissary of divine grace, and his return is part of the revival of those simpler faiths associated with Dante's earlier trust in Beatrice. And yet, of course, Virgil by himself is insufficient. It cannot be said that Dante rejects Virgil; rather he sadly found that nowhere in Virgil's work, that is, in his consciousness, was there any sense of personal liberation from the enthrallment of history and its processes. Virgil had provided Dante with moral instruction in survival as an exile, which is the theme of his own poem as well as Dante's, but he clung to his faith in the processes of history, which, given their culmination in the Roman Empire, were deeply consoling. Dante, on the other hand, was determined to go beyond history because it had become for him a nightmare.

In the *Paradiso* true heroic fulfillment is achieved. Dante's poem gives expression to those figures from the past who seem to defy death. Their historical impact continues and the totality of their commitment inspires in their followers a feeling of exaltation and a desire for identification. In his encounters with such characters as his great-great-grandfather Cacciaguida and SS. Francis, Dominic, and Bernard, Dante is carried beyond himself. The *Paradiso* is consequently a poem of fulfillment and of completion. It is the fulfillment of what is prefigured in the earlier canticles. Aesthetically it completes the poem's elaborate system of anticipation and retrospection.

*G*UILLAUME DE *M*ACHAUT

(b. *c.* 1300, Machault, France—d. 1377, Reims)

A poet and musician, Guillaume de Machaut (also spelled Machault) was greatly admired by contemporaries as a master of French versification and regarded as one of the leading French composers of the Ars Nova musical style of the 14th century. It is on his shorter poems and his musical compositions that his reputation rests. He was the last great poet in France to think of the lyric and its musical setting as a single entity.

He took holy orders and in 1323 entered the service of John of Luxembourg, king of Bohemia, whom he accompanied on his wars as chaplain and secretary. He was rewarded for this service by his appointment in 1337 as canon (clergyman) of Reims cathedral. After the king's death, he found another protector in the king's daughter, Bonne of Luxembourg, wife of the future king John II of France, and in 1349 in Charles II, king of Navarre. Honours and patronage continued to be lavished by kings and princes on Machaut at Reims until his death.

In his longer poems Machaut did not go beyond the themes and genres already widely employed in his time. Mostly didactic and allegorical exercises in the well-worked courtly love tradition, they are of scant interest to the modern reader. An exception among the longer works is *Voir-Dit*, which relates how a young girl of high rank falls in love with the poet because of his fame and creative accomplishments. The difference in age is too great, however, and the idyll ends in disappointment. Machaut's lyric poems also are based on the courtly love theme but reworked into a deft form with a verbal music that is often perfectly achieved. His influence—most significantly his technical innovations—spread beyond the borders of France. In England, Geoffrey Chaucer drew heavily upon Machaut's poetry for elements of *The Book of the Duchesse.*

All of Machaut's music has been preserved in 32 manuscripts, representing a large part of the surviving music from his period. He was the first composer to write single-handedly a polyphonic setting of the mass ordinary, a work that has been recorded in modern performance. In most of this four-part setting he employs the characteristic Ars Nova technique of isorhythm (repeated overlapping of a rhythmic pattern in varying melodic forms).

Machaut's secular compositions make up the larger part of his music. His three- and four-part motets (polyphonic songs in which each voice has a different text) number 23. Of these, 17 are in French, 2 are Latin mixed with French, and 4, like the religious motets of the early 13th century, are in Latin. Love is often the subject of their texts, and all but 3 employ isorhythm. Machaut's 19 lais are usually for unaccompanied voice, although two are for three parts, and one is for two parts. They employ a great variety of musical material, frequently from the popular song and dance. Of his 33 virelais, 25 consist solely of a melody, and they, along with the bulk of his lais, represent the last of such unaccompanied songs composed in the tradition of the trouvères. The rest of his virelais have one or two additional parts for instrumental accompaniment, and these are typical of the accompanied solo song that became popular in the 14th century. The polyphonic songs he wrote, in addition to his motets, consist of 21 rondeaux and 41 of his 42 ballades. The wide distribution of his music in contemporary manuscripts reveals that he was esteemed not only in France but also in Italy, Spain, and much of the rest of Europe.

𝒫ETRARCH

(b. July 20, 1304, Arezzo, Tuscany [Italy]—d. July 18/19, 1374, Arquà, near Padua, Carrara)

Francesco Petrarca (better known as Petrarch) was an Italian scholar, poet, and humanist whose poems addressed to Laura, an idealized beloved, contributed to the Renaissance flowering of lyric poetry.

Education and Early Poems

Petrarch's father, a lawyer, had been obliged to leave Florence in 1302 and had moved to Arezzo, where Petrarch was born. The family eventually moved to Avignon (1312), in the Provence region of southern France, the home of the exiled papal court, at which an Italian lawyer might hope to find employment. Petrarch's first studies were at Carpentras, France, and at his father's insistence he was sent to study law at Montpellier, France (1316). From there he returned to Italy with his younger brother Gherardo to continue these studies at Bologna (1320). But already he was developing what, in a later letter, he described as "an unquenchable thirst for literature."

Petrarch's earliest surviving poems, on the death of his mother, date from the Montpellier and Bologna period, though like all Petrarch's work they were heavily revised

PETRARCA.

Petrarch. DEA/Veneranda Biblioteca Ambrosiana/De Agostini/ Getty Images

later. Meanwhile, his knowledge and love of the Classical authors increasing, he made his acquaintance with the new vernacular poetry that was being written. After his father's death, in 1326, Petrarch was free to abandon his law studies and pursue his own interests. Returning to Avignon, he took minor ecclesiastical orders and entered the household of the influential cardinal Giovanni Colonna.

As well as a love of literature, Petrarch also had during his early youth a deep religious faith, a love of virtue, and an unusually deep perception of the transitory nature of human affairs. There now followed the reaction—a period of dissipation—which also coincided with the beginning of his famous chaste love for a woman known now only as Laura. Vain attempts have been made to identify her, but Petrarch himself kept silent about everything concerning her civil status, as though he thought it unimportant. He first saw her in the Church of St. Clare at Avignon on April 6, 1327, and loved her, although she was outside his reach, almost until his death. From this love there springs the work for which he is most celebrated, the Italian poems (*Rime*), which he affected to despise as mere trifles in the vulgar tongue but which he collected and revised throughout his life.

Classical Studies and Early Career

He spent the summer of 1330 at Lombez, France, the bishop of which was an old friend from Bologna, Giacomo Colonna. In 1335 he received a canonry there but continued to reside at Avignon in the service of the cardinal, with whom he stayed until 1337. Quite apart from his love for Laura, this period was an important one for Petrarch. These were years of ambition and unremitting study. They were also years of travel. In 1333 his journeying took him through France, Flanders, Brabant, and the Rhineland, where he visited men of learning and searched monastic libraries for "lost" Classical manuscripts.

These experiences bring Petrarch's mission as a stubborn advocate of the continuity between Classical culture and the Christian message more sharply into focus. By making a synthesis of the two seemingly conflicting ideals—regarding the one as the rich promise and the other as its divine fulfillment—he can claim to be the founder and great representative of the movement known as European humanism. He rejected the sterile argumentation and endless dialectical subtleties to which medieval Scholasticism had become prey and turned back for values and illumination to the moral weight of the Classical world. In 1337 he visited Rome for the first time, to be stirred among its ruins by the evident grandeur of its past. On returning to Avignon he sought a refuge from its corrupt life—the papacy at this time was wholly absorbed in secular matters—and a few miles to the east found his "fair transalpine solitude" of Vaucluse, which was afterward to become a much-loved place of retreat.

Moral and Literary Evolution

Meanwhile, his reputation as a scholar was spreading; in September 1340 he received invitations from Paris and Rome to be crowned as poet. He had perhaps sought out this honour, partly from ambition but mainly in order that the rebirth of the cult of poetry after more than 1,000 years might be fittingly celebrated. He had no hesitation in choosing Rome, and accordingly he was crowned on the Capitoline Hill on April 8, 1341, afterward placing his laurel wreath on the tomb of the Apostle in St. Peter's Basilica: again, the symbolic gesture linking the Classical tradition with the Christian message.

From Rome he went to Parma and the nearby solitude of Selvapiana, returning to Avignon in the autumn of 1343. It is generally believed that he went through some kind of moral crisis at this time, rooted in his inability to make his life conform to his religious faith and possibly heightened by his brother's decision to enter a Carthusian monastery. At any rate, this is a common reading of the *Secretum meum* (1342–43). It is an autobiographical treatise consisting of three dialogues between Petrarch and St. Augustine in the presence of Truth. In it he maintains hope that, even amidst worldly preoccupations and error, even while absorbed in himself and his own affairs, a man might still find a way to God. Thus, Petrarch's spiritual "problem" found a coherent solution, one that can be said to express the Petrarchan vision and the humanist's religious and moral outlook.

It was therefore an evolution—both moral and literary—rather than a "crisis" that made Petrarch decide his love for Laura was love for the creature rather than for the Creator and therefore wrong—proof of his attachment to the world. It was an evolution in his thinking that led him to break through the barriers of his too-exclusive admiration for antiquity and to admit other authoritative voices. It was now, for example, that *De viris* was enlarged to include material from sacred as well as secular history, while in the *De vita solitaria* (1346) he developed the theoretical basis and description of the "solitary life" whereby man enjoys the consolations of nature and study together with those of prayer.

Break with His Past

The events of the next few years are fundamental to his biography, both as a man and as a writer. In the first place, he became enthusiastic for the efforts of Cola di Rienzo to revive the Roman Republic and restore popular government in Rome—a sympathy that divided him still more sharply from the Avignon court and in 1346 even led to the loss of Cardinal Colonna's friendship. The plague of 1348, known as the Black Death, saw many friends fall victim, including Laura, who died on April 6, the anniversary of Petrarch's first seeing her. Finally, in the jubilee year of 1350 he made a pilgrimage to Rome and later assigned to this year his renunciation of sensual pleasures.

These are the landmarks of Petrarch's career, but the time in between was filled with diplomatic missions, study, and immense literary activity. In Verona in 1345 he made his great discovery of the letters of Cicero to Atticus, Brutus, and Quintus. The letters spurred him on to write epistles to the ancient authors whom he loved and to make a collection of his own letters that he had scattered among his friends. These great collections record not only Petrarch's genius for friendship but also all those shifts in attitude by which he left behind the Middle Ages and prepared for the Renaissance. Toward the end of 1345 he returned again to the peace of Vaucluse and spent two years there, chiefly revising *De vita solitaria* but also developing the theme of solitude in a specifically monastic context, in *De otio religioso*. Between November 1347 and his pilgrimage to Rome in 1350 he was also in Verona, Parma, and Padua. Much of the time was spent in advancing his career in the church; the manoeuvring and animosities this involved resulted in an intense longing for the peace of Vaucluse; not even a visit from his lifelong friend the poet Giovanni Boccaccio, who offered him a chair to be established under his guidance in the University of Florence, could deflect him. He left Rome in May 1351 for Vaucluse.

Here he worked on a new plan for the *Rime*. The project was divided into two parts: the *Rime in vita di Laura* ("Poems During Laura's Life") and the *Rime in morte di Laura* ("Poems After Laura's Death"), which he now selected and arranged to illustrate the story of his own spiritual growth. The choice of poems was further governed by an exquisite aesthetic taste and by a preference for an approximately chronological arrangement, from the description of his falling in love to his final invocation to the Virgin; from his "youthful errors" to his realization that "all worldly pleasure is a fleeting dream"; from his love for this world to his final trust in God. The theme of his *Canzoniere* (as the poems are usually known) therefore goes beyond the apparent subject matter, his love for Laura. For the first time in the history of the new poetry, lyrics are held together in a marvellous new tapestry, possessing its own unity. By selecting all that was most polished and at the same time most vigorous in the lyric tradition of the preceding two centuries and filtering it through his new appreciation of the classics, he not only bequeathed to humanity the most limpid and yet passionate, precise yet suggestive, expression of love and grief, of the ecstasies and sorrows of man, but also created with his marvellous sensibility the form and language of the modern lyric, to provide a common stock for lyric poets of the whole of Europe.

He also continued work on the *Metricae*, begun in 1350; he embarked on a polemic against the conservative enemies of his new conception of education, which rejected the prevailing Aristotelianism of the schools and restored the spiritual worth of Classical writers — the new studies to be called *litterae humanae*, "humane letters." He also began work on his poem *Trionfi*, a more generalized version of the story of the human soul in its progress from earthly passion toward fulfillment in God.

Later Years

But the death of his closest friends, dislike of the newly elected pope, Innocent VI, and increasingly bitter relations with the Avignon court all finally convinced Petrarch to leave Provence. He found rooms in Milan and stayed there for most of the next eight years. During these eight years he also completed the first proper edition of the *Rime*, continued assiduously with the *Familiares*, worked on the *Trionfi*, and set in order many of his earlier writings.

Early in 1361 he went to Padua, hoping to escape the plague. He remained there until September 1362, when, again a fugitive from the Black Death, he sought shelter in Venice. He was given a house, and in return Petrarch promised to bequeath all his books to the republic. He was joined by his daughter Francesca, and the tranquil happiness of her little family gave him great pleasure. He was visited by his dearest and most famous friends (including the great chancellor Benintendi de' Ravegnani and Boccaccio, who presented him with a long-desired Latin translation of Homer's poems); he was invited to play an honourable part in the life and politics of the city; he worked peacefully but with great concentration at the definitive versions of his various writings. Nevertheless, after receiving an insult from four young men who followed the Arab "naturalist" interpretation of Aristotle's work, Petrarch was induced to move back to Padua in 1367. There he wrote the defense of his humanism against the critical attack from Venice, *De sui ipsius et multorum ignorantia*. He was still in great demand as a diplomat; in 1370 he was called to Rome by Urban V, and he set off eager to see the fulfillment of his great dream of a new Roman papacy, but at Ferrara he was seized by a stroke. Yet he did not stop working; in addition to revision he composed more minor works and added new sections to his *Posteritati*, an autobiographical letter to posterity that was to have formed the conclusion to his *Seniles*; he also composed the final sections of the *Trionfi*. Petrarch died in 1374 while working in his study at Arquà and was found the next morning, his head resting on a manuscript of Virgil.

GIOVANNI BOCCACCIO

(b. 1313, Paris, France—d. December 21, 1375, Certaldo, Tuscany [Italy])

The Italian poet and scholar Giovanni Boccaccio is best remembered as the author of the earthy tales in the *Decameron*. With Petrarch he laid the foundations for the humanism of the Renaissance and raised vernacular literature to the level and status of the classics of antiquity.

Youth

Boccaccio was the son of a Tuscan merchant, Boccaccio di Chellino (called Boccaccino), and a mother who was probably French. He passed his early childhood rather unhappily in Florence. His father had no sympathy for Boccaccio's literary inclinations and sent him, not later than 1328, to Naples to learn business, probably in an office of the Bardi, who dominated the court of Naples by means of their loans. In this milieu Boccaccio experienced the aristocracy of the commercial world as well as all that survived of the splendours of courtly chivalry and feudalism. He also studied canon law and mixed with the learned men of the court and the friends and admirers of Petrarch, through whom he came to know the work of Petrarch himself.

These years in Naples, moreover, were the years of Boccaccio's love for a Neopolitan woman, who dominates all his literary activity as the character Fiammetta up to the *Decameron*, in which there also appears a Fiammetta who somewhat resembles that of the Fiammetta of his earlier works. Attempts to use passages from Boccaccio's writings to identify Fiammetta with a supposedly historical Maria, natural daughter of King Robert and wife of a count of Aquino, are untrustworthy—the more so since there is no documentary proof that this Maria ever existed.

Early Works

It was probably in 1340 that Boccaccio was recalled to Florence by his father, involved in the bankruptcy of the Bardi. The sheltered period of his life thus came to an end, and thenceforward there were to be only difficulties and occasional periods of poverty. From Naples, however, the young Boccaccio brought with him a store of literary work already completed. *La caccia di Diana* ("Diana's Hunt"), his earliest work, is a short poem, in terza rima (an iambic verse consisting of stanzas of three lines), of no great merit. Much more important are two works with themes derived from medieval romances: *Il filocolo* (*c.* 1336; "The Love Afflicted"), a prose work in five books on the loves and adventures of Florio and Biancofiore (Floire and Blanchefleur); and *Il filostrato* (*c.* 1338; "The Love Struck"), a short poem in ottava rima (a stanza form composed of eight 11-syllable lines) telling the story of Troilus and the faithless Criseida. The *Teseida* (probably begun in Naples and finished in Florence, 1340–41) is an ambitious epic of 12 cantos in ottava rima in which the wars of Theseus serve as a background for the love of two friends, Arcita and Palemone, for the same woman, Emilia; Arcita finally wins her in a tournament but dies immediately.

While the themes of chivalry and love in these works had long been familiar in courtly circles, Boccaccio enriched them with the fruits of his own acute observation of real life and sought to present them nobly and illustriously by a display of learning and rhetorical ornament, so as to make his Italian worthy of comparison with the monuments of Latin literature. It was Boccaccio, too, who raised to literary dignity ottava rima, the verse metre of the popular minstrels, which was eventually to become the characteristic vehicle for Italian verse. Boccaccio's early works had an immediate effect outside Italy: Geoffrey Chaucer drew inspiration from *Il filostrato* for his own *Troilus and Criseyde* (as William Shakespeare was later to do for *Troilus and Cressida*) and from Boccaccio's *Teseida* for his "Knight's Tale" in *The Canterbury Tales*.

The 10 or 12 years following Boccaccio's return to Florence are the period of his full maturity, culminating in the *Decameron*. From 1341 to 1345 he worked on *Il ninfale d'Ameto* ("Ameto's Story of the Nymphs"), in prose and terza rima; *L'amorosa visione* ("The Amorous Vision"; 1342–43), a mediocre allegorical poem of 50 short cantos in terza rima; the prose *Elegia di Madonna Fiammetta* (1343–44); and the poem *Il ninfale fiesolano* (perhaps 1344–45; "Tale of the Fiesole Nymph"), in ottava rima, on the love of the shepherd Africo for the nymph Mensola.

The Decameron

It was probably in the years 1348–53 that Boccaccio composed the *Decameron* in the form in which it is read today. In the broad sweep of its range and its alternately tragic and comic views of life, it is rightly regarded as his masterpiece. Stylistically, it is the most perfect example of Italian classical prose, and its influence on Renaissance literature throughout Europe was enormous.

The *Decameron* begins with the flight of 10 young people (7 women and 3 men) from plague-stricken Florence in 1348. They retire to a rich, well-watered countryside, where, in the course of a fortnight, each member of the party has a turn as king or queen over the others, deciding in detail how their day shall be spent and directing their leisurely walks, their outdoor conversations, their dances and songs, and, above all, their alternate storytelling. This storytelling occupies 10 days of the fortnight (the rest being set aside for personal adornment or for religious devotions); hence the title of the book itself, *Decameron*, or "Ten Days' Work." The stories thus amount to 100 in all. Each of the days, moreover, ends with a *canzone* (song) for dancing sung by one of the storytellers, and these *canzoni* include some of Boccaccio's finest lyric poetry. In addition to the 100 stories, Boccaccio has a master theme, namely, the way of life of the refined bourgeoisie, who combined respect for conventions with an open-minded attitude to personal behaviour.

The sombre tones of the opening passages of the book, in which the plague and the moral and social chaos that accompanies it are described in the grand manner, are in sharp contrast to the scintillating liveliness of Day I, which is spent almost entirely in witty disputation, and to the playful atmosphere of intrigue that characterizes the tales of adventure or deception related on Days II and III. With Day IV and its stories of unhappy love, the gloomy note returns; but Day V brings some relief, though it does not entirely dissipate the echo of solemnity, by giving happy endings to stories of love that does not at first run smoothly. Day VI reintroduces the gaiety of Day I and constitutes the overture to the great comic score, Days VII, VIII, and IX, which are given over to laughter, trickery, and license. Finally, in Day X, all the themes of the preceding days are brought to a high pitch, the impure made pure and the common made heroic.

The prefaces to the days and to the individual stories and certain passages of especial magnificence based on classical models, with their select vocabulary and elaborate periods, have long held the attention of critics. But there is also another Boccaccio: the master of the spoken word and of the swift, vivid, tense narrative free from the proliferation of ornament. These two aspects of the *Decameron* made it the fountainhead of Italian literary prose for the following centuries.

The whole corpus of Boccaccio's work is basically medieval in subject matter, form, and taste, at least in its point of departure. It is the spirit in which Boccaccio treats his subjects and his forms that is new. For the first time in the Middle Ages, Boccaccio in the *Decameron* deliberately shows humans striving with fortune and learning to overcome it. To be truly noble, according to the *Decameron*, individuals must accept life as it is, without bitterness, must accept, above all, the consequences of their actions, however contrary to expectation or even tragic those actions may be. To realize earthly happiness, a person must confine his desire to what is humanly possible and renounce the absolute without regret. Thus Boccaccio insists both on an individual's powers and on the inescapable limitations of those powers, without reference to the possible intervention of divine grace. A sense of spiritual realities and an affirmation of moral values underlying the frivolity even in the most licentious passages of the *Decameron* are features of Boccaccio's work that modern critics have brought to light and that make it no longer possible to regard him only as an obscene mocker or sensual cynic.

During the years in which Boccaccio is believed to have written the *Decameron*, the Florentines appointed him ambassador to the lords of Romagna in 1350; municipal councillor and also ambassador to Louis, duke of Bavaria, in the Tirol in 1351; and ambassador to Pope Innocent VI in 1354.

Petrarch and Boccaccio's Mature Years

Of far more lasting importance than official honours was Boccaccio's first meeting with Petrarch, in Florence in 1350, which helped to bring about a decisive change in Boccaccio's literary activity. Boccaccio revered the older man as his master, and Petrarch proved himself a serene and ready counselor and a reliable helper. Together, through the exchange of books, news, and ideas, the two men laid the foundations for the humanist reconquest of classical antiquity.

After the *Decameron*, of which Petrarch remained in ignorance until the very last years of his life, Boccaccio wrote nothing in Italian except *Il Corbaccio* (1354–55; a satire on a widow who had jilted him), his late writings on Dante, and perhaps an occasional lyric. Turning instead to Latin, he devoted himself to humanist scholarship rather than to imaginative or poetic creation. His encyclopaedic *De genealogia deorum gentilium* ("On the Genealogy of the Gods of the Gentiles"), medieval in structure but humanist in spirit, was probably begun in the very year of his meeting with Petrarch but was continuously corrected and revised until his death. His *Bucolicum carmen* (1351–66), a series of allegorical eclogues (short pastoral poems) on contemporary events, follows classical models on lines already indicated by Dante and Petrarch.

The meeting with Petrarch, however, was not the only cause of the change in Boccaccio's writing. A premature weakening of his physical powers and disappointments in love may also have contributed to it. Some such occurrence would explain how Boccaccio, having previously written always in praise of women and love, came suddenly to write the bitterly misogynistic *Corbaccio* and then turn his genius elsewhere. Furthermore, there are signs that he may have begun to feel religious scruples. Petrarch describes how the Carthusian monk Pietro Petrone, on his deathbed in 1362, sent another Carthusian, Gioacchino Ciani, to exhort Boccaccio to renounce his worldly studies; and it was Petrarch who then dissuaded Boccaccio from burning his own works and selling his library. As early as 1360, moreover, Boccaccio's way of life was regarded as austere enough to justify his being entrusted with a pastoral cure of souls in a cathedral. He had taken minor orders many years earlier, perhaps at first only in the hope of being given benefices.

Last Years

All of Boccaccio's studies were pursued in poverty, sometimes almost in destitution, and he had to earn most of his income by transcribing his own works or those of others. In 1363 poverty compelled him to retire to the village of Certaldo. In October 1373, however, he began public readings of Dante's *Divina commedia* in the Church of San Stefano di Badia in Florence. A revised text of the commentary that he gave with these readings is still extant but breaks off at the point that he had reached when, early in 1374, ill health made him lose heart. Petrarch's death in July 1374 was another grief to him, and he retired again to Certaldo. There Boccaccio died the following year and was buried in the Church of SS. Michele e Jacopo.

ḤĀFEẒ

(b. 1325/26, Shīrāz, Iran—d. 1389/90, Shīrāz)

Mohammad Shams al-Dīn Ḥāfeẓ (also spelled Ḥāfiz) was one of the finest lyric poets of Persia.

Ḥāfeẓ received a classical religious education, lectured on Qur'ānic and other theological subjects ("Ḥāfeẓ" designates one who has learned the Qur'ān [also spelled Koran] by heart), and wrote commentaries on religious classics. As a court poet, he enjoyed the patronage of several rulers of Shīrāz.

About 1368–69 Ḥāfeẓ fell out of favour at the court and did not regain his position until 20 years later, just before his death. In his poetry there are many echoes of historical events as well as biographical descriptions and details of life in Shīrāz. One of the guiding principles of his life was Sufism, the Islamic mystical movement that demanded of its adherents complete devotion to the pursuit of union with the ultimate reality.

Ḥāfeẓ's principal verse form, one that he brought to a perfection never achieved before or since, was the ghazal, a lyric poem of 6 to 15 couplets linked by unity of subject and symbolism rather than by a logical sequence of ideas. Traditionally the ghazal had dealt with love and wine, motifs that, in their association with ecstasy and freedom from restraint, lent themselves naturally to the expression of Sufi ideas. Ḥāfeẓ's achievement was to give these conventional subjects a freshness and subtlety that completely relieves his poetry of tedious formalism. An important innovation credited to Ḥāfeẓ was the use of the ghazal instead of the qasida (ode) in panegyrics. Ḥāfeẓ also reduced the panegyric element of his poems to a mere one or two lines, leaving the remainder of the poem for his ideas. The extraordinary popularity of Ḥāfeẓ's poetry in all Persian-speaking lands stems from his simple and often colloquial though musical language, free from artificial virtuosity, and his unaffected use of homely images and proverbial expressions. Above all, his poetry is characterized by love of humanity, contempt for hypocrisy and mediocrity, and an ability to universalize everyday experience and to relate it to the mystic's unending search for union with God. His appeal in the West is indicated by the numerous translations of his poems. Ḥāfeẓ is most famous for his *Dīvān*.

WILLIAM LANGLAND

(b. *c.* 1330 — d. *c.* 1400)

William Langland is the presumed author of one of the greatest examples of Middle English alliterative poetry, generally known as *Piers Plowman*, an allegorical work with a complex variety of religious themes. One of the major achievements of *Piers Plowman* is that it translates the language and conceptions of the cloister into symbols and images that could be understood by the layman. In general, the language of the poem is simple and colloquial, but some of the author's imagery is powerful and direct.

There were originally thought to be three versions of *Piers Plowman*: the A version of the text, which was the earliest, followed by the B and C versions that consisted of revisions and further amplifications of the major themes of A. However, a fourth version, called Z, has been suggested and the order of issue questioned. The version described here is from the B text, which consists of (1) a prologue and seven passus (divisions) concerned primarily with the life of man in society, the dangers of Meed (love of gain), and manifestations of the seven capital sins; and (2) 13 passus ostensibly dealing with the lives of three characters who have the phonically revelatory names of Do-wel, Do-bet, and Do-best. In effect, the text explores the growth of the individual Christian in self-knowledge, grace, and charity.

In its general structure the poem mirrors the complexity of the themes with which it deals, particularly in the recurring concepts of Do-wel, Do-bet, and Do-best, all in the end seen as embodied in Christ. They are usually identified with the active, contemplative, and "mixed" religious life, but the allegory of the poem is often susceptible to more than one interpretation, and some critics have related it to the traditional exegetical (explanatory) way of interpreting the Scriptures historically, allegorically, anagogically, and topologically.

Little is known of Langland's life: he is thought to have been born somewhere in the region of the Malvern Hills, in Worcestershire, and if he is to be identified with the "dreamer" of the poem, he may have been educated at the Benedictine school in Great Malvern. References in the poem suggest that he knew London and Westminster as well as Shropshire, and he may have been a cleric in minor orders in London.

Langland clearly had a deep knowledge of medieval theology and was fully committed to all the implications of Christian doctrine. He was interested in the asceticism of St. Bernard of Clairvaux, and his comments on the defects of churchmen and the religious in his day are nonetheless concomitant with his orthodoxy.

JOHN GOWER

(b. 1330?—d. 1408, London?)

A medieval English poet in the tradition of courtly love and moral allegory, John Gower strongly influenced the writing of other poets of his day. His reputation once matched that of his contemporary and friend Geoffrey Chaucer, but after the 16th century his popularity waned and interest in him did not revive until the middle of the 20th century.

It is thought from Gower's language that he was of Kentish origin, though his family may have come from Yorkshire, and he was clearly a man of some wealth. Allusions in his poetry and other documents, however, indicate that he knew London well and was probably a court official. At one point, he professed acquaintance with Richard II, and in 1399 he was granted two pipes (casks) of wine a year for life by Henry IV as a reward for complimentary references in one of his poems. In 1397, living as a layman in the priory of St. Mary Overie, Southwark, London, Gower married Agnes Groundolf, who survived him. In 1400 Gower described himself as "senex et cecus" ("old and blind"), and on October 24, 1408, his will was proved; he left bequests to the Southwark priory, where he is buried.

Gower's three major works are in French, English, and Latin, and he also wrote a series of French *balades* intended for the English court. The *Speculum meditantis*, or *Mirour de l'omme*, in French, is composed of 12-line stanzas and opens impressively with a description of the devil's marriage to the seven daughters of sin; continuing with the marriage of reason and the seven virtues, it ends with a searing examination of the sins of English society just before the Peasants' Revolt of 1381: the denunciatory tone is relieved at the very end by a long hymn to the Virgin.

Gower's major Latin poem, the *Vox clamantis*, owes much to Ovid; it is essentially a homily (short sermon), being in part a criticism of the three estates of society, in part a mirror for a prince, in elegiac form. The poet's political doctrines are traditional, but he uses the Latin language with fluency and elegance.

Gower's English poems include *In Praise of Peace*, in which he pleads urgently with the king to avoid the horrors of war, but his greatest English work is the *Confessio amantis (The Lover's Confession)*, essentially a collection of exemplary tales of love, whereby Venus's priest, Genius, instructs the poet, Amans, in the art of both courtly and Christian love. The stories are chiefly adapted from classical and medieval sources and are told with a tenderness and the restrained narrative art that constitute Gower's main appeal today.

JEAN FROISSART

(b. 1333?, Valenciennes, Brabant—d. *c.* 1400, Chimay, Hainaut)

Jean Froissart was a medieval poet and court historian whose *Chronicles* of the 14th century remain the most important and detailed document of feudal times in Europe and the best contemporary exposition of chivalric and courtly ideals.

As a scholar, Froissart lived among the nobility of several European courts. In England he served Queen Philippa of Hainaut, King Edward III, and his sons the Black Prince and the Duke of Clarence. He became the chaplain of Guy II de Chatillon, comte de Blois, under

Battle of Sluys during the Hundred Years' War, illustration from Jean Froissart's Chronicles, *14th century.* Universal Images Group/ Getty Images

whose auspices he was ordained canon of Chimay. He travelled to Scotland, Italy, France, and the Iberian Peninsula.

The main subject of Froissart's *Chronicles* was the "honourable adventures and feats of arms" of the Hundred Years' War. He used his privileged position to question central figures and observe key events. The firsthand narrative covers weddings, funerals, and great battles from 1325 to 1400. Book I was based on the work of the Flemish writer Jean le Bel and later rewritten. Book II concerns the events in Flanders and the Peace of Tournai. Book III concerns Spain and Portugal. Book IV is based on the

Battle of Poitiers and a final visit to England, where he was shocked by the weakness of the royal government.

Froissart cites exact dialogues and all available facts, allowing readers to draw their own conclusions. The splendour and pageantry are emphasized, however, according to the courtly traditions of his patrons, while the victims and causes of suffering are overlooked. A didactic moral tone urges readers to aspire to the ideals of chivalry. While the *Chronicles* contain historical errors and lapses of judgment, they are the best information available to modern readers interested in the 14th century.

Froissart's allegorical poetry celebrates courtly love. *L'Horloge amoureux* compares the heart to a clock, and *Méliador* is a chivalrous romance. His ballades and rondeaux expose the poet's personal feelings. Despite his fame during his lifetime, Froissart apparently died in obscurity.

GEOFFREY CHAUCER

(b. *c.* 1342/43, London?, England—d. October 25, 1400, London)

The outstanding English poet before Shakespeare and "the first finder of our language," Geoffrey Chaucer is the author of *The Canterbury Tales*, which ranks as one of the greatest poetic works in English. He also contributed importantly in the second half of the 14th century to the management of public affairs as courtier, diplomat, and civil servant.

Early Years

Although *c.* 1340 is customarily given as Chaucer's birth date, 1342 or 1343 is probably a closer guess. No information exists concerning his early education, although

Geoffrey Chaucer, from the 15th-century Ellesmere manuscript of The Canterbury Tales. *Photos.com/Thinkstock*

doubtless he would have been as fluent in French as in the Middle English of his time. He also became competent in Latin and Italian.

Chaucer first appears in the records in 1357, as a member of the household of Elizabeth, countess of Ulster, wife of Lionel, third son of Edward III. Geoffrey's father presumably had been able to place him among the group of young men and women serving in that royal household, a customary arrangement whereby families who could do so provided their children with opportunity for the necessary courtly education and connections to advance their careers. By 1359 Chaucer was a member of Edward III's army in France and was captured during the unsuccessful siege of Reims. The king contributed to his ransom, and Chaucer served as messenger from Calais to England during the peace negotiations of 1360. Chaucer does not appear in any contemporary record during 1361–65. On February 22, 1366, the king of Navarre issued a certificate of safe-conduct for Chaucer, three companions, and their servants to enter Spain. This occasion is the first of a number of diplomatic missions to the continent of Europe over the succeeding 10 years, and the wording of the document suggests that here Chaucer served as "chief of mission."

By 1366 Chaucer had married. Probably his wife was Philippa Pan, who had been in the service of the countess of Ulster and entered the service of Philippa of Hainaut, queen consort of Edward III, when Elizabeth died in 1363. In 1366 Philippa Chaucer received an annuity, and later annuities were frequently paid to her through her husband. These and other facts indicate that Chaucer married well.

In 1367 Chaucer received an annuity (annual payment) for life as yeoman of the king, and in the next year he was listed among the king's esquires. Such officers lived at court and performed staff duties of considerable importance. In 1368 Chaucer was abroad on a diplomatic mission, and in 1369 he was on military service in France. Also in 1369 he and his wife were official mourners for the death of Queen Philippa. Obviously, Chaucer's career was prospering, and his first important poem—*Book of the Duchess*—seems further evidence of his connection with persons in high places.

That poem of more than 1,300 lines, probably written in late 1369 or early 1370, is an elegy for Blanche, duchess of Lancaster, John of Gaunt's first wife, who died of plague in September 1369. Chaucer's close relationship with John, which continued through most of his life, may have commenced as early as Christmas 1357 when they, both about the same age, were present at the countess of Ulster's residence in Yorkshire. For this first of his important poems, Chaucer used the dream-vision form, a genre made popular by the highly influential 13th-century French poem of courtly love, the *Roman de la rose (The Romance of the Rose)*. In addition, the *Duchess* foreshadows Chaucer's skill at presenting the rhythms of natural conversation within the confines of Middle English verse and at creating realistic characters within courtly poetic conventions.

Diplomat and Civil Servant

During the decade of the 1370s, Chaucer was at various times on diplomatic missions in Flanders, France, and Italy. Several times during the 1370s, Chaucer and his wife received generous monetary grants from the king and from John of Gaunt. On May 10, 1374, he obtained rent-free a dwelling above Aldgate, in London, and on June 8 of that year he was appointed comptroller of the customs and subsidy of wools, skins, and tanned hides for the Port of London. In 1375 he was granted two wardships, which paid well, and in 1376 he received a sizable sum from a fine. When Richard II became king in June 1377, he confirmed Chaucer's comptrollership and, later, the annuities granted by Edward III to both Geoffrey and Philippa.

Chaucer's most important work of the 1370s was *Hous of Fame*, a poem of more than 2,000 lines, also in dream-vision form. In some ways it is a failure—it is unfinished, its theme is unclear, and the diversity of its parts seems to overshadow any unity of purpose—but it gives considerable evidence of Chaucer's advancing skill as a poet. The eight-syllable metre is handled with great flexibility; the light, bantering, somewhat ironic tone—later to become one of Chaucer's chief effects—is established; and a wide variety of subject matter is included.

The Middle Years: Political and Personal Anxieties

Chaucer continued to work at the Customs House, and in 1382 he was additionally appointed comptroller of the petty customs for wine and other merchandise, but in October 1386 his dwelling in London was leased to another man, and in December of that year successors were named for both of his comptrollerships in the customs; whether he resigned or was removed from office is not clear. In October 1385 he was appointed a justice of the peace for Kent, and in August 1386 he became knight of the shire for Kent, to attend Parliament in October. Philippa Chaucer apparently died in 1387.

The period 1386–89 was clearly difficult for Chaucer. Although he was reappointed justice of the peace for 1387, he was not returned to Parliament after 1386. In 1388 a series of suits against him for debts began, and he sold his royal pension for a lump sum. Also, from February 3 to June 4, 1388, the so-called Merciless Parliament, controlled by the barons, caused many leading members of the court party—some of them Chaucer's close friends—to be executed. In May 1389, however, the 23-year-old King Richard II regained control, ousted his enemies, and began appointing his supporters to office. Almost certainly, Chaucer owed his next public office to that political change. On July 12, 1389, he was appointed clerk of the king's works, with executive responsibility for repair and maintenance of royal buildings.

Although political events of the 1380s, from the Peasants' Revolt of 1381 through the Merciless Parliament of 1388, must have kept Chaucer steadily anxious, he produced a sizable body of writings during this decade, some of very high order. Surprisingly, these works do not in any way reflect the tense political scene. Indeed, one is tempted to speculate that during this period Chaucer turned to his reading and writing as escape from the difficulties of his public life. *The Parlement of Foules*, a poem of 699 lines, is a dream-vision for St. Valentine's Day. Beneath its playfully humorous tone, it seems to examine the value of various kinds of love within the context of "common profit" as set forth in the introductory abstract from the *Somnium Scipionis* (*The Dream of Scipio*) of Cicero. The narrator searches unsuccessfully for an answer and concludes that he must continue his search in other books.

The *Consolation of Philosophy*, written by the Roman philosopher Boethius (early 6th century), a Christian, was one of the most influential of medieval books. Its discussion of free will, God's foreknowledge, destiny, fortune, and true and false happiness had a deep and lasting effect upon Chaucer's thought and art. His prose translation of the *Consolation* is carefully done, and in his next poem—*Troilus and Criseyde*—the influence of Boethius's book is pervasive.

Some critics consider *Troilus and Criseyde* Chaucer's finest work, greater even than the far more widely read

Canterbury Tales. But the two works are so different that comparative evaluation seems fruitless. The state of the surviving manuscripts of *Troilus* shows Chaucer's detailed effort in revising this poem. Against the background of the legendary Trojan War, the love story of Troilus, son of the Trojan king Priam, and Criseyde, widowed daughter of the deserter priest Calkas, is recounted. The poem moves in leisurely fashion, with introspection and much of what would now be called psychological insight dominating many sections. Aided by Criseyde's uncle Pandarus, Troilus and Criseyde are united in love about halfway through the poem; but then she is sent to join her father in the Greek camp outside Troy. Despite her promise to return, she gives her love to the Greek Diomede, and Troilus, left in despair, is killed in the war. These events are interspersed with Boethian discussion of free will and determinism. At the end of the poem, when Troilus's soul rises into the heavens, the folly of complete immersion in sexual love is viewed in relation to the eternal love of God. The effect of the poem is controlled throughout by the direct comments of the narrator, whose sympathy for the lovers—especially for Criseyde—is ever present.

Also in the 1380s Chaucer produced his fourth and final dream-vision poem, *The Legend of Good Women*, which is not a success. Perhaps the most important fact about the *Legend* is that it shows Chaucer structuring a long poem as a collection of stories within a framework. Seemingly the static nature of the framing device for the *Legend* and the repetitive aspect of the series of stories with a single theme led him to give up this attempt as a poor job. But the failure here must have contributed to his brilliant choice, probably about this same time, of a pilgrimage as the framing device for the stories in *The Canterbury Tales*.

Last Years and The Canterbury Tales

Chaucer's service as clerk of the king's works lasted only from July 1389 to June 1391, when he was appointed sub-forester of the king's park in North Petherton, Somerset, an office that he held until his death. The records show his close relationship during 1395–96 with John of Gaunt's son, the earl of Derby, later King Henry IV. The new king confirmed Chaucer's grants from Richard II and added an additional generous annuity. In December 1399 Chaucer took a lease on a house in the garden of Westminster Abbey. But in October of the following year he died. He was buried in the Abbey, a signal honour for a commoner.

Chaucer's great literary accomplishment of the 1390s was *The Canterbury Tales*. In it a group of about 30 pilgrims gather at the Tabard Inn in Southwark, across the Thames from London, and agree to engage in a storytelling contest as they travel on horseback to the shrine of Thomas à Becket in Canterbury, Kent, and back. Interspersed between the 24 tales told by the pilgrims are short dramatic scenes presenting lively exchanges, called links and usually involving the host and one or more of the pilgrims. Chaucer did not complete the full plan for his book: the return journey from Canterbury is not included, and some of the pilgrims do not tell stories. The work is nevertheless sufficiently complete to be considered a unified book rather than a collection of unfinished fragments. Use of a pilgrimage as a framing device for the collection of stories enabled Chaucer to bring together people from many walks of life: knight, prioress (nun), monk; merchant, man of law, franklin (landowner of free but not noble birth), scholarly clerk; miller, reeve (administrator to the king), pardoner; wife of Bath and many others. Also, the pilgrimage and the storytelling contest allowed presentation of a highly varied collection of literary genres: courtly romance, racy fabliau, saint's life, allegorical tale, beast fable, medieval sermon, alchemical account, and, at times, mixtures of these genres. Because of this structure, the sketches, the links, and the tales all fuse as complex presentations of the pilgrims, while at the same time the tales present remarkable examples of short stories in verse, plus two expositions in prose. In addition, the pilgrimage, combining a fundamentally religious purpose with its secular aspect of vacation in the spring, made possible extended consideration of the relationship between the pleasures and vices of this world and the spiritual aspirations for the next, that seeming dichotomy with which Chaucer, like Boethius and many other medieval writers, was so steadily concerned.

Over the whole expanse of this intricate dramatic narrative, he presides as Chaucer the poet, Chaucer the civil servant, and Chaucer the pilgrim: somewhat slow-witted in his pose and always intrigued by human frailty but always questioning the complexity of the human condition and always seeing both the humour and the tragedy in that condition. At the end, in the Retractation with which *The Canterbury Tales* closes, Chaucer as poet and pilgrim states his conclusion that the concern for this world fades into insignificance before the prospect for the next; in view of the admonitions in The Parson's Tale, he asks forgiveness for his writings that concern "worldly vanities" and remembrance for his translation of the *Consolation* and his other works of morality and religious devotion. On that note he ends his finest work and his career as poet.

ZEAMI

(b. 1363, Japan—d. September 1, 1443, Kyōto?)

Zeami (also spelled Seami) is the greatest playwright and theorist of the Japanese Noh theatre. (Noh dramas present classic Japanese legends using movement, music, and words.) Zeami and his father, Kan'ami (1333–84), were the creators of the Noh drama in its present form.

Under the patronage of the shogun Ashikaga Yoshimitsu, whose favour Zeami enjoyed after performing before him in 1374, the Noh was able to shake off the crudities of its past and to develop as a complex and aristocratic theatre. After his father's death, Zeami became the chief figure in the Noh. He directed the Kanze school of Noh that his father had established and that had profound and lasting influence. Zeami not only continued to perform brilliantly but also wrote and revised plays prolifically. He is credited with about 90 (and most of the greatest) of the approximately 230 plays in the present repertoire. In 1422 he became a Zen monk, and his son Motomasa succeeded him. But Ashikaga Yoshinori, who became shogun (military governor) in 1429, favoured On'ami (Zeami's nephew) and refused to allow the son to perform before him. Motomasa died in 1432, and Yoshinori exiled Zeami to the island of Sado in 1434. After the shogun died in 1441, Zeami returned to Kyōto.

In his treatises—of which the most important is the collection *Fūshi kaden* (1400–18; "The Transmission of the Flower of Acting Style," also known as the *Kaden sho*), "flower" representing the freshness and appropriateness of fine acting—written as manuals for his pupils, Zeami said the actor must master three basic roles: the warrior, the woman, and the old person, including the singing and dancing appropriate to each. The two main elements in Noh acting were *monomane*, "an imitation of things," or the representational aspect, and *yūgen*, the symbolic aspect and spiritual core of the Noh, which took precedence and which became the touchstone of excellence in the Noh. Zeami wrote, "The essence of *yūgen* is true beauty and gentleness," but not mere outward beauty: it had to suggest behind the text of the plays and the noble gestures of the actors a world impossible to define yet ultimately real. Such plays as *Matsukaze*, written by Kan'ami and adapted by Zeami, have a mysterious stillness that seems to envelop the visible or audible parts of the work. In other of Zeami's dramas there is less *yūgen* and more action and, occasionally, even realism.

ANONYMOUS: SIR GAWAYNE THE GRENE KNIGHT

Sir Gawayne and the Grene Knight (also spelled *Sir Gawain and the Green Knight*) is a Middle English alliterative poem of unknown authorship, dating from the second half of the 14th century (perhaps 1375). It is a chivalric romance that tells a tale of enchantment in an Arthurian setting. Its hero, Sir Gawayne (Gawain), is presented as a devout but humanly imperfect Christian who wins a test of arms, resists temptation by a lord's wife, but succumbs to an offer of invulnerability.

The poem is technically brilliant. Its alliterative lines (some 2,500) are broken up into irregular stanzas by short rhyming passages; they are tautly constructed, and the vocabulary is astonishingly rich—influenced by French in the scenes at court but strengthened by many dialect words, often of Scandinavian origin, that belonged to northwest England. The blend of sophisticated atmosphere, psychological depth, and vivid language produces an effect superior to that found in any other work of the time.

Preserved in the same manuscript with *Sir Gawayne* were three other poems, now generally accepted as the work of its author. These are two alliterative poems of moral teaching, *Patience* and *Purity*, and an intricate elegiac poem, *Pearl*. The author of *Sir Gawayne* and the other poems is frequently referred to as "the Pearl Poet."

ALAIN CHARTIER

(b. *c.* 1385, Bayeux, Normandy, France—d. *c.* 1433, Avignon, Provence?)

The French poet and political writer Alain Chartier wrote in a didactic, elegant, and Latinate style that was regarded as a model by succeeding generations of poets and prose writers.

Educated at the University of Paris, Chartier entered the royal service, acting as secretary and notary to both Charles VI and the dauphin, later Charles VII. He carried out various diplomatic missions for Charles VII, and in 1428 he was sent to Scotland to negotiate the marriage of Margaret of Scotland with the future Louis XI.

His work, written mainly from 1415 to 1430, is distinguished by its variety of subject matter and form. Chartier was a poet, orator, historian, moralist, and pamphleteer who wrote in Latin and French. His earliest-known poem, the *Livre des quatre dames* (1415 or 1416; "Book of the Four Ladies"), is a discussion among four ladies who have lost their lovers at the Battle of Agincourt. The same technique is used in the prose *Quadrilogue invectif*, written in 1422, the dialogue being between France and the three estates of the realm (clergy, nobility, and commoners). This work exposes the sufferings of the peasantry, the misdeeds of the church, and the abuses of the feudal army but maintains that France could yet be saved if the kingdom's contending factions would lay aside their differences in the face of the common enemy.

Chartier's poems are mostly allegories in the courtly tradition but show the influence of his classical learning in their frequent Latinisms. They include *La Belle Dame sans merci* ("The Beautiful Lady Without Mercy"), *Le Lay de paix* ("The Lay of Peace"), and *Le Bréviaire des nobles* (roughly, "The Nobleman's Prayerbook"), the first of which, a tale of unrequited love, is the best known and was translated into English in the 15th century.

Leon Battista Alberti

(b. February 14, 1404, Genoa—d. April 25, 1472, Rome)

Leon Battista Alberti was an Italian humanist, architect, and principal initiator of Renaissance art theory. In his personality, works, and breadth of learning, he is considered the prototype of the Renaissance "universal man."

Childhood and Education

The society and class into which Alberti was born endowed him with the intellectual and moral tendencies he was to articulate and develop over a lifetime. He belonged to one of the wealthy merchant-banker families of Florence. At the time of his birth, the Alberti were in exile, expelled from Florence by the oligarchical government then dominated by the Albizzi family. Alberti's father, Lorenzo, was managing the family's concerns in Genoa, where Battista was born. Shortly thereafter he moved to Venice, where he raised Battista (Leo or Leon was a name adopted in later life) and his elder brother, Carlo.

It was from his father that Battista received his mathematical training. The useful intellectual tools of the businessman inspired in him a lifelong love for the regular, for rational order, and a lasting delight in the practical application of mathematical principles. As in Leonardo da Vinci's case, mathematics led Alberti into several seemingly disparate fields of learning and practice. At one stroke, it resolved a diversity of problems and awakened an appreciation of the rational structure and processes of the physical world.

His early formal education was humanistic. At the age of 10 or 11, Alberti was sent to boarding school in Padua. There he was given classical Latin training that was largely literary, and Alberti emerged from the school an accomplished Latinist and literary stylist. Relishing his skill as a classicist, he wrote a Latin comedy at the age of 20 that was acclaimed as the "discovered" work of a Roman playwright—and was still published as a Roman work in 1588 by the famous Venetian press of Aldus Manutius. But it was the content rather than the form of the classical authors that absorbed Alberti as a youth and throughout his life. As for most humanists, the literature of ancient Rome opened up for him the vision of an urbane, secular, and rational world that seemed remarkably similar to the emerging life of the Italian cities and met its cultural needs. He brought his own emotional and intellectual tendencies to "the ancients," but from them he drew the conceptual substance of his thought.

Alberti completed his formal education at the University of Bologna in an apparently joyless study of law. After receiving his doctorate in canon law in 1428, he chose to accept a "literary" position as a secretary rather than pursue a legal career. By 1432 he was a secretary in the Papal Chancery in Rome (which supported several humanists), and he had a commission from a highly placed ecclesiastical patron to rewrite the traditional lives of the saints and martyrs in elegant "classical" Latin. From this point on, the church was to provide him with his livelihood. He took holy orders, thus receiving in addition to his stipend as a papal secretary an ecclesiastical benefice, the priory of Gangalandi in the diocese of Florence, and some years later Nicholas V conferred upon him as well the rectory of Borgo San Lorenzo in Mugello. Although he led an exemplary, and apparently a celibate, life, there is almost nothing in his subsequent career to remind one of the fact that Alberti was a churchman. His interests and activities were wholly secular and began to issue in an impressive series of humanistic and technical writings.

Contribution to Philosophy, Science, and the Arts

The treatise "Della famiglia" ("On the Family"), which he began in Rome in 1432, is the first of several dialogues on moral philosophy upon which his reputation as an ethical thinker and literary stylist largely rests. He wrote these dialogues in the vernacular, expressly for a broad urban public that would not be skilled in Latin: for the *non litteratissimi cittadini*, as he called them. Based upon classical models, chiefly Cicero and Seneca, these works brought to the day-to-day concerns of a bourgeois society the reasonable counsel of the ancients—on the fickleness of fortune, on meeting adversity and prosperity, on husbandry, on friendship and family, on education and obligation to the common good. They are didactic and derivative, yet fresh with the tone and life-style of the Quattrocento (the 1400s). In Alberti's dialogues the ethical ideals of the ancient world are made to foster a distinctively modern outlook: a morality founded upon the idea of work. Virtue has become a matter of action, not of right thinking. It arises not out of serene detachment but out of striving, labouring, producing.

The basilica of the Church of San Andrea in Mantua, Italy, designed by Leon Battista Alberti. Alinari Archives/Getty Images

This ethic of achievement, which corresponds to the social reality of his youth, found ready acceptance in the urban society of central and northern Italy in which Alberti moved after 1434. Travelling with the papal court of Eugenius IV to Florence (the ban of exile against his family was lifted with the restoration of Medici influence), Bologna, and Ferrara, Alberti made several congenial and fruitful contacts. The writings, both the Latin and vernacular ones, that he dedicated to his new associates are imbued with his characteristic notions of work, practice, and productive activity.

At the Este court in Ferrara, where Alberti was first made a welcome guest in 1438, the Marchese Leonello encouraged (and commissioned) him to direct his talents toward another field of endeavour: architecture. Alberti's earliest effort at reviving classical forms of building still stands in Ferrara, a miniature triumphal arch that supports an equestrian statue of Leonello's father. Leonello inspired a great humanistic undertaking as well as a mode of artistic practice on Alberti's part by urging him to restore the classic text of Vitruvius, architect and architectural theorist of the age of the Roman emperor Augustus. With customary thoroughness, Alberti embarked upon a study of the architectural and engineering practices of antiquity that he continued when he returned to Rome in 1443 with the papal court. By the time Nicholas V became pope in 1447, Alberti was knowledgeable enough to become the Pope's architectural adviser. The collaboration between Alberti and Nicholas V gave rise to the first grandiose building projects of Renaissance Rome, initiating among other works the reconstruction of St. Peter's and the Vatican Palace. As the Este prince was now dead, it was to Nicholas V that Alberti dedicated in 1452 the monumental theoretical result of his long study of Vitruvius. This was his *De re aedificatoria*

(*Ten Books on Architecture*), not a restored text of Vitruvius but a wholly new work, that won him his reputation as the "Florentine Vitruvius." It became a bible of Renaissance architecture, for it incorporated and made advances upon the engineering knowledge of antiquity, and it grounded the stylistic principles of classical art in a fully developed aesthetic theory of proportionality and harmony.

In all his projects, Alberti employed his intellectual gifts in some "useful" work—useful to the artistic, cultivated, and courtly circles in which he moved, including painters and builders, mapmakers and astronomers, humanists, princes, and popes. In all of his work, his versatility remained bound to the social outlook that characterized the "civic Humanism" of Florence.

It is fitting that his final and finest dialogue should be set in Florence and be written in the clear Tuscan prose he had helped to regularize and refine. Although the republicanism of Florence was now eclipsed, and Alberti now moved as a familiar in the circle of the princely Lorenzo de' Medici, *De iciarchia* ("On the Man of Excellence and Ruler of His Family") represents in full flower the public-spirited Humanism of the earlier bourgeois age to which he belonged. Alberti is its chief protagonist, and no more appropriate figure is conceivable. For this dialogue, more than any other, celebrates the union of theory and practice that Florentine Humanism had attained and the ethic of achievement and public service that he himself had come to exemplify. *De iciarchia* was completed just a few years before his death.

SIR THOMAS MALORY

(fl. *c.* 1470)

Original drawing by Aubrey Beardsley for an 1893 edition of Le Morte Darthur *by Sir Thomas Malory.* Rosenwald Collection, Library of Congress, Washington, D.C.

Sir Thomas Malory was an English writer whose identity remains uncertain but whose name is famous as that of the author of *Le Morte Darthur (The Death of Arthur)*, the first prose account in English of the rise and fall of the legendary king Arthur and the fellowship of the Round Table.

Even in the 16th century Malory's identity was unknown, although there was a tradition that he was a Welshman. In the colophon to *Le Morte Darthur* the author, calling himself "Syr Thomas Maleore knyght," says that he finished the work in the ninth year of the reign of Edward IV (i.e., March 4, 1469–March 3, 1470) and adds a prayer for "good delyueraunce" from prison. The only known knight at this time with a name like Maleore was Thomas Malory of Newbold Revell in the parish of Monks Kirby, Warwickshire. This Malory was jailed on various occasions during the period 1450–60, but it is not recorded that he was in prison about 1470, when the colophon was written.

A "Thomas Malorie (or Malarie), knight" was excluded from four general pardons granted by Edward IV to the Lancastrians in 1468 and 1470. This Malorie, who may have been Malory of Newbold Revell, was probably the author of *Le Morte Darthur*. According to Sir William Dugdale's *Antiquities of Warwickshire* (1656), Malory of Newbold Revell served in the train of Richard Beauchamp, earl of Warwick, at the siege of Calais (presumably 1436, but possibly 1414); was knight of the shire in 1445; and died on March 14, 1471. He was buried in the Chapel of St. Francis at Grey Friars, near Newgate. (He had been imprisoned in Newgate in 1460.)

Malory completed *Le Morte Darthur* about 1470; it was printed by William Caxton in 1485. The only extant manuscript that predates Caxton's edition is in the British Library, London. It retells the adventures of the knights of the Round Table in chronological sequence from the birth of Arthur. Based on French romances, Malory's account differs from his models in its emphasis on the brotherhood of the knights rather than on courtly love and on the conflicts of loyalty (brought about by the adultery of Lancelot and Guinevere) that finally destroy the fellowship.

IIO SŌGI

(b. 1421, Japan—d. September 1, 1502, Hakone, Japan)

The Buddhist monk and greatest master of renga (linked verse) Iio Sōgi was the supreme Japanese poet of his age.

Sōgi was born of humble stock, and nothing is known of his career before 1457. His later writings suggest that, after serving as a Zen monk in Kyōto, he became, in his 30s, a professional renga poet. His teachers included not only provincial renga masters but also court nobles, and though his training undoubtedly benefited his poetry, it also exerted an inhibiting influence. Sōgi's own selection of his best work shows him at his most ingenious in the aristocratic tradition; but his modern reputation is based on the deeply moving vein found in his simpler and more personal poems.

Sōgi is known as a traveler-poet. His life for 40 years was divided between the capital and the provinces. From 1466 to 1472, a period when warfare ravaged Kyōto, he lived mainly in eastern Japan. His return to Kyōto in 1473 ushered in his most fruitful period. His residence became the centre of literary activity in the city, and he compiled several collections of his poetry. In 1480 he made a journey to Kyushu (recorded in his *Tsukushi no michi no ki*; "A Record of the Road to Tsukushi"), not in the traditional manner as a wandering priest but as a celebrity, feted everywhere by his admirers.

Sōgi's reputation derives mainly from two renga sequences, *Minase Sangin Hyakuin* (1486; *Minase Sangin Hyakuin: A Poem of One Hundred Links Composed by Three Poets at Minase*) and *Yuyama Sangin Hyakuin* (1491; "One

Hundred Poems Composed by Three Poets at Yuyama");
in each of these, three poets led by Sōgi took turns at composing short stanzas (links) to form a single poem with
many shifts of mood and direction. Sōgi left over 90 works
including renga anthologies, diaries, poetic criticism, and
manuals.

FRANÇOIS VILLON

(b. 1431, Paris—d. after 1463)

O ne of the greatest French lyric poets, François
Villon (a pseudonym of François de Montcorbier
or François des Loges) was known for his life of criminal
excess, spending much time in prison or in banishment
from medieval Paris. His chief works include *Le Lais* (*Le
Petit Testament*) (*The Legacy [The Small Testament]*), *Le Grand
Testament* (known as *The Testament* or *The Grand Testament*),
and various ballades, chansons, and rondeaux.

Life

Villon's father died while he was still a child, and he was
brought up by the canon Guillaume de Villon, chaplain
of Saint-Benoît-le-Bétourné. The register of the faculty
of arts of the University of Paris records that in March
1449 Villon received the degree of bachelor, and in May–
August 1452, that of master. On June 5, 1455, a violent
quarrel broke out in the cloisters of Saint-Benoît among
himself, some drinking companions, and a priest, Philippe
Sermoise, whom Villon killed with a sword thrust. He was
banished from the city but, in January 1456, won a royal
pardon. Just before Christmas of the same year, however,

he was implicated in a theft from the Collège de Navarre and was again obliged to leave Paris.

At about this time he composed the poem his editors have called *Le Petit Testament*, which he himself entitled *Le Lais* (*The Legacy*). It takes the form of a list of "bequests," ironically conceived, made to friends and acquaintances before leaving them and the city. To his barber he leaves the clippings from his hair; to three well-known local usurers, some small change; to the clerk of criminal justice, his sword (which was in pawn).

After leaving Paris, he probably went for a while to Angers. He certainly went to Blois and stayed on the estates of Charles, duc d'Orléans, who was himself a poet. Here, further excesses brought him another prison sentence, this time remitted because of a general amnesty declared at the birth of Charles's daughter, Marie d'Orléans, on December 19, 1457. Villon entered his ballade "Je meurs de soif auprès de la fontaine" ("I die of thirst beside the fountain") in a poetry contest organized by the prince, who is said to have had some of Villon's poems (including the "letter" dedicated to the young child, "Épître à Marie d'Orléans") transcribed into a manuscript of his own work.

At some later time, Villon is known to have been in Bourges and in the Bourbonnais, where he possibly stayed at Moulins. But throughout the summer of 1461 he was once more in prison. He was not released until October 2, when the prisons were emptied because King Louis XI was passing through.

Free once more, Villon wrote his longest work, *Le Testament* (or *Le Grand Testament*, as it has since been known). It contains 2,023 octosyllabic lines in 185 *huitains* (eight-line stanzas). These *huitains* are interspersed with a number of fixed-form poems, chiefly ballades (usually poems of three 10-line stanzas, plus an envoi of between 4 and 7 lines) and chansons (songs written in a variety of metres and with varied verse patterns), some of which he had composed earlier.

In *Le Testament* Villon reviews his life and expresses his horror of sickness, prison, old age, and his fear of death. It is from this work especially that his poignant regret for his wasted youth and squandered talent is known. He re-creates the taverns and brothels of the Paris under-world, recalling many of his old friends in drunkenness and dissipation, to whom he had made various "bequests" in *Le Lais*. But Villon's tone is here much more scathing than in his earlier work, and he writes with greater ironic detachment.

Shortly after his release from the prison at Meung-sur-Loire he was arrested, in 1462, for robbery and detained at the Châtelet in Paris. He was freed on November 7 but was in prison the following year for his part in a brawl in the rue de la Parcheminerie. This time he was condemned to be *pendu et etranglé* ("hanged and strangled"). While under the sentence of death he wrote his superb *Ballade des pendus,* or *L'Épitaphe Villon*, in which he imagines himself hanging on the scaffold, his body rotting, and he makes a plea to God against the "justice" of men. At this time, too, he wrote his famous wry quatrain *Je suis Françoys, dont il me poise* ("I am François, they have caught me"). He also made an appeal to the Parlement, however, and on January 5, 1463, his sentence was commuted to banishment from Paris for 10 years. He was never heard from again.

Poetry

The criminal history of Villon's life can all too easily obscure the scholar, trained in the rigorous intellectual disciplines of the medieval schools. While it is true that his poetry makes a direct unsentimental appeal to our emotions, it is also true that it displays a remarkable control of rhyme and reveals a disciplined composition that suggests a deep concern with form, and not just random inspiration. For example, the ballade *Fausse beauté, qui tant me couste chier* ("False beauty, for which I pay so dear a price"), addressed to his friend, a prostitute, not only supports a double rhyme pattern but is also an acrostic, with the first letter of each line of the first two stanzas spelling out the names Françoys and Marthe. Even the arrangement of stanzas in the poem seems to follow a determined order, difficult to determine, but certainly not the result of happy accident. An even higher estimate of Villon's technical ability would probably be reached if more were known about the manner and rules of composition of the time.

A romantic notion of Villon's life as some sort of medieval *vie de bohème*—a conception reinforced by the 19th-century Symbolist poet Arthur Rimbaud, who saw him as the "accursed poet"—has been challenged by modern critical studies. David Kuhn has examined the way most texts were made to yield literal, allegorical, moral, and spiritual meanings, following a type of biblical exegesis prevalent in that theocentric age. He has discovered in *Le Testament* a numerical pattern according to which Villon distributed the stanzas. If his analysis is correct, then it would seem *Le Testament* is a poem of cosmic significance, to be interpreted on many levels. Kuhn believes, for example, that the stanza numbered 33—the number of years Jesus Christ lived—refers directly to Jesus, which, if true, could hardly be regarded as the random inspiration of a "lost child." The critic Pierre Guiraud sees the poems as codes that, when broken, reveal the satire of a Burgundian cleric against a corps of judges and attorneys in Paris.

That Villon was a man of culture familiar with the traditional forms of poetry and possessing an acute sense of the past is evident from the poems themselves. There is the ballade composed in Old French, parodying the language of the 13th century; *Le Testament*, which stands directly in the tradition of Jehan Bodel's *Congés* ("Leave-takings"), poetry that poets such as Adam de la Halle and Bodel before him had composed when setting out on a journey; best of all, perhaps, there is his *Ballade des dames du temps jadis* ("Ballade of the Ladies of Bygone Times," included in *Le Testament*), with its famous, incantatory refrain "Mais où sont les neiges d'antan?" ("But where are the snows of yesteryear?").

However farfetched some of these insights into Villon may appear to be, it is not surprising that the poet—given the historical context of learning—should inform his own work with depth of thought, meaning, and significance. But an "intellectual" approach to Villon's work should not distract from its burning sincerity nor contradict the accepted belief that fidelity to genuine, often painful, personal experience was the source of the harsh inspiration whereby he illuminated his largely traditional subject matter—the procession of shattered illusions, the regrets for a lost past, the bitterness of love betrayed, and, above all, the hideous fear of death so often found in literature and art at that time of pestilence and plague, massacre and war.

The little knowledge of Villon's life that has come down to the present is chiefly the result of the patient research of the 19th-century French scholar Auguste Longnon, who brought to light a number of historical documents—most of them judicial records—relating to the poet. But after Villon's banishment by the Parlement in 1463 all trace of him vanishes. Still, it is a wonder that any of his poetry should have survived, and there exist about 3,000 lines, the greater part published as early as 1489 by the Parisian bookseller Pierre Levet, whose edition served as the basis for some 20 more in the next century. Apart from the works mentioned, there are also 12 single ballades and rondeaux (basically 13-line poems with a sophisticated double rhyme pattern), another 4 of doubtful authenticity, and 7 ballades in jargon and jobelin—the slang of the day. Two stories about the poet were later recounted by François Rabelais: one told of his being in England, the other of his seeking refuge at the monastery of Saint-Maixent in Poitou. Neither is credible, nor is it known when or where Villon died.

ʿAlī Shīr Navāʾī

(b. 1441, Herāt, Timurid Afghanistan—d. January 3, 1501, Herāt)

The Turkish poet and scholar Mir ʿAlī Shīr Navāʾī (also spelled Nevāʾī) was the greatest representative of Chagatai literature (Chagatai being a classical Turkic literary language).

Born into an aristocratic military family, Navāʾī studied in Herāt and in Meshed. After his school companion, the sultan Ḥusayn Bayqarah, succeeded to the throne of Herāt, Navāʾī held a number of offices at court. He was also a member of the Naqshbandī dervish order, and under his master, the renowned Persian poet Jāmī, he read and studied the works of the great mystics. As a philanthropist, he was responsible for much construction in the city. His other interests included miniature painting, music, architecture, and calligraphy.

Navāʾī devoted the latter part of his life to poetry and scholarship, writing first in Persian and then in Chagatai. He left four great divans, or collections of poems, belonging to different phases of his life. He wrote five *masnawis* (series of rhymed couplets), collected in his *Khamseh*, that are based on conventional themes in Islamic literature, such as the story of Farhād and Shīrīn. His *Lisān ul-tayr* (1498; "The Language of the Birds"), an adaptation of

Manṭeq al-ṭayr (*The Conference of the Birds*) by the Persian poet Farīd al-Dīn 'Aṭṭār, is also a *masnawi*. One of Navā'ī's most important prose works is *Majālis-i nefa'īs* (1491; "The Exquisite Assemblies"), a *tezkire* (literary dictionary) that contains much autobiographical information and facts about the lives of Turkish poets. He also wrote a treatise on Turkish prosody. Navā'ī's mastery of the Chagatai language was such that it came to be known as "the language of Navā'ī."

SEBASTIAN BRANT

(b. 1457, Strassburg [now Strasbourg, France] —
d. May 10, 1521, Strassburg)

The satirical poet Sebastian Brant (also spelled Brandt) is best known for his *Das Narrenschiff* (1494; *The Ship of Fools*), the most popular German literary work of the 15th century.

Brant studied in Basel, where he received his B.A. in 1477 and doctor of laws in 1489; he taught in the law faculty there from 1484 to 1500. In 1500, when Basel joined the Swiss Confederation (1499), he returned to Strassburg, where in 1503 he was made municipal secretary. Maximilian I appointed him imperial councillor and count palatine.

Brant's writings are varied: legal; religious; political (in support of Maximilian, against the French and Turks); and, especially, moral (adaptations of the aphorisms of Cato, Faceto, and Freidank). His chief work, however, is *Das Narrenschiff*, an allegory telling of a ship laden with fools and steered by fools setting sail for Narragonia, the "fool's paradise." The ship allegory is not sustained; instead Brant presents more than 100 fools representing every contemporary shortcoming, serious and trivial.

Criminals, drunkards, ill-behaved priests and lecherous monks, spendthrifts, bribe-taking judges, busybodies, and lusty women are included in this unsparing, bitter, sweeping satire. Brant's aims are the improvement of his fellows and the regeneration of church and empire. The language is popular, the verse rough but vigorous; each chapter is accompanied by a woodcut, many ascribed to Albrecht Dürer; they are beautifully executed but often only loosely connected with the text. Brant's work was an immediate sensation and was widely translated.

Two English versions appeared in 1509, one in verse by Alexander Barclay (*The Shyp of Folys of the Worlde*) and another in prose by Henry Watson, and it gave rise to a whole school of fool's literature. Yet Brant essentially looks backward; he is not a forerunner of the Reformation nor even a true humanist but rather a representative of medieval thought and ideals.

GIL VICENTE

(b. *c.* 1465, Portugal — d. 1536/37)

Sometimes called the Portuguese Plautus (one of ancient Rome's great comic dramatists), Gil Vicente was the chief dramatist of Portugal. He was also a noted lyric poet, in both Portuguese and Spanish.

The record of much of Vicente's life is vague, to the extent that his identity is still uncertain. Some have identified him with a goldsmith of that name at the court of Evora; the goldsmith is mentioned in royal documents from 1509 to 1517 and worked for the widow of King John II, Dona Leonora. Others believe he was the master of rhetoric of the future King Manuel. His first known work was produced June 7, 1502, on the occasion of the birth of the future John III. This was a short play entitled *Monológo del Vaquero* ("The Herdsman's Monologue"), which was presented in Castilian in the apartment of Queen Maria. Later that year he produced for Christmas a longer but equally simple *Auto Pastoril Castelhano* ("Castilian Pastoral Play").

For the next 34 years he was a kind of poet laureate, accompanying the court from Lisbon to Almeirim, Thomar, Coimbra, or Evora and staging his plays to celebrate great events and the solemn occasions of Christmas, Easter, and Holy Thursday. The departure of a Portuguese fleet on the expedition against Azamor in 1513 turned his attention to more national themes; and in the *Auto da Exhortação da Guerra* (1513; "Play of Exhortation to War") and *Auto da Fama* (1515; "Play of Fame"), inspired by the victories of Albuquerque in the East, he wrote fervent patriotic verse. In 1514 he produced the charming *Comédia do Viúvo* ("The Widower's Comedy").

After the death of King Manuel in 1521, Vicente frequently complained of poverty, but he received various pensions in the new reign and enjoyed the personal friendship of King John III.

On the occasion of the departure by sea of King Manuel's daughter Beatriz to wed the duke of Savoy in August 1521, Vicente's *Cortes de Júpiter* ("Jupiter's Courts") was acted in a large room "adorned with tapestry of gold," a fact chronicled by his friend, the poet Garcia de Resende. The *Frágua de Amor* (1524; "The Forge of Love") was also written for a court occasion, the betrothal of King John III to the sister of the Holy Roman emperor Charles V. In the *Auto Pastoril Português* (1523; "Portuguese Pastoral Play"), the farce *Juiz da Beira* (1525; "The Judge of Beira"), the *Tragi-comédia Pastoril da Serra da Estrela* (1527; "The Pastoral Tragicomedy of Serra da Estrela"), and the satirical *Clérigo da Beira* (1529–30; "The Priest of Beira"), he returned to the peasants and shepherds of the Beira mountain country that he knew so intimately.

He devoted himself more and more to the stage and multiplied his output in answer to the critics of Sá de Miranda's school. In 1526 came the *Templo de Apolo* ("The Temple of Apollo"), followed in rapid succession by the biblical play *Breve sumário da história de Deus* ("A Brief Summary of the Story of God"), *Nao de amores* ("The Ship of Love"), *Divisa da Cidade de Coimbra* ("The Coat of Arms of the City of Coimbra"), and *Farsa dos Almocreves* ("The Muleteers' Farce," a muleteer being one who drives mules). These last three plays, with the *Serra da Estrella*, were all produced before the court in 1527 at Lisbon and Coimbra. On the other hand the *Auto da Festa* (1525; "The Festival Play") appears to have been acted in a private house at Evora.

Vicente was now over 60, but he retained his vigour and versatility. The brilliant scenes of two of his last plays, *Romagem de Agravados* (1533) and *Floresta de Enganos* (1536; "The Forest of Lies"), are loosely put together, and may well be earlier work; but the lyrical power of *Triunfo do Inverno* (1529; "The Triumph of Summer") and the long, compact *Amadis de Gaula* (1532) show that he retained his creative powers in his last decade. *Auto da Mofina Mendes* (1534), partly a religious allegory, shows his old lightness of touch and penetrating charm. *Auto da Lusitânia*, which was acted in the presence of the court in 1532, may with some plausibility be identified with the *Caça de Segredos* ("The Hunt for Secrets") at which Vicente tells us he was at work in 1525. It was the last of his plays to be staged at Lisbon in his lifetime; in Lent of 1534, by request of the abbess of the neighbouring convent of Odivelas, he produced there his religious *Auto da Cananéia* ("The Canaanite Play"), but the remainder of his plays were acted before the king and court at Evora; and it was probably at Evora that Vicente died in the year of his last play (1536).

Vicente's 44 plays admirably reflect the change and upheaval of his era in all its splendour and squalor. Eleven are written exclusively in Spanish, 14 in Portuguese; the rest are multilingual; scraps of church or medical or law Latin, of French and Italian, of the dialect or slang of peasants, gypsies, sailors, fairies, and devils frequently occur. His drama may be divided into religious plays, foreshadowing the Calderon *autos*, court plays, pastoral plays, popular farces, and romantic comedy. They were often elaborately staged: a ship was rowed on the scene, or a tower opened to display some splendid allegory; here too he anticipated the later Spanish drama.

The various plays of the years 1513–19, composed when he was about 50, show Vicente at the height of his genius. He possessed a genuine comic vein, an incomparable lyric gift, and the power of seizing touches of life or literature and transforming them into something new by the magic of his phrase and his satiric force, under which lay a strong moral and patriotic purpose.

ELIJAH BOKHER LEVITA

(b. February 13, 1469, Neustadt an der Aisch, Nürnberg [Germany]—d. January 28, 1549, Venice [Italy]),

Elijah Bokher Levita was a German-born Jewish grammarian whose writings and teaching furthered the study of Hebrew in European Christendom at a time of widespread hostility toward the Jews.

Levita went to Italy early in life and in 1504 settled at Padua. There he wrote a manual of Hebrew (1508) that was appropriated by his transcriber, Benjamin Colbo, who made interpolations and published it under his own name. The work enjoyed wide popularity among both Jewish and Christian students, but Levita did not receive credit for writing it until 1546, when he published a corrected edition.

Forced to flee Padua when it was taken and sacked by the League of Cambrai in 1509, he settled in Venice and in 1513 went to Rome, where he enjoyed the patronage of Gilles of Viterbo, general of the Augustinian religious order and later a cardinal. Encouraged by Gilles to write a treatise on Hebrew grammar, Levita produced *Sefer ha-Baḥur [Bokher]* (1518; "Book of Baḥur"), which was widely used and went into many editions. About the same time, he published a table of paradigms and an annotated dictionary of irregular word forms found in the Bible. A work on phonetics and various aspects of Hebrew grammar, *Pirqe Eliyahu* ("Chapters of Elijah"), appeared in 1520.

In 1527 Levita again lost his property and many of his manuscripts and was forced to leave Rome when it was sacked by the imperial army. He went back to Venice, where he employed himself in correcting Hebrew works for a printer, teaching, and completing the work that he considered his masterpiece, *Sefer ha-zikhronot* ("Book of Memoirs"), a Masoretic, or Hebrew biblical, concordance. Though never published, the manuscript brought him offers of professorships from church prelates, princes, and the king of France, Francis I. He declined all of them, however. Another Masoretic work, *Massarot ha-massarot* (1538; "Tradition of Tradition"), remained a subject of debate among Hebraists for nearly three centuries.

During the last years of his life Levita produced, among other writings, two major works. *Sefer meturgeman* (1541; "A Translator's Book") was the first dictionary of the Targums, or Aramaic books of the Hebrew Bible. His lexicon *Tishbi* (1542) explained much of the Mishnaic Hebrew language and was a supplement to two important earlier dictionaries.

Levita also wrote in Yiddish. He is noted for the *Bove-bukh* (written in 1507 and printed in 1541; "The Book of Bove"), based on an Italian version of an Anglo-Norman tale about a queen who betrays her husband and causes his death. He may also have written *Pariz un Viene* (printed in 1594; "Paris and Vienna"), about a poor knight seeking to marry a princess.

NICCOLÒ MACHIAVELLI

(b. May 3, 1469, Florence, Italy—d. June 21, 1527, Florence)

Niccolò Machiavelli was a political philosopher and statesman, secretary of the Florentine republic, whose most famous work, *The Prince* (*Il Principe*), brought him a reputation as an atheist and an immoral cynic.

Early Life and Political Career

From the 13th century onward, Machiavelli's family was wealthy and prominent, holding on occasion Florence's most important offices. His father, Bernardo, a doctor of laws, was nevertheless among the family's poorest members. Barred from public office in Florence as an insolvent debtor, Bernardo lived frugally, administering his small landed property near the city and supplementing his meagre income from it with earnings from the restricted and almost clandestine exercise of his profession.

Bernardo kept a library in which Niccolò must have read, but little is known of Niccolò's education and early life in Florence, at that time a thriving centre of

An oil portrait of the political philosopher Niccolò Machiavelli by Santi di Tito, in the Palazzo Vecchio in Florence. Imagno/Hulton Fine Art Collection/Getty Images

philosophy and a brilliant showcase of the arts. He learned Latin well and probably knew some Greek, and he seems to have acquired the typical humanist education that was expected of officials of the Florentine Chancery.

Emerging from obscurity in 1498 at the age of 29, Machiavelli became head of the second chancery (*cancelleria*), a post that placed him in charge of the republic's foreign affairs in subject territories. How so young a man could be entrusted with so high an office remains a mystery, particularly because Machiavelli apparently never served an apprenticeship in the chancery. He held the post until 1512, having gained the confidence of Piero Soderini (1452–1522), the gonfalonier (chief magistrate) for life in Florence from 1502.

In 1503 Machiavelli wrote a short work, *Del modo di trattare i sudditi della Val di Chiana ribellati* (*On the Way to Deal with the Rebel Subjects of the Valdichiana*). Anticipating his later *Discourses on Livy*, a commentary on the ancient Roman historian, in this work he contrasts the errors of Florence with the wisdom of the Romans and declares that in dealing with rebellious peoples one must either benefit them or eliminate them.

In 1503 Machiavelli was sent to Rome for the duration of the conclave that elected Pope Julius II, an enemy of the Borgias, whose election Cesare had unwisely aided. Machiavelli watched Cesare's decline and, in a poem (*First Decennale*), celebrated his imprisonment, a burden that "he deserved as a rebel against Christ." Altogether, Machiavelli embarked on more than 40 diplomatic missions during his 14 years at the chancery.

In 1512 the Florentine republic was overthrown and the gonfalonier deposed by a Spanish army that Julius II had enlisted into his Holy League. The Medici family returned to rule Florence, and Machiavelli, suspected of conspiracy, was imprisoned, tortured, and sent into exile in 1513 to his father's small property in San Casciano, just south of Florence. There he wrote his two major works, *The Prince* and *Discourses on Livy*, both of which were published after his death.

Machiavelli was first employed in 1520 by Cardinal Giulio de' Medici to resolve a case of bankruptcy in Lucca, where he took the occasion to write a sketch of its government and to compose his *The Life of Castruccio Castracani of Lucca* (1520; *La vita di Castruccio Castracani da Lucca*). Later that year the cardinal agreed to have Machiavelli elected official historian of the republic, a post to which he was appointed in November 1520. In the meantime, he was commissioned by the Medici pope Leo X (reigned 1513–21) to write a discourse on the organization of the government of Florence. Machiavelli criticized both the Medici regime and the succeeding republic he had served and boldly advised the pope to restore the republic, replacing the unstable mixture of republic and principality then prevailing.

After the death of Pope Leo X in 1521, Cardinal Giulio, Florence's sole master, was inclined to reform the city's government and sought out the advice of Machiavelli, who replied with the proposal he had made to Leo X. In 1523, following the death of Pope Adrian VI, the cardinal became Pope Clement VII, and Machiavelli worked with renewed enthusiasm on an official history of Florence. In June 1525 he presented his *Florentine Histories* (*Istorie Fiorentine*) to the pope, receiving in return a gift of 120 ducats. In April 1526 Machiavelli was made chancellor of the Procuratori delle Mura to superintend Florence's fortifications. At this time the pope had formed a Holy League at Cognac against Holy Roman emperor Charles V (reigned 1519–56), and Machiavelli went with the army to join his friend Francesco Guicciardini (1482–1540), the pope's lieutenant, with whom he remained until the sack of Rome by the emperor's forces brought the war to an end in May 1527. Now that Florence had cast off the Medici, Machiavelli hoped to be restored to his old post at the chancery. But the few favours that the Medici had doled out to him caused the supporters of the free republic to look upon him with suspicion. Denied the post, he fell ill and died within a month.

Writings

In office Machiavelli wrote a number of short political discourses and poems (the *Decennali*) on Florentine history. It was while he was out of office and in exile, however, that the "Florentine Secretary," as Machiavelli came to be called, wrote the works of political philosophy for which he is remembered.

About the same time that Machiavelli wrote *The Prince* (1513), he was also writing a very different book, *Discourses on Livy* (or, more precisely, *Discourses on the First Ten Books of Titus Livy* [*Discorsi sopra la prima deca di Tito Livio*]). Both books were first published only after Machiavelli's death, the *Discourses on Livy* in 1531 and *The Prince* in 1532. The two works differ in substance and manner. Whereas *The Prince* is mostly concerned with princes—particularly new princes—and is short, easy to read, and, according to many, dangerously wicked, the *Discourses on Livy* is a "reasoning" that is long, difficult, and full of advice on how to preserve republics. Every thoughtful treatment of Machiavelli has had to come to terms with the differences between his two most important works.

The Prince

The first and most persistent view of Machiavelli is that of a teacher of evil. *The Prince* is in the tradition of the

"Mirror for Princes"—i.e., books of advice that enabled princes to see themselves as though reflected in a mirror—which began with the *Cyropaedia* by the Greek historian Xenophon (431–350 BCE) and continued into the Middle Ages. Prior to Machiavelli, works in this genre advised princes to adopt the best prince as their model, but Machiavelli's version recommends that a prince go to the "effectual truth" of things and forgo the standard of "what should be done" lest he bring about his ruin. To maintain himself a prince must learn how not to be good and use or not use this knowledge "according to necessity." An observer would see such a prince as guided by necessity, and from this standpoint Machiavelli can be interpreted as the founder of modern political science, a discipline based on the actual state of the world as opposed to how the world might be.

Machiavelli divides principalities into those that are acquired and those that are inherited. In general, he argues that the more difficult it is to acquire control over a state, the easier it is to hold on to it. The reason for this is that the fear of a new prince is stronger than the love for a hereditary prince; hence, the new prince, who relies on "a dread of punishment that never forsakes you," will succeed, but a prince who expects his subjects to keep their promises of support will be disappointed. The prince will find that "each wants to die for him when death is at a distance," but, when the prince needs his subjects, they generally decline to serve as promised. Thus, every prince, whether new or old, must look upon himself as a new prince and learn to rely on "one's own arms," both literally in raising one's own army and metaphorically in not relying on the goodwill of others.

The new prince relies on his own virtue, but, if virtue is to enable him to acquire a state, it must have a new meaning distinct from the New Testament virtue of seeking peace. Machiavelli's notion of *virtù* requires the prince to be concerned foremost with the art of war and to seek not merely security but also glory, for glory is included in necessity. *Virtù* for Machiavelli is virtue not for its own sake but rather for the sake of the reputation it enables princes to acquire. Virtue, according to Machiavelli, aims to reduce the power of fortune over human affairs because fortune keeps men from relying on themselves. At first Machiavelli admits that fortune rules half of men's lives, but then, in an infamous metaphor, he compares fortune to a woman who lets herself be won more by the impetuous and the young, "who command her with more audacity," than by those who proceed cautiously. A prince who possesses the virtue of mastery can command fortune and manage people to a degree never before thought possible.

The Discourses on Livy

Like *The Prince*, the *Discourses on Livy* admits of various interpretations. One view stresses the work's republicanism and locates Machiavelli in a republican tradition that starts with Aristotle (384–322 BCE) and continues through the organization of the medieval city-states, the renewal of classical political philosophy in Renaissance humanism, and the establishment of the contemporary American republic. This interpretation focuses on Machiavelli's various pro-republican remarks, such as his statement that the multitude is wiser and more constant than a prince and his emphasis in the *Discourses on Livy* on the republican virtue of self-sacrifice as a way of combating corruption. Yet Machiavelli's republicanism does not rest on the usual republican premise that power is safer in the hands of many than it is in the hands of one. To the contrary, he asserts that, to found or reform a republic, it is necessary to "be alone." Any ordering must depend on a single mind; thus, Romulus "deserves excuse" for killing Remus, his brother and partner in the founding of Rome, because it was for the common good. This statement is as close as Machiavelli ever came to saying "the end justifies the means," a phrase closely associated with interpretations of *The Prince*.

Republics need the kind of leaders that Machiavelli describes in *The Prince*. These "princes in a republic" cannot govern in accordance with justice, because those who get what they deserve from them do not feel any obligation. Nor do those who are left alone feel grateful. Thus, a prince in a republic will have no "partisan friends" unless he learns "to kill the sons of Brutus," using violence to make examples of enemies of the republic and, not incidentally, of himself. To reform a corrupt state presupposes a good man, but to become a prince presupposes a bad man. Good men, Machiavelli claims, will almost never get power, and bad men will almost never use power for a good end. Yet, since republics become corrupt when the people lose the fear that compels them to obey, the people must be led back to their original virtue by sensational executions reminding them of punishment and reviving their fear. The apparent solution to the problem is to let bad men gain glory through actions that have a good outcome, if not a good motive.

Throughout his two chief works, Machiavelli sees politics as defined by the difference between the ancients and the moderns: the ancients are strong, the moderns weak. The moderns are weak because they have been formed by Christianity, and, in three places in the *Discourses on Livy*, Machiavelli boldly and impudently criticizes the Roman Catholic Church and Christianity itself. For Machiavelli the church is the cause of Italy's disunity; the clergy is dishonest and leads people to believe "that it is evil to say evil of evil"; and Christianity glorifies suffering and makes the world effeminate. But Machiavelli leaves it unclear whether he prefers atheism, paganism, or a reformed Christianity, writing later, in a letter dated April 16, 1527 (only two months before his death): "I love my fatherland more than my soul."

DESIDERIUS ERASMUS

(b. October 27, 1469, Rotterdam, Holland [now in the Netherlands] — d. July 12, 1536, Basel, Switzerland)

The humanist Desiderius Erasmus was the greatest scholar of the northern Renaissance, the first editor of the New Testament, and also an important figure in classical literature and in patristics (the study of early writings by Christians).

Early Life and Career

Erasmus was the second illegitimate son of Roger Gerard, a priest, and Margaret, a physician's daughter. He advanced as far as the third-highest class at the chapter school of St. Lebuin's in Deventer. One of his teachers, Jan Synthen, was a humanist, as was the headmaster, Alexander Hegius. The schoolboy Erasmus was clever enough to write classical Latin verse that impresses a modern reader as cosmopolitan.

After both parents died, the guardians of the two boys sent them to a school in 's-Hertogenbosch conducted by the Brethren of the Common Life, a lay religious movement that fostered monastic vocations. Erasmus would remember this school only for a severe discipline intended, he said, to teach humility by breaking a boy's spirit.

Having little other choice, both brothers entered monasteries. Erasmus chose the Augustinian canons regular

Desiderius Erasmus, oil on panel by Hans Holbein the Younger, 1523–24; in the Louvre, Paris. Photos.com/Thinkstock

at Steyn, near Gouda, where he seems to have remained about seven years (1485–92). While at Steyn he paraphrased Lorenzo Valla's *Elegantiae*, which was both a compendium of pure classical usage and a manifesto against the scholastic "barbarians" who had allegedly corrupted it. Erasmus' monastic superiors became "barbarians" for him by discouraging his classical studies. Thus, after his ordination to the priesthood (April 1492), he was happy to escape the monastery by accepting a post as Latin secretary to the influential Henry of Bergen, bishop of Cambrai. Erasmus' *Antibarbarorum liber*, extant from a revision of 1494–95, is a vigorous restatement of patristic arguments for the utility of the pagan classics, with a polemical thrust against the cloister he had left behind: "All sound learning is secular learning."

Erasmus was not suited to a courtier's life, nor did things improve much when the bishop was induced to send him to the University of Paris to study theology (1495). He disliked the quasi-monastic regimen of the Collège de Montaigu, where he lodged initially, and pictured himself to a friend as sitting "with wrinkled brow and glazed eye" through Scotist lectures. To support his classical studies, he began taking in pupils; from this period (1497–1500) date the earliest versions of those aids to elegant Latin— including the *Colloquia* and the *Adagia*—that before long would be in use in humanist schools throughout Europe.

The Wandering Scholar

In 1499 a pupil, William Blount, Lord Mountjoy, invited Erasmus to England. There he met Thomas More, who became a friend for life. John Colet quickened Erasmus' ambition to be a "primitive theologian," one who would expound Scripture not in the argumentative manner of the scholastics but in the manner of Jerome and the other Church Fathers, who lived in an age when men still understood and practiced the classical art of rhetoric. The impassioned Colet besought him to lecture on the Hebrew Bible at Oxford, but the more cautious Erasmus was not ready. He returned to the Continent with a Latin copy of St. Paul's Epistles and the conviction that "ancient theology" required mastery of Greek.

On a visit to Artois, France (1501), Erasmus met the fiery preacher Jean Voirier, who, though a Franciscan, told him that "monasticism was a life more of fatuous men than of religious men." Admirers recounted how Voirier's disciples faced death serenely, trusting in God, without the solemn reassurance of the last rites. Voirier lent Erasmus a copy of works by Origen, the early Greek Christian writer who promoted the allegorical, spiritualizing mode of scriptural interpretation, which had roots in Platonic philosophy. By 1502 Erasmus had settled in the university town of Leuven (Brabant [now in Belgium]) and was reading Origen and St. Paul in Greek. The fruit of his labours was *Enchiridion militis Christiani* (1503/04; *Handbook of a Christian Knight*). In this work Erasmus urged readers to "inject into the vitals" the teachings of Christ by studying and meditating on the Scriptures, using the spiritual interpretation favoured by the "ancients" to make the text pertinent to moral concerns. The *Enchiridion* was a manifesto of lay piety in its assertion that "monasticism is not piety."

Erasmus sailed for England in 1505, hoping to find support for his studies. Instead he found an opportunity to travel to Italy, the land of promise for northern humanists, as tutor to the sons of the future Henry VIII's physician. In Venice Erasmus was welcomed at the celebrated printing house of Aldus Manutius, where Byzantine émigrés enriched the intellectual life of a numerous scholarly company. For the Aldine press Erasmus expanded his *Adagia*, or annotated collection of Greek and Latin adages, into a monument of erudition with over 3,000 entries; this was the book that first made him famous.

De pueris instituendis, written in Italy though not published until 1529, is the clearest statement of Erasmus' enormous faith in the power of education. With strenuous effort the very stuff of human nature could be molded, so as to draw out peaceful and social dispositions while discouraging unworthy appetites. Erasmus, it would almost be true to say, believed that one is what one reads. Thus the "humane letters" of classical and Christian antiquity would have a beneficent effect on the mind, in contrast to the disputatious temper induced by scholastic logic-chopping or the vengeful sense of self-esteem bred into young aristocrats by chivalric literature, "the stupid and tyrannical fables of King Arthur."

The celebrated *Moriae encomium*, or *Praise of Folly*, conceived as Erasmus crossed the Alps on his way back to England and written at Thomas More's house, expresses a very different mood. For the first time the earnest scholar saw his own efforts along with everyone else's as bathed in a universal irony, in which foolish passion carried the day: "Even the wise man must play the fool if he wishes to beget a child."

Little is known of Erasmus' long stay in England (1509–14), except that he lectured at Cambridge and worked on scholarly projects, including the Greek text of the New Testament. Having returned to the Continent, Erasmus made connections with the printing firm of Johann Froben and traveled to Basel to prepare a new edition of the *Adagia* (1515). In this and other works of about the same time Erasmus showed a new boldness in commenting on the ills of Christian society—popes who in their warlike ambition imitated Caesar rather than Christ; princes who hauled whole nations into war to avenge a personal slight; and preachers who looked to their own interests by pronouncing the princes' wars just or by nurturing superstitious observances among the faithful. To remedy these evils Erasmus looked to education. In particular, the training of preachers should be based on "the philosophy of Christ" rather than on scholastic methods. Erasmus tried to show the way with his annotated text of the Greek New Testament and his edition of St. Jerome's *Opera omnia*, both of which appeared from the Froben press in 1516.

Erasmus' home base was now in Brabant, where he had influential friends at the Habsburg court of the Netherlands in Brussels, notably the grand chancellor, Jean Sauvage. Through Sauvage he was named honorary councillor to the 16-year-old archduke Charles, the future Charles V, and was commissioned to write *Institutio principis Christiani* (1516; *The Education of a Christian Prince*) and *Querela pacis* (1517; *The Complaint of Peace*). These works expressed Erasmus' own convictions, but they also did no harm to Sauvage's faction at court, which wanted to maintain peace with France. It was at this time too that he began his *Paraphrases* of the books of the New Testament, each one dedicated to a monarch or a prince of the church. He was accepted as a member of the theology faculty at nearby Leuven, and he also took keen interest in a newly founded Trilingual College, with endowed chairs in Latin, Greek, and Hebrew. *Ratio verae theologiae* (1518) provided the rationale for the new theological education based on the study of languages. Revision of his Greek New Testament, especially of the copious annotations, began almost as soon as the first edition appeared. Though Erasmus certainly made mistakes as a textual critic, in the history of scholarship he is a towering figure, intuiting philological principles that in some cases would not be formulated explicitly until 150 years after his death.

The Protestant Challenge

From the very beginning of the momentous events sparked by Martin Luther's challenge to papal authority, Erasmus' clerical foes blamed him for inspiring Luther, just as some of Luther's admirers in Germany found that he merely proclaimed boldly what Erasmus had been hinting. In fact, Luther's first letter to Erasmus (1516) showed an important disagreement over the interpretation of St. Paul, and in 1518 Erasmus privately instructed his printer, Froben, to stop printing works by Luther, lest the two causes be confused. As he read Luther's writings, at least those prior to *The Babylonian Captivity of the Church* (1520), Erasmus found much to admire, and he could even describe Luther, in a letter to Pope Leo X, as "a mighty trumpet of Gospel truth." Being of a suspicious nature, however, he also convinced himself that Luther's fiercest enemies were men who saw the study of languages as the root of heresy and thus wanted to be rid of both at once. Hence he tugged at the slender threads of his influence, vainly hoping to forestall a confrontation that could only be destructive to "good letters." When he quit Brabant for Basel (December 1521), he did so lest he be faced with a personal request from the emperor to write a book against Luther, which he could not have refused.

When Pope Adrian VI, whom Erasmus had known at Leuven, was succeeded by Clement VII in 1523, Erasmus could no longer avoid "descending into the arena" of theological combat, though he promised the Swiss reformer Huldrych Zwingli that he would attack Luther in a way that would not please the "pharisees." *De libero arbitrio* (1524) defended the place of human free choice in the process of salvation and argued that the consensus of the church through the ages is authoritative in the interpretation of

Scripture. In reply Luther wrote one of his most important theological works, *De servo arbitrio* (1525), to which Erasmus responded with a lengthy, two-part *Hyperaspistes* (1526–27). In this controversy Erasmus lets it be seen that he would like to claim more for free will than St. Paul and St. Augustine seem to allow.

The years in Basel (1522–29) were filled with polemics, some of them rather tiresome by comparison to the great debate with Luther. Irritated by Protestants who called him a traitor to the Gospel as well as by hyper-orthodox Catholic theologians who repeatedly denounced him, Erasmus showed the petty side of his own nature often enough. Although there is material in his apologetic writings that scholars have yet to exploit, there seems no doubt that on the whole he was better at satiric barbs, such as the colloquy representing one young "Pseudo-Evangelical" of his acquaintance as thwacking people over the head with a Gospel book to gain converts.

Final Years

In 1529, when Protestant Basel banned Catholic worship altogether, Erasmus and some of his humanist friends moved to the Catholic university town of Freiburg im Breisgau. He refused an invitation to the Diet of Augsburg, where Philipp Melanchthon's Augsburg Confession was to initiate the first meaningful discussions between Lutheran and Catholic theologians. He nonetheless encouraged such discussion in *De sarcienda ecclesiae concordia* (1533), which suggested that differences on the crucial doctrine of justification might be reconciled by considering a *duplex justitia*, the meaning of which he did not elaborate. Having returned to Basel to see his manual on preaching (*Ecclesiastes*, 1535) through the press, he lingered on in a city he found congenial; it was there he died in 1536.

BARTOLOMÉ DE LAS CASAS

(b. August 1474, Sevilla? — d. July 17, 1566, Madrid)

An early Spanish historian and Dominican missionary in the Americas, Bartolomé de Las Casas was the first to expose the oppression of the Indian by the European and to call for the abolition of Indian slavery. His several works include *Historia de las Indias* (first printed in 1875). A prolific writer and in his later years an influential figure of the Spanish court, Las Casas nonetheless failed to stay the progressive enslavement of the indigenous races of Latin America.

The son of a small merchant, Las Casas is believed to have gone to Granada as a soldier in 1497 and to have enrolled to study Latin in the academy at the cathedral in Sevilla (Seville). In 1502 he left for Hispaniola, in the West Indies, with the governor, Nicolás de Ovando. As a reward for his participation in various expeditions, he was given an *encomienda* (a royal land grant including Indian inhabitants), and he soon began to evangelize the Indians, serving as *doctrinero*, or lay teacher of catechism. Perhaps the first person in America to receive holy orders, he was ordained priest in either 1512 or 1513. In 1513 he took part in the bloody conquest of Cuba and, as priest-*encomendero* (land grantee), received an allotment of Indian serfs.

Although during his first 12 years in America Las Casas was a willing participant in the conquest of the Caribbean, he did not indefinitely remain indifferent to the fate of the natives. In a famous sermon on August 15, 1514, he announced that he was returning his Indian serfs to the governor. Realizing that it was useless to attempt to defend the Indians at long distance in America, he returned to Spain in 1515 to plead for their better treatment. The most influential person to take up his cause was Francisco Jiménez de Cisneros, the archbishop of Toledo and future co-regent of Spain. With the help of the archbishop, the *Plan para la reformación de las Indias* was conceived, and Las Casas, named priest-procurator of the Indies, was appointed to a commission to investigate the status of the Indians. He sailed for America in November 1516.

Las Casas returned to Spain the next year. In addition to studying the juridical problems of the Indies, he began to work out a plan for their peaceful colonization by recruiting farmers as colonists. His stirring defense of the Indians before the Spanish Parliament in Barcelona in December 1519 persuaded King Charles I (the emperor Charles V), who was in attendance, to accept Las Casas's project of founding "towns of free Indians"—i.e., communities of both Spaniards and Indians who would jointly create a new civilization in America. The location selected for the new colony was on the Gulf of Paria in the northern part of present-day Venezuela. Las Casas and a group of farm labourers departed for America in December 1520. The failure to recruit a sufficient number of farmers, the opposition of the *encomenderos* of Santo Domingo, and, finally, an attack by the Indians themselves all were factors that brought disaster to the experiment in January 1522.

Upon his return to Santo Domingo, the unsuccessful priest and political reformer abandoned his reforming activities to take refuge in religious life; he joined the Dominican order in 1523. Four years later, while serving as prior of the convent of Puerto de Plata, a town in northern Santo Domingo, he began to write the *Historia apologética*. One of his major works, the *Apologética* was to serve as the introduction to his masterpiece, the *Historia de las Indias*.

The *Historia*, which by his request was not published until after his death, is an account of all that had happened in the Indies just as he had seen or heard of it. But, rather than a chronicle, it is a prophetic interpretation of events. The purpose of all the facts he sets forth is the exposure of the "sin" of domination, oppression, and injustice that the European was inflicting upon the newly discovered colonial peoples. It was Las Casas's intention to reveal to Spain the reason for the misfortune that would inevitably befall her when she became the object of God's punishment.

Las Casas interrupted work on the book only to send to the Council of the Indies in Madrid three long letters (in 1531, 1534, and 1535), in which he accused persons and institutions of the sin of oppressing the Indian, particularly through the *encomienda* system. After various adventures in Central America, where his ideas on the treatment of the natives invariably brought him into conflict with the Spanish authorities, Las Casas wrote *De único modo* (1537; "Concerning the Only Way of Drawing All Peoples to the True Religion"), in which he set forth the doctrine of peaceful evangelization of the Indian. Together with the Dominicans, he then employed this new type of evangelization in a "land of war" (a territory of still-unconquered Indians)—Tuzutlan, near the Golfo Dulce (Sweet Gulf) in present-day Costa Rica. Encouraged by the favourable outcome of this experiment, Las Casas set out for Spain late in 1539, arriving there in 1540.

While awaiting an audience with Charles V, Las Casas conceived the idea of still another work, the *Brevísima relación de la destrucción de las Indias* ("A Short Account of the Destruction of the Indies"), which he wrote in 1542 and in which the historical events described are in themselves of less importance than their theological interpretation: "The reason why the Christians have killed and destroyed such an infinite number of souls is that they have been moved by their wish for gold and their desire to enrich themselves in a very short time."

Las Casas's work finally seemed to be crowned with success when King Charles signed the so-called New Laws (Leyes Nuevas). According to these laws, the *encomienda* was not to be considered a hereditary grant; instead, the owners had to set free their Indians after the span of a single generation. To ensure enforcement of the laws, Las Casas was named bishop of Chiapas in Guatemala, and in July 1544 he set sail for America, together with 44 Dominicans. Upon his arrival in January 1545, he immediately issued *Avisos y reglas para confesores de españoles* ("Admonitions and Regulations for the Confessors of Spaniards"), the famous *Confesionario*, in which he forbade absolution (the remission of sins) to be given to those who held Indians in *encomienda*. The rigorous enforcement of his regulations led to vehement opposition on the part of the Spanish faithful during Lent of 1545 and forced Las Casas to establish a council of bishops to assist him in his task. But soon his uncompromisingly pro-Indian position alienated his colleagues, and in 1547 he returned to Spain.

Las Casas then entered upon the most fruitful period of his life. He became an influential figure at court and at the Council of the Indies. In addition to writing numerous *memoriales* (petitions), he came into direct confrontation with the learned Juan Ginés de Sepúlveda, an increasingly important figure at court by reason of his *Democrates II* ("Concerning the Just Cause of the War Against the Indians"), in which he maintained, theoretically in accordance with Aristotelian principles, that the Indians "are inferior to the Spaniards just as children are to adults, women to men, and, indeed, one might even say, as apes are to men." Las Casas finally confronted him in 1550 at the Council of Valladolid, which was presided over by famous theologians. The argument was continued in 1551, and its repercussions were enormous.

The servitude of the Indians was already irreversibly established, and, despite the fact that Sepúlveda's teachings had not been officially approved, they were, in effect, those that were followed in the Indies. But Las Casas continued to write books, tracts, and petitions, testimony to his unwavering determination to leave in written form his principal arguments in defense of the American Indian.

During his final years Las Casas came to be the indispensable adviser both to the Council of the Indies and to the king on many of the problems relating to the Indies. In 1562 he had the final form of the *Prólogo* to the *Historia de las Indias* published, although in 1559 he had left written instructions that the work itself should be published only "after forty years have passed, so that, if God determines to destroy Spain, it may be seen that it is because of the destruction that we have wrought in the Indies and His just reason for it may be clearly evident." At the age of 90 Las Casas completed two more works on the Spanish conquest in the Americas. Two years later he died in the Dominican convent of Nuestra Señora de Atocha de Madrid, having continued to the end his defense of his beloved Indians, oppressed by the colonial system that Europe was organizing.

At the suggestion of Francisco de Toledo, the viceroy of Peru, the king ordered all the works, both published and unpublished, of Las Casas to be collected. Although his influence with Spain and the Indies declined sharply, his name became well known in other parts of Europe, thanks to the translations of the *Destrucción* that soon appeared in various countries. In the early 19th century the Latin American revolutionary Simón Bolívar himself was inspired by some of the letters of Las Casas in his struggle against Spain, as were some of the heroes of

Mexican independence. His name came into prominence again in the latter half of the 20th century, in connection with the so-called Indigenistas (indigenous) movements in Peru and Mexico. The modern significance of Las Casas lies in the fact that he was the first European to perceive the economic, political, and cultural injustice of the colonial or neocolonial system maintained by the North Atlantic powers since the 16th century for the control of Latin America, Africa, and Asia.

LUDOVICO ARIOSTO

(b. September 8, 1474, Reggio Emilia, duchy of Modena [Italy]—
d. July 6, 1533, Ferrara)

The Italian poet Ludovico Ariosto is remembered for his epic poem *Orlando furioso* (1516; *Mad Orlando*), which is generally regarded as the finest expression of the literary tendencies and spiritual attitudes of the Italian Renaissance.

Ariosto's father, Count Niccolò, was commander of the citadel at Reggio Emilia. When Ludovico was 10, the family moved to his father's native Ferrara, and the poet always considered himself a Ferrarese. He showed an inclination toward poetry from an early age, but his father intended him for a legal career, and so he studied law, unwillingly, at Ferrara from 1489 to 1494. Afterward he devoted himself to literary studies until 1499. Count Niccolò died in 1500, and Ludovico, as the eldest son, had to give up his dream of a peaceful life devoted to humanistic studies in order to provide for his four brothers and five sisters. In 1502 he became commander of the citadel of Canossa and in 1503 entered the service of Cardinal Ippolito d'Este, son of Duke Ercole I.

Ludovico Ariosto wearing a laurel crown, engraving. © Photos.com/ Thinkstock

Ariosto's duties as a courtier were sharply at odds with his own simple tastes. He was expected to be in constant attendance on the cardinal and to accompany him on dangerous expeditions as well as travel on diplomatic missions. In 1509 he followed the cardinal in Ferrara's campaign against Venice. In 1512 he went to Rome with the cardinal's brother Alfonso, who had succeeded Ercole as duke in 1505 and had sided with France in the Holy League war in an attempt to placate Pope Julius II. In this they were totally unsuccessful and were forced to flee over the Apennines to avoid the pope's wrath. In the following year, after the election of Leo X, hoping to find a situation that would allow him more time to pursue his literary ambitions, Ariosto again went to the Roman court. But his journey was in vain, and he returned to Ferrara.

So far Ariosto had produced a number of Latin verses inspired by the Roman poets Tibullus and Horace. They do not compare in technical skill with those by Pietro Bembo, a contemporary poet and outstanding scholar, but they are much more genuine in feeling. Since about 1505, however, Ariosto had been working on *Orlando furioso*, and, indeed, he continued to revise and refine it for the rest of his life. The first edition was published in Venice in 1516. This version and the second (Ferrara, 1521) consisted of 40 cantos written in the metrical form of the ottava rima (an eight-line stanza, keeping to a tradition that had been followed since Giovanni Boccaccio in the 14th century through such 15th-century poets as Politian and Matteo Maria Boiardo). The second edition shows signs of Bembo's influence in matters of language and style that is still more evident in the third edition.

Orlando furioso is an original continuation of Boiardo's poem *Orlando innamorato* (*Orlando in Love*). Its hero is Orlando, whose name is the Italian form of Roland.

Orlando furioso consists of a number of episodes derived from the epics, romances, and heroic poetry of the Middle Ages and Early Renaissance. The poem, however, achieves homogeneity by the author's skill and economy in handling the various episodes. Despite complete disregard of unity of action (which was to become compulsory in the second half of the century), it is possible to identify three principal nuclei around which the various stories are grouped: Orlando's unrequited love for Angelica, which makes him go mad (*furioso*); the war between Christians (led by Charlemagne) and Saracens (led by Agramante) near Paris; and the secondary love story of Ruggiero and Bradamante. The first is the most important, particularly in the first part of the poem; the second represents the epic background to the whole narrative; and the third is merely introduced as a literary courtesy, since the Este family was supposed to owe its origin to the union of the two lovers. The main unifying element, however, is the personality of Ariosto himself, who confers his own refined spirituality on all his characters. Sensual love is the prevailing sentiment, but it is tempered by the author's ironical attitude and artistic detachment. Upon its publication in 1516, *Orlando furioso* enjoyed immediate popularity throughout Europe, and it was to influence greatly the literature of the Renaissance.

In 1517 Cardinal Ippolito was created bishop of Buda. Ariosto refused to follow him to Hungary, however, and in the following year he entered the personal service of Duke Alfonso, the cardinal's brother. He was thus able to remain in Ferrara near his mistress, Alessandra Benucci, whom he had met in 1513. But, in 1522, financial necessity compelled him to accept the post of governor of the Garfagnana, a province in the wildest part of the Apennines. It was torn by rival political factions and overrun by brigands, but

Ariosto showed great administrative ability in maintaining order there.

During this period, from 1517 to 1525, he composed his seven satires (titled *Satire*), modeled after the *Sermones* (satires) of Horace. The first (written in 1517 when he had refused to follow the cardinal to Buda) is a noble assertion of the dignity and independence of the writer; the second criticizes ecclesiastical corruption; the third moralizes on the need to refrain from ambition; the fourth deals with marriage; the fifth and sixth describe his personal feelings at being kept away from his family by his masters' selfishness; and the seventh (addressed to Pietro Bembo) points out the vices of humanists and reveals his sorrow at not having been allowed to complete his literary education in his youth.

Ariosto's five comedies, *Cassaria* (1508), *I suppositi* (1509), *Il negromante* (1520), *La lena* (1529), and *I studenti* (completed by his brother Gabriele and published posthumously as *La scolastica*), are based on the Latin classics but were inspired by contemporary life. Though minor works in themselves, they were among the first of those imitations of Latin comedy in the vernacular that would long characterize European comedy.

By 1525 Ariosto had managed to save enough money to return to Ferrara, where he bought a little house with a garden. Probably between 1528 and 1530 he married Alessandra Benucci (though secretly, so as not to forego certain ecclesiastical benefices to which he was entitled). He spent the last years of his life with his wife, cultivating his garden and revising the *Orlando furioso*. The third edition of his masterpiece (Ferrara, 1532) contained 46 cantos (a *giunta*, or appendix, known as the *Cinque canti*, or "Five Cantos," was published posthumously in 1545). This final version at last achieved perfection and was published a few months before Ariosto's death.

BALDASSARE CASTIGLIONE

(b. December 6, 1478, Casatico, near Mantua [Italy]—d. February 2, 1529, Toledo [Spain])

An Italian courtier, diplomat, and writer, Baldassare Castiglione is best known for his dialogue *Il cortegiano* (*The Courtier*).

The son of a noble family, Castiglione was educated at the humanist school of Giorgio Merula and Demetrius Chalcondyles, and at the court of Ludovico Sforza in Milan. He returned to Mantua in 1499 to enter the service of the marquis, Francesco Gonzaga, transferring to the service of Guidobaldo da Montefeltro, duke of Urbino, in 1504. Among his duties was a mission to England to receive the Order of the Garter as a proxy for Guidobaldo. It was at Urbino that Castiglione collaborated with his cousin on a pastoral drama, *Tirsi*, in which the speeches of nymphs and shepherds conceal references to the court. Castiglione was sent to Rome in 1513 as ambassador of the new duke of Urbino, Francesco Maria della Rovere, and later entered papal service. He knew the master painter and architect Raphael and collaborated with him on a memorandum regarding the preservation of the city's antiquities. Castiglione was posted to Spain as papal nuncio (ambassador) in 1525 and apparently impressed Emperor Charles V as a perfect gentleman.

Il cortegiano (written 1513–18 and published in Venice in 1528) is a discussion of the qualities of the ideal courtier, put into the mouths of such friends as Pietro Bembo, Ludovico da Canossa, Bernardo da Bibbiena, and Gasparo Pallavicino. The dialogue claims to represent conversations

Baldassare Castiglione, portrait by Raphael, 1516; in the Louvre, Paris. DEA/J.E. Bulloz/De Agostini/Getty Images

at the court of Urbino on four successive evenings in 1507, with the duchess Elisabetta Gonzaga and her "lieutenant," Lady Emilia, in the chair. Its main themes include the nature of graceful behaviour, especially the impression of effortlessness (*sprezzatura*); the essence of humour; the best form of Italian to speak and write; the relation between the courtier and his prince (stressing the need to speak frankly and not to flatter); the qualities of the ideal court lady (notably "a discreet modesty"); and the definition of honourable love. As was common in the Renaissance, the text freely imitates the work of ancient writers such as Plato (on the ideal republic) and Cicero (on the ideal orator), as well as discussing the problem of creative imitation. It also has its place in a late medieval tradition of courtesy books, manuals of noble behaviour. At the same time, it is a nostalgic evocation of the court of Urbino as it was in Castiglione's youth, a "portrait" in the manner of Raphael of the duchess and of his friends, many of whom were dead by the time the book was published. Further, Castiglione invests *Il cortegiano* with an unusual lightness that both describes *sprezzatura* and exemplifies it, and a lively dialogue that brings his leading characters to life.

Il cortegiano was a great publishing success by the standards of the time. It was written for and read by noblewomen, including the poet Vittoria Colonna, Isabella d'Este, Marchioness of Mantua, and the author's mother, as well as by men. In the century after its publication, it averaged an edition a year and was translated into Spanish (1534), French (1537), Latin (1561), and German (1565), besides the English version by Sir Thomas Hoby, *The Courtyer* (1561), and the Polish adaptation by Łukasz Górnicki, *Dworzanin polski* (1566; "The Polish Courtier"). Copies of the text can be found in libraries from Portugal to Hungary and from Sweden to Sicily. English readers included politicians such as Thomas Cromwell and Sir

Christopher Hatton, intellectuals such as Roger Ascham, Robert Burton, and Francis Bacon, and perhaps writers such as Sir Philip Sidney and William Shakespeare. The book remains a classic of Italian literature.

The apparent intention of the author was to raise problems (Does a courtier need to be of noble birth? Is his primary occupation warfare? and so on), leaving them deliberately unresolved. However, his 16th-century readers, responding to the cues given by editors who furnished the book with marginal notes and summaries as well as indexes, appear to have read the book as a treatise on the art of shining in society. It was studied by lawyers and merchants who wished to appear well-bred (whether the author would have approved of this use of his dialogue is doubtful). The underlining in surviving copies suggests that some readers paid closer attention to the jokes and instructions on how to ride or dance with elegance than the more philosophical debates.

The text survived the Counter-Reformation with minor expurgations, such as the deletion of anticlerical jokes and references to the pagan goddess Fortune. Eclipsed by rival and more up-to-date treatises on behaviour in the 17th and 18th centuries (despite interest in the book on the part of Lord Chesterfield, Samuel Johnson, and the actor David Garrick), *Il cortegiano* was rediscovered in the late 19th century as a typical or representative text of the Renaissance.

FRANCISCO DE SÁ DE MIRANDA

(b. August 28, 1481?, Coimbra, Portugal—d. May? 1558, Tapada)

Francisco de Sá de Miranda was the Portuguese poet who introduced Renaissance poetic forms to Portugal.

The illegitimate son of a canon of Coimbra, Gonçalo Mendes de Sá, and Dona Inês de Melo, he was made legitimate in 1490. He studied at the university, which was then in Lisbon, and seems to have lived mainly in the capital until 1521, frequenting the royal court and taking part in the poetical improvisations there and, possibly, teaching at the university. The years from 1521 to 1526 he spent in Italy, visiting Milan, Venice, Florence, Rome, Naples, and Sicily. He made the acquaintance of Giovanni Ruccellai, Lattanzio Tolomei, and Jacopo Sannazzaro; he met the illustrious Vittoria Colonna, a distant connection of his family, and in her house he probably talked with Cardinal Pietro Bembo and Ariosto. By the time he returned home in 1526 he had become familiar with Italian verse forms and metres: the sonnet and *canzone* of Petrarch, the tercet of Dante, the ottava rima of Ariosto, the eclogue in the manner of Sannazzaro, and Italian hendecasyllabic verse. He did not, however, abandon the short national metre, which he carried to perfection in his *Cartas*, or epistles in verse.

His play *Os estrangeiros* ("The Foreigners"), written about 1527, was the first Portuguese prose comedy in the classical manner, and he wrote another, *Os vilhalpandos*, about 1528 (published 1560). His *Cleópatra* (written *c.* 1550), of which only a dozen lines are extant, was probably the first Portuguese classical tragedy. About 1528 Sá de Miranda made his first attempt to introduce the new Renaissance forms of verse by writing in Spanish a *canzone* entitled *Fábula do Mondego* ("Fable of the Mondego"), and this was followed a year or two later by the eclogue *Alexo*.

About 1530, the year he married, he left Lisbon finally and settled on his country estate in the Minho. It is in this later period that he produced his best work: the eclogue *Basto*, the *Cartas*, and the satires, in which he shows himself a stern critic of contemporary society. Some of the sonnets of this period combine a grave tenderness of feeling and refinement of thought with simplicity of expression.

Under Sá de Miranda's influence, Portuguese poetry became higher in aim, purer in tone, and broader in sympathy. As well as introducing the poetic and dramatic forms and spirit of the Renaissance into Portugal, he made an austere stand against the growing materialism of this time.

PIETRO ARETINO

(b. April 20, 1492, Arezzo, Republic of Florence [Italy]—d. October 21, 1556, Venice)

The Italian poet, prose writer, and dramatist Pietro Aretino was celebrated throughout Europe in his time for his bold and insolent literary attacks on the powerful. His fiery letters and dialogues are of great biographical and topical interest.

Although Aretino was the son of an Arezzo shoemaker, he later pretended to be the bastard son of a nobleman and derived his adopted name ("the Aretine") from that of his native city (his real name is unknown). While still very young, he went to Perugia and painted for a time and then moved on to Rome in 1517, where he wrote a series of viciously satirical lampoons supporting the candidacy of Giulio de' Medici for the papacy (Giulio became Pope Clement VII in 1523). Despite the support of the pope and another patron, Aretino was finally forced to leave Rome because of his general notoriety and his 1524 collection of *Sonetti lussuriosi* ("Lewd Sonnets"). From Rome he went to Venice (1527), where he became the object of great adulation and lived in a grand and dissolute style for the rest of his life.

One of Aretino's closest friends in Venice was the painter Titian, for whom he sold many paintings to Francis I, king of France; a great gold chain that Aretino wears in Titian's portrait (*c.* 1545; Pitti Palace, Florence) was a gift from the king.

Among Aretino's many works, the most characteristic are his satirical attacks, often amounting to blackmail, on the powerful. He grew wealthy on gifts from kings and nobles who feared his satire and coveted the fame accruing from his adulation. His six volumes of letters (published 1537–57) show his power and cynicism and give ample justification for the name he gave himself, "*flagello dei principe*" ("scourge of princes"). Aretino was particularly vicious in his attacks on Romans because they had forced him to flee to Venice. In his *Ragionamenti* (1534–36; modern edition, 1914; "Discussions"), Roman prostitutes reveal to each other the moral failings of many important men of their city, and in *I dialoghi* and other dialogues he continues the examination of carnality and corruption among Romans.

Only Aretino's dramas were relatively free of such venomous assaults. His five comedies are acutely perceived pictures of lower-class life, free from the conventions that burdened other contemporary dramas. Of the five comedies, written between 1525 and 1544 (modern collection, *Commedie*, 1914), the best known is *Cortigiana* (published 1534, first performed 1537, "The Courtesan"), a lively and amusing panorama of the life of the lower classes in papal Rome. Aretino also wrote a tragedy, *Orazia* (published 1546; "The Horatii"), which has been judged by some the best Italian tragedy written in the 16th century.

FRANÇOIS RABELAIS

(b. *c.* 1494, Poitou, France—d. probably April 9, 1553, Paris)

François Rabelais was a French writer and priest who for his contemporaries was an eminent physician and humanist and for posterity is the author of the comic masterpiece *Gargantua and Pantagruel*. The four novels composing this work are outstanding for their rich use of Renaissance French as well as their comedy, which ranges from gross burlesque to profound satire. The adjective *Rabelaisian* applied to scatological humour is misleading; Rabelais used scatology aesthetically, not gratuitously, for comic condemnation. His creative exuberance, colourful and wide-ranging vocabulary, and literary variety continue to ensure his popularity.

Life

Details of Rabelais's life are sparse and difficult to interpret. He was the son of Antoine Rabelais, a rich Touraine landowner and a prominent lawyer who deputized for the *lieutenant-général* of Poitou in 1527. After apparently studying law, Rabelais became a Franciscan novice at La Baumette (1510?) and later moved to the Puy-Saint-Martin convent at Fontenay-le-Comte in Poitou. By 1521 (perhaps earlier) he had taken holy orders.

Rabelais early acquired a reputation for profound humanist learning among his contemporaries, but the elements of religious satire and scatological humour in his comic novels eventually left him open to persecution. He depended throughout his life on powerful political figures and on high-ranking liberal ecclesiastics for protection in those dangerous and intolerant times in France.

Rabelais was closely associated with Pierre Amy, a liberal Franciscan humanist of international repute. In 1524 the Greek books of both scholars were temporarily confiscated by superiors of their convent, because Greek was suspect to hyperorthodox Roman Catholics as a "heretical" language that opened up the original New Testament to study. Rabelais then obtained a temporary dispensation from Pope Clement VII and was removed to the Benedictine house of Saint-Pierre-de-Maillezais, the prior of which was his bishop, Geoffroy d'Estissac. He never liked his new order, however, and he later satirized the Benedictines, although he passed lightly over Franciscan shortcomings.

Rabelais studied medicine, probably under the aegis of the Benedictines in their Hôtel Saint-Denis in Paris. In 1530 he broke his vows and left the Benedictines to study medicine at the University of Montpellier, probably with the support of his patron, Geoffroy d'Estissac. As a doctor he placed great reliance on classical authority, siding with the Platonic school of Hippocrates but also following the Greek physician and philosopher Galen and the Muslim physician and philosopher Avicenna. During this period an unknown widow bore him two children (François and Junie), who were given their father's name and were legitimated by Pope Paul IV in 1540.

Gargantua eating pilgrims, as illustrated by artist Gustave Dore for François Rabelais's comic novel. Apic/Hulton Archive/Getty Images

After practicing medicine briefly in Narbonne, Rabelais was appointed physician to the hospital of Lyon, the Hôtel-Dieu, in 1532. In the same year, he edited the medical letters of Giovanni Manardi, a contemporary Italian physician. It was during this period that he discovered his true talent. Fired by the success of an anonymous popular chapbook, *Les Grandes et inestimables cronicques du grant et énorme géant Gargantua* ("The Grand and Inestimable Chronicles of the Grand and Enormous Giant Gargantua"), he published his first novel, *Les horribles et épouvantables faits et prouesses du très renommé Pantagruel, roy des Dipsodes* (1532; "The Horrible and Terrifying Deeds and Words of the Renowned Pantagruel, King of the Dipsodes"), under the pseudonym Alcofribas Nasier (an obvious anagram of his real name). *Pantagruel* is slighter in length and intellectual depth than his later novels, but nothing of this quality had been seen before in French in any similar genre. Rabelais displayed his delight in words, his profound sense of the comedy of language itself, his mastery of comic situation, monologue, dialogue, and action, and his genius as a storyteller who was able to create a world of fantasy out of words alone. Within the framework of a mock-heroic, chivalrous romance, he laughed at many types of sophistry, including legal obscurantism and hermeticism, which he nevertheless preferred to the scholasticism of the Sorbonne. One chapter stands out for its sustained seriousness, praising the divine gift of fertile matrimony as a compensation for death caused by Adam's fall. *Pantagruel* borrows openly from Sir Thomas More's *Utopia* in its reference to the war between Pantagruel's country, Utopia, and the Dipsodes, but it also preaches a semi-Lutheran doctrine—that no one but God and his angels may spread the gospel by force. *Pantagruel* is memorable as the book in which Pantagruel's companion, Panurge, a cunning and witty rogue, first appears.

Though condemned by the Sorbonne in Paris as obscene, *Pantagruel* was a popular success. It was followed in 1533 by the *Pantagrueline Prognostication*, a parody of the almanacs, astrological predictions that exercised a growing hold on the Renaissance mind. In 1534 Rabelais left the Hôtel-Dieu to travel to Rome with the bishop of Paris, Jean du Bellay. He returned to Lyon in May of that year and published an edition of Bartolomeo Marliani's description of Rome, *Topographia antiquae Romae*. He returned to the Hôtel-Dieu but left it again in February 1535, upon which the authorities of the Lyon hospital appointed someone else to his post.

La vie inestimable du grand Gargantua ("The Inestimable Life of the Great Gargantua") belongs to this period. The second edition is dated 1535; the first edition was probably published in 1534, though it lacks the title page in the only known copy. In *Gargantua* Rabelais continues to exploit medieval romances mock-heroically, telling of the birth, education, and prowesses of the giant Gargantua, who is Pantagruel's father. Much of the satire — for example, mockery of the ignorant trivialization of the mystical cult of emblems and of erroneous theories of heraldry — is calculated to delight the court; much also aims at delighting the learned reader — for example, Rabelais sides with humanist lawyers against legal traditionalists and doctors who accepted 11-month, or even 13-month, pregnancies. Old-fashioned scholastic pedagogy is ridiculed and contrasted with the humanist ideal of the Christian prince, widely learned in art, science, and crafts and skilled in knightly warfare. The war between Gargantua and his neighbour, the "biliously choleric" Picrochole, is partly a private satire of an enemy of Rabelais's father and partly a mocking of Charles V, the Holy Roman emperor, and the imperial design of world conquest. Gargantua commands the military operations, but some of the exploits are carried out by Frère Jean (the Benedictine). Though he is lean, lecherous, dirty, and ignorant, Frère Jean is redeemed by his jollity and active virtue; for his fellow monks are timorous and idle, delighting in "vain repetitions" of prayers. *Gargantua*'s last major episode centres on the erection of the Abbey of Thélème, a monastic institution that rejects poverty, celibacy, and obedience; instead it welcomes wealth and the well-born, praises the aristocratic life, and rejoices in good marriages.

After *Gargantua*, Rabelais published nothing new for 11 years, though he prudently expurgated his two works of overbold religious opinions. He continued as physician to Jean du Bellay, who had become a cardinal, and his powerful brother Guillaume, and in 1535 Rabelais accompanied the cardinal to Rome. There he regularized his position by making a "supplication" to the pope for his "apostasy" (i.e., his unauthorized departure from the Benedictine monastery); the pope issued a bull freeing Rabelais from ecclesiastical censure and allowing him to reenter the Benedictine order. Rabelais then arranged to enter the Benedictine convent at Saint-Maur-les-Fossés, where Cardinal Jean du Bellay was abbot. The convent was secularized six months later, and Rabelais became a secular priest, authorized to exercise his medical profession.

In May 1537 Rabelais was awarded the doctorate of medicine of Montpellier; and he delivered, with considerable success, a course of lectures on Hippocrates' *Prognostics*. He was at Aigues-Mortes in July 1538 when Charles V met the French king Francis I, but his movements are obscure until he followed Guillaume du Bellay to the Piedmont in 1542. Guillaume died in January 1543, and to Rabelais his death meant the loss of an important patron. That same year Geoffroy d'Estissac died as well, and Rabelais's novels were condemned by the Sorbonne and the Parlement of Paris. Rabelais sought protection from the French king's sister Margaret, queen of Navarre, dedicating to her the third book of the Gargantua-Pantagruel series, *Tiers livre des faits et dits héroïques du noble Pantagruel* (1546; "Third Book of the Heroic Deeds and Words of the Noble Pantagruel"). Despite its royal *privilège* (i.e., license to print), the book was immediately condemned for heresy by the Sorbonne, and Rabelais fled to Metz (an imperial city), remaining there until 1547.

The *Tiers livre* is Rabelais's most profound work. Pantagruel has now deepened into a Stoico-Christian inerrant sage; Panurge, a lover of self and deluded by the devil, is now an adept at making black seem white. He consults numerous prognostications, both good Platonic ones and less reputable ones—all to no effect because of his self-love. Panurge trusts in no one, least of all in himself. It is therefore decided to consult the oracle of the Dive Bouteille ("Sacred Bottle"), and the travelers set out for the temple. The *Tiers livre* ends enigmatically with a mock eulogy in which hemp is praised for its myriad uses.

From 1547 onward, Rabelais found protection again as physician to Cardinal Jean du Bellay and accompanied him to Rome via Turin, Ferrara, and Bologna. Passing through Lyon, he gave his printer his incomplete *Quart livre* ("Fourth Book"), which, as printed in 1548, finishes in the middle of a sentence but contains some of his most delightful comic storytelling. In Rome Rabelais sent a story to his newest protector in the Guise family, Charles of Lorraine, 2nd Cardinal de Lorraine; the story described the "Sciomachie" ("Simulated Battle") organized by Cardinal Jean to celebrate the birth of Louis of Orléans, second son of Henry II of France.

In January 1551 the Cardinal de Guise presented him with two benefices at Meudon and Jambet, though Rabelais never officiated or resided there. In 1552, through the influence of the cardinal, Rabelais was able to publish—with a new prologue—the full *Quart livre des faits et dits héroïques du noble Pantagruel* ("Fourth Book of the Heroic Deeds and Words of the Noble Pantagruel"), his longest book. Despite its royal *privilège*, this work, too, was condemned by the Sorbonne and banned by Parlement, but Rabelais's powerful patrons soon had the censorship lifted. In 1553 Rabelais resigned his benefices. He died shortly thereafter and was buried in Saint-Paul-des-Champs, Paris.

Gargantua and Pantagruel

Rabelais's purpose in the four books of his masterpiece was to entertain the cultivated reader at the expense of the follies and exaggerations of his times. If he points lessons, it is because his life has taught him something about the evils of comatose monasticism, the trickery of lawyers, the pigheaded persistence of litigants, and the ignorance of grasping physicians. Though it is an entertainment, therefore, *Gargantua and Pantagruel* is also serious. Its principal narrative is devoted to a voyage of discovery that parodies the travelers' tales current in Rabelais's day. Rabelais begins lightheartedly; his travelers merely set out to discover whether Panurge will be cuckolded if he marries. A dozen oracles have already hinted at Panurge's inevitable fate, yet each time he has reasoned their verdict away; and the voyage itself provides a number of amusing incidents. Yet, like Don Quixote's, it is a fundamentally serious quest directed toward a true goal, the discovery of the secret of life.

Intoxication—with life, with learning, with the use and abuse of words—is the prevailing mood of the book. Rabelais himself provides the model of the exuberant creator. His four books provide a cunning mosaic of scholarly, literary, and scientific parody. One finds this in its simplest form in the catalog of the library of St. Victor, in the list of preposterous substantives or attributes in which Rabelais delights, and in the inquiry by means of Virgilian lots into the question of Panurge's eventual cuckoldom. But at other times the humour is more complicated and works on several levels. Gargantua's campaign against King Picrochole (book 1), for instance, contains personal, historical, moral, and classical points closely interwoven. The battles are fought in Rabelais's home country, in which each hamlet is magnified into a fortified city. Moreover, they also refer to the feud between Rabelais the elder and his neighbour. They also comment on recent historical events involving France and the Holy Roman Empire, however, and can even be read as propaganda against war, or at least in favour of the more humane conduct of hostilities. On yet another level, Rabelais's account of this imaginary warfare can be taken as mockery of the classical historians.

Despite these complex levels of reference, Rabelais was not a self-conscious writer; he made his book out of the disorderly contents of his mind. As a result it is ill-constructed, and the same thoughts are repeated in *Gargantua* that he had already set down in *Pantagruel*; the nature of an ideal education, for example, is examined in both books. Moreover, the main action of the story, which arises from the question of Panurge's intended marriage, only begins in the third book.

The third and fourth books pursue the story of the inquiry and voyage, and in them Rabelais's invention is at its height. The first two books contain incidents close in feeling to the medieval *fabliaux*, but the third and fourth books are rich in a new, learned humour. Rabelais was a writer molded by one tradition, the medieval Roman Catholic, whose sympathies lay to a greater extent with another, the Renaissance or classical. Yet when he writes in praise of the new humanist ideals—in the chapters on education, on the foundation of Thélème, or in praise of drinking from the "sacred bottle" of learning or enlightenment—he easily becomes sententious. His head is for the new learning, while his flesh and heart belong to the old. It is in his absurd, earthy, and exuberant inventions, which are medieval in spirit even when they mock at medieval acceptances, that Rabelais is a great, entertaining, and worldly wise writer.

CLÉMENT MAROT

(b. 1496?, Cahors, France—d. September 1544, Turin, Savoy [now in Italy])

One of the greatest poets of the French Renaissance, Clément Marot used the forms and imagery of Latin poetry, which had marked influence on the style of his successors. His father, Jean, was a poet and held a post at the court of Anne de Bretagne and later served Francis I.

In 1514 Marot became page to Nicolas de Neufville, seigneur de Villeroi, secretary to the king. Wishing to follow in his father's footsteps by obtaining a place as court poet, he entered the service of Margaret of Angoulême, sister of Francis I and later queen of Navarre. On his father's death, he became valet de chambre to Francis I, a post he held, except for his years of exile (1534–36), until 1542.

Marot was arrested in 1526 for defying Lenten abstinence regulations, behaviour that put him under suspicion of being a Lutheran. A short imprisonment inspired some of his best-known works, especially "L'Enfer" ("The Inferno"), an allegorical satire on justice, and an epistle to his friend Lyon Jamet (1526). In 1527 he was again imprisoned, this time for attacking a prison guard and freeing a prisoner; an epistle, addressed to the king and begging for his deliverance, won his release. In 1531 Marot was again arrested for eating meat during Lent, but this time he avoided imprisonment. By 1530, in any event, his fame had become firmly established, and his many poems seem to have enjoyed a wide circulation.

After the Affaire des Placards, when placards attacking the Mass were posted in the major cities and on the door of the king's bedchamber (1534), Marot fled to Navarre, where he was protected by Margaret. When persecution of the Protestants increased, he again fled, this time to the court of Renée de France in Ferrara, Italy. Marot subsequently returned to Paris in 1537 after Francis I had stopped the persecutions.

When he was not engaged in writing the official poems that his duties at the French court compelled him to write, Marot spent most of his time translating the Psalms; a first edition of some of these appeared in 1539, the *Trente Pseaulmes de Davíd* in 1542. These translations were notable for their sober and solemn musicality. Their condemnation by the Sorbonne caused Marot to go into exile again. But they were greatly admired by John Calvin, who gave Marot sanctuary in Geneva. Marot's behaviour became unacceptable in that strict and sober city, however, and he was forced to return to Italy.

Although Marot's early poems were composed entirely in the style of the late medieval poets known as *rhétoriqueurs*, he soon abandoned the established genres of that school as well as its conceits, its didactic use of allegory, and its complicated versification. Instead, his knowledge of the Latin classics and his contacts with Italian literary forms enabled him to learn to imitate the styles and themes of antiquity. He introduced the elegy, the eclogue, the epigram, the epithalamium (nuptial poem), and the one-stanza Italian satiric *strambotto* (French *estrabot*) into French poetry, and he was one of the first French poets to attempt the Petrarchan sonnet form. His epigrams and epistolary poems (*épîtres*), in particular, display those qualities of wit, intellectual refinement, and sincerity and naturalness that were to characterize the French use of these genres for the next two centuries. He was also a master of the chant royal and infused some Horatian wit into the old forms of the ballade and the rondeau.

Marot attempted to create new or to improve existing lyrical forms, composing chansons and *cantiques* and originating the *blason* (1536), a satiric verse describing, as a rule, some aspect of the female body in minute detail. The *blason* found immediate popularity and was so widely imitated that it was possible to publish an anthology in 1555. Marot translated Catullus, Virgil, and Ovid and edited the works of François Villon and the *Roman de la rose*. He added grace, elegance, and personal warmth to French light verse. Much of his achievement was temporarily eclipsed by La Pléiade, a group of poets who dominated the literary scene for a period shortly after his death. But the influence of Marot was evident in England among the Elizabethans, notably Edmund Spenser, and was revived in France in the 17th century.

Wu Cheng'en

(b. *c.* 1500, Shanyang, Huaian [now in Jiangsu province], China — d. *c.* 1582, Huaian)

The novelist and poet of the Ming dynasty (1368–1644) Wu Cheng'en (Wu Ch'eng-en) is generally acknowledged as the author of the Chinese folk novel *Xiyouji* (*Journey to the West*, also partially translated as *Monkey*).

Wu received a traditional Confucian education and was appointed a resident scholar at the imperial university in Nanjing in 1544. From 1546 to 1552 Wu lived in

Beijing, where he was a member of a small literary circle and became known for his cleverness in the composition of poetry and prose in the classical style. He later traveled extensively before settling back in Huai'an in 1570. Throughout his life he displayed a marked interest in bizarre stories, such as the set of oral and written folktales that formed the basis of *Xiyouji*. In its 100 chapters *Xiyouji* details the adventures of a cunningly resourceful monkey who accompanies the Buddhist priest Xuanzang on a journey to India. One of the most popular Chinese folk novels, *Xiyouji* is notable for its multiple rhetorical styles that reflect the dialects and regional cultural idiosyncrasies that Xuanzang and the monkey encounter on their journey. The local colour gives added weight to the cutting satire of Chinese culture found throughout the work. Like all novels of its time, *Xiyouji* was written in the vernacular, as opposed to the officially accepted classical style, and therefore had to be published anonymously to protect the author's reputation. As a result, the identity of the novelist was long unknown outside of Wu's native district. Only two volumes of Wu's other writings have survived; these were discovered in the imperial palaces and were reprinted in 1930.

GARCILASO DE LA VEGA

(b. 1503, Toledo, Spain—d. October 14, 1536, Nice, duchy of Savoy [now in France])

Garcilaso de la Vega was the first major poet in the Golden Age of Spanish literature (*c.* 1500–1650).

Garcilaso was born into an aristocratic family that had been prominent in Spanish letters and politics for several centuries. Entering court life at an early age, he distinguished himself as a soldier, serving Emperor Charles V in Rhodes, Tunis, and Pavia. After a brief imprisonment in 1532 for conspiring to marry his brother's son to a prominent lady-in-waiting against the emperor's wishes, he was released into the service of the viceroy, the Marqués de Villafranca. Serving under the viceroy in southern France, he was mortally wounded in an assault on a fortified position and died several days later.

After writing poetry in rather conventional Spanish metres for a short period, Garcilaso had become acquainted with the poet Juan Boscán Almogáver, who quickly introduced him to Italianate metres, to the use of which he was further attracted by his close study of such Italian Renaissance poets as Petrarch, Giovanni Boccaccio, and Jacopo Sannazzaro. Garcilaso was a consummate craftsman, and he transformed the Italianate metres into Spanish verse of high lyric quality. His most important innovations in this regard were the verse stanzas of the *silva* and *liva* (both using combinations of 7- and 11-syllable lines), which allowed him a new concern with the analytical expression of thought and emotion. Garcilaso's major theme is the melancholy laments and misfortunes of romantic love as conventionally portrayed in pastoral poetry. He continually rewrote and polished his poetry, lifting his work high above that of his contemporaries and profoundly influencing the development of Spanish verse.

Garcilaso's small body of work—38 sonnets, 5 canciones, 3 eclogues, 2 elegies, 1 epistle, and 8 coplas (songs)—was published with that of Boscán, by the latter's widow, in 1543. These works were soon accepted as classics and largely determined the course of lyric poetry throughout Spain's Golden Age.

Garcilaso de la Vega. Hulton Archive/Getty Images

SAINT TERESA OF ÁVILA

(b. March 28, 1515, Ávila, Spain—d. October 4, 1582, Alba de Tormes; canonized 1622; feast day October 15)

The Spanish nun Saint Teresa of Ávila was one of the great mystics and religious women of the Roman Catholic Church, and author of spiritual classics. She was the originator of the Carmelite Reform, which restored and emphasized the austerity and contemplative character of primitive Carmelite life. St. Teresa was elevated to doctor of the church in 1970 by Pope Paul VI, the first woman to be so honoured.

Her mother died in 1529, and, despite her father's opposition, Teresa de Cepeda y Ahumada entered, probably in 1535, the Carmelite Convent of the Incarnation at Ávila. Within two years her health collapsed, and she was an invalid for three years, during which time she developed a love for mental prayer. After her recovery, however, she stopped praying. She continued for 15 years in a state divided between a worldly and a divine spirit, until, in 1555, she underwent a religious awakening.

In 1558 Teresa began to consider the restoration of Carmelite life to its original observance of austerity, which had relaxed in the 14th and 15th centuries. Her reform required utter withdrawal so that the nuns could meditate on divine law and, through a prayerful life of penance, exercise what she termed "our vocation of reparation" for the sins of mankind. In 1562, with Pope Pius IV's authorization, she opened the first convent (St. Joseph's) of the Carmelite Reform. A storm of hostility came from municipal and religious personages, especially because the convent existed

Portrait of Saint Teresa of Ávila. Archive Photos/Getty Images

without endowment, but she staunchly insisted on poverty and subsistence only through public alms.

John Baptist Rossi, the Carmelite prior general from Rome, went to Ávila in 1567 and approved the reform, directing Teresa to found more convents and to establish monasteries. In the same year, while at Medina del

Campo, Spain, she met a young Carmelite priest, Juan de Yepes (later St. John of the Cross, the poet and mystic), who she realized could initiate the Carmelite Reform for men. A year later Juan opened the first monastery of the Primitive Rule at Duruelo, Spain.

Despite frail health and great difficulties, Teresa spent the rest of her life establishing and nurturing 16 more convents throughout Spain. In 1575, while she was at the Sevilla (Seville) convent, a jurisdictional dispute erupted between the friars of the restored Primitive Rule, known as the Discalced (or "Unshod") Carmelites, and the observants of the Mitigated Rule, the Calced (or "Shod") Carmelites. Although she had foreseen the trouble and endeavoured to prevent it, her attempts failed. The Carmelite general, to whom she had been misrepresented, ordered her to retire to a convent in Castile and to cease founding additional convents; Juan was subsequently imprisoned at Toledo in 1577.

In 1579, largely through the efforts of King Philip II of Spain, who knew and admired Teresa, a solution was effected whereby the Carmelites of the Primitive Rule were given independent jurisdiction, confirmed in 1580 by a rescript of Pope Gregory XIII. Teresa, broken in health, was then directed to resume the reform. In journeys that covered hundreds of miles, she made exhausting missions and was fatally stricken en route to Ávila from Burgos.

Teresa's ascetic doctrine has been accepted as the classical exposition of the contemplative life, and her spiritual writings are among the most widely read. Her *Life of the Mother Teresa of Jesus* (1611) is autobiographical; the *Book of the Foundations* (1610) describes the establishment of her convents. Her writings on the progress of the Christian soul toward God are recognized masterpieces: *The Way of Perfection* (1583), *The Interior Castle* (1588), *Spiritual Relations, Exclamations of the Soul to God* (1588), and *Conceptions on the Love of God.* Of her poems, 31 are extant; of her letters, 458.

HENRY HOWARD, EARL OF SURREY

(b. 1517, Hunsdon, Hertfordshire, England? —
d. January 13, 1547, London)

Henry Howard, Earl of Surrey, was a poet who, with Sir Thomas Wyatt (1503–42), introduced into England the styles and metres of the Italian humanist poets and so laid the foundation of a great age of English poetry.

The eldest son of Lord Thomas Howard, Henry took the courtesy title of Earl of Surrey in 1524 when his father succeeded as 3rd Duke of Norfolk. It was Surrey's fate, because of his birth and connections, to be involved (though usually peripherally) in the jockeying for place that accompanied Henry VIII's policies. From 1530 until 1532 he lived at Windsor with his father's ward, Henry Fitzroy, Duke of Richmond, who was the son of Henry VIII and his mistress Elizabeth Blount. In 1532, after talk of marriage with the princess Mary (daughter of Henry VIII and Catherine of Aragon), he married Lady Frances de Vere, the 14 year-old daughter of the Earl of Oxford, but they did not live together until 1535. Despite this marriage, an alliance between him and the princess Mary was still discussed. In 1533 Richmond married Surrey's sister Mary, but the two did not live together because Mary preferred to stay in the country. Richmond died three years later, under suspicious circumstances.

Surrey was confined at Windsor (1537–39) after being charged by the Seymours (high in favour since the king's marriage to Jane Seymour in 1536) with having secretly favoured the Roman Catholics in the rebellion of 1536. He had in fact joined his father against the insurgents.

In 1540 he was a champion in court jousts, and his prospects were further improved by the marriage of his cousin Catherine Howard to the king. He served in the campaign in Scotland in 1542 and in France and Flanders from 1543 to 1546. He acted as field marshal in 1545 but was reprimanded for exposing himself unnecessarily to danger.

Returning to England in 1546, he found the king dying and his old enemies the Seymours incensed by his interference in the projected alliance between his sister Mary and Sir Thomas Seymour, Jane's brother; he made matters worse by his assertion that the Howards were the obvious regents for Prince Edward, Henry VIII's son by Jane Seymour. The Seymours, alarmed, accused Surrey and his father of treason and called his sister, the Duchess of Richmond, to witness against him. She made the disastrous admission that he was still a close adherent to the Roman Catholic faith. Because Surrey's father, the Duke of Norfolk, had been considered heir apparent if Henry VIII had had no issue, the Seymours urged that the Howards were planning to set Prince Edward aside and assume the throne. Surrey defended himself unavailingly and at the age of 30 was executed on Tower Hill. His father was saved only because the king died before he could be executed.

Most of Surrey's poetry was probably written during his confinement at Windsor; it was nearly all first published in 1557, 10 years after his death. He acknowledged Wyatt as a master and followed him in adapting Italian forms to English verse. He translated a number of Petrarch's sonnets already translated by Wyatt. Surrey achieved a greater smoothness and firmness, qualities that were to be important in the evolution of the English sonnet. Surrey was the first to develop the sonnet form used by William Shakespeare.

In his other short poems he wrote not only on the usual early Tudor themes of love and death but also of life in London, of friendship, and of youth. The love poems have little force except when, in two "Complaint[s] of the absence of her lover being upon the sea," he wrote, unusual for his period, from the woman's point of view.

The short poems were printed by Richard Tottel in his *Songes and Sonettes, Written by the Ryght Honorable Lorde Henry Haward Late Earle of Surrey and Other* (1557; usually known as *Tottel's Miscellany*). "Other" included Wyatt, and critics from George Puttenham onward have coupled their names.

Surrey's translation of Books II and IV of the *Aeneid*, published in 1557 as *Certain Bokes of Virgiles Aenaeis*, was the first use in English of blank verse, a style adopted from Italian verse.

PIERRE DE RONSARD

(b. September 11, 1524, La Possonnière, near Couture, France—d. December 27, 1585, Saint-Cosme, near Tours)

Pierre de Ronsard was a poet, chief among the French Renaissance group of poets known as La Pléiade.

Ronsard was a younger son of a noble family of the county of Vendôme. He entered the service of the royal family as a page in 1536 and accompanied Princess Madeleine to Edinburgh after her marriage to James V of Scotland. On his return to France two years later, a court appointment or a military or diplomatic career seemed to be open before him, and in 1540 he accompanied the diplomat Lazare de Baïf on a mission to an international conference at Haguenau in Alsace. An illness contracted on this expedition left him partially deaf, however, and his ambitions were deflected to scholarship and literature. For someone in his position, the church provided the only future, and he accordingly took minor orders, which entitled him to hold ecclesiastical benefices, though he was never an ordained priest. A period of enthusiastic study of the classics followed his convalescence; during this time he learned Greek from the brilliant tutor Jean Dorat, read all the Greek and Latin poetry then known, and gained some familiarity with Italian poetry. With a group of fellow students he formed a literary school that came to be called La Pléiade, in emulation of the seven ancient Greek poets of Alexandria: its aim was to produce French poetry that would stand comparison with the verse of classical antiquity.

The title of his first collection of poems, *Odes* (4 books, 1550), emphasizes that he was attempting a French counterpart to the odes of the ancient Roman poet Horace. In *Les Amours* (1552) he also proved his skill as an exponent of the Italian *canzoniere*, animating the compliments to his beloved, entreaties, and lamentations traditional to this poetic form by the vehemence of his manner and the wealth of his imagery. Always responsive to new literary influences, he found fresh inspiration in the recently discovered verse of the Greek poet Anacreon (6th century BCE). The more playful touch encouraged by this model is to be felt in the *Bocage* ("Grove") of poetry of 1554 and in the *Meslanges* ("Miscellany") of that year, which contain some of his most exquisite nature poems, and in the *Continuation des amours* and *Nouvelles Continuations*, addressed to a country girl, Marie. In 1555 he began to write a series of long poems, such as the "Hymne du Ciel" ("Hymn of the Sky"), celebrating natural phenomena, abstract ideas such as death or justice, or gods and heroes of antiquity; these poems, published as *Hymnes* (following the 3rd-century-BCE Greek poet Callimachus, who had inspired them), contain passages of stirring eloquence and vivid description, though few of them can hold the modern reader's interest from beginning to end. Reminiscences of his boyhood inspired other poems, such as his "Complainte contre fortune," published in the second book of the *Meslanges* (1559), which contains a haunting description of his solitary wanderings as a child in the woods and the discovery of his poetic vocation. This poem is also notable for a celebrated denunciation of the colonization of the New World, whose people he imagined to be noble savages living in an unspoiled state of nature comparable to his idealized memories of childhood.

The outbreak of the religious wars found him committed to an extreme royalist and Catholic position, and he drew upon himself the hostility of the Protestants. To this period belong the *Discours des misères de ce temps* (1562; "Discourse on the Miseries of These Times") and other *Discours* attacking his opponents, whom he dismissed as traitors and hypocrites with ever-increasing bitterness. Yet he also wrote much court poetry during this period, encouraged by the young king Charles IX, a sincere admirer, and, on the king's marriage to Elizabeth of Austria in 1571, he was commissioned to compose verses and plan the scheme of decorations for the state entry through the city of Paris. If he was by now in some sense the poet laureate of France, he made slow progress with *La Franciade*, which he intended to be the national epic; this somewhat halfhearted imitation of Virgil's great Latin epic, the *Aeneid*, was abandoned after the death of Charles IX, the four completed books being published in 1572. After the accession of Henry III, who did not favour Ronsard so much, he lived in semi-retirement, though his creativity was undiminished. The collected edition of his works published in 1578 included some remarkable new works, among them the so-called "Elegy

Against the Woodcutters of Gâtine" ("Contre les bucherons de la forêt de Gastine"), lamenting the destruction of the woods near his old home; a sequel to *Les Amours de Marie*; and the *Sonnets pour Hélène*. In the latter, which is now perhaps the most famous of his collections, the veteran poet demonstrates his power to revivify the stylized patterns of courtly love poetry. Even in his last illness, Ronsard still wrote verse that is sophisticated in form and rich with classical allusions. His posthumous collection, *Les Derniers Vers* ("The Final Verses"), poignantly expresses the anguish of the incurable invalid in nights spent alone in pain, longing for sleep, watching for the dawn, and praying for death.

Ronsard perfected the 12-syllable, or alexandrine, line of French verse, hitherto despised as too long and pedestrian, and established it as the classic medium for scathing satire, elegiac tenderness, and tragic passion. During his lifetime he was recognized in France as the prince of poets and a figure of national significance. This prominence, scarcely paralleled until Victor Hugo in the 19th century, faded into relative neglect in the 17th and 18th centuries; but his reputation was reinstated by the critic C.-A. Sainte-Beuve, and it has remained secure.

To the modern reader Ronsard is perhaps most appealing when celebrating his native countryside, reflecting on the brevity of youth and beauty, or voicing the various states of unrequited love, though he is also effective when identifying himself imaginatively with some classical mythological character and when expressing sentiments of fiery patriotism or deep humanity. He was a master of lyric themes and forms, and his poetry remains attractive to composers; some of his odes, such as "Mignonne, allons voir si la rose . . . ," were set to music repeatedly and have become as familiar to the general public in France as folk songs.

LUÍS DE CAMÕES

(b. *c.* 1524/25, Lisbon, Portugal—d. June 10, 1580, Lisbon)

Portugal's great national poet, Luís Vaz de Camões is the author of the epic poem *Os Lusíadas* (1572; *The Lusiads*), which describes Vasco da Gama's discovery of the sea route to India. Camões had a permanent and unparalleled impact on Portuguese and Brazilian literature alike, due not only to his epic but also to his posthumously published lyric poetry.

Life

What little information there is about Camões in a strict biographical sense falls into three categories: statements by his first biographers in the 17th century, a few documents unearthed in the 19th century and scant subsequent research, and very abstract allusions (some chronologically uncertain) to his own life in his works. Successive biographers have woven the few concrete facts known about Camões' life into a bewildering complexity of fantasy and theory that is unsupported by concrete documentary evidence.

It is supposed that Camões was born in Lisbon around 1524 or 1525, when Portuguese expansion in the East was at its peak. Research has shown him to be a member of the impoverished old aristocracy but well-related to the grandees of Portugal and Spain. A tradition that Camões studied at the University of Coimbra or that he followed any regular studies, for that matter, remains unproved, though few other European poets of that time achieved

Luís de Camões. Apic/Hulton Archive/Getty Images

such a vast knowledge of both classical and contemporary culture and philosophy. He is supposed to have been, in his youth, in territories held by the Portuguese in Morocco, but it is uncertain whether he had been exiled or was there because it was simply the place for a young Portuguese aristocrat to start a military career and to qualify for royal favours. It is also assumed that his youth in Lisbon was less than subdued. King John III pardoned him in 1553, when he was under arrest for taking part in a street brawl in which a royal officer was assaulted. The pardon hints that Camões would go to India in the king's service, but none of his wanderings for nearly 17 years there has been documented. He was certainly there, judging from references in his works that reveal an intimate knowledge of the area's social conditions. He surely did not make his fortune there, since he complains often in his poetry about his bad luck and the injustices he met with. While in the East, he took part in one or two military naval expeditions and, as he alludes to it in his epic, underwent shipwreck in the Mekong Delta. His years in the East can be assumed to have been like those of thousands of Portuguese scattered at the time from Africa to Japan, whose survival and fortunes were, as he says, always hanging from divine providence's very thin thread. Diogo do Couto, a 16th-century historian of the Portuguese East, who never included Camões among the nobles he carefully listed for every skirmish, did note, however, that he found "that great poet and old friend of mine" stranded penniless in Mozambique and helped to pay his trip back to Lisbon.

Camões returned to Portugal in 1570, and his *Os Lusíadas* was published in Lisbon in early 1572. In July of that year he was granted a royal pension, probably in recompense for both his service in India and his having written *Os Lusíadas*. His mother, a widow, survived him and had the pension renewed in her name. Documents related to payments due and to the renewal are known, and through them the date of his death in 1580 has been accepted. It is not certain that he died of anything more than premature old age brought on by illnesses and hardships.

Literary Works

Camões' poetical works may conveniently be discussed under three headings: lyric, epic, and dramatic.

The first edition of Camões' *Rimas* was published in 1595, 15 years after his death. The editor, Fernão Rodrigues Lobo Soropita, had exercised scrupulous care in collecting the poems from manuscript songbooks, but even so he could not avoid the inclusion of some apocryphal poems. The increasing fame of Camões' epic during the early 17th century also swept the lyrics into fame, and in the 17th century many efforts, not all of them praise-worthy, were made to unearth more poems. Prominent in this enterprise, but in a manner condemned by modern criticism, was Manuel de Faria e Sousa. Even in the 19th century, the Visconde de Juromenha added to the already excessive collection of lyrics, introducing into his edition of 1860–69 many poems from the songbooks, which were still comparatively unstudied. As a result the sonnets increased from 65 in the first edition to 352 in the Juromenha edition; the total number of poems, including sonnets, sextets, odes, octets, eclogues, elegies, and the Portuguese forms known as *canções*, *redondilhas*, *motos*, *esparsas*, and *glosas* had risen from 170 in the first edition to 593 by 1860.

With the work of Wilhelm Storck and Carolina Michaelis de Vasconcelos in the late 19th and early 20th centuries, there began a critical reaction which led to the elimination of many apocryphal poems. Although a complete restoration of Camões' lyrics appears impossible, scholars continue the work of purifying the texts. Fortunately there are sufficient authentic poems to confirm Camões' position as Portugal's finest lyric poet. If he had remained at the Portuguese court, he would not have reached this high pinnacle despite his consummate artistry. But he exchanged the vanity and superficiality of court life for the hardships of a soldier's life in Africa and India, and the exchange immeasurably enriched his poetry. He no longer needed to conform to the standards of brevity required in court circles, and, more important still, so profound was the anguish he experienced because of his exile from home and the trials he underwent in the East that his anguish became an integral part of his being, enabling him to give to "yearning fraught with loneliness" (*saudade-soledade*) a new and convincing undertone unique in Portuguese literature. His best poems vibrate with the unmistakable note of genuine suffering and deep sincerity of feeling. It is this note that places him far above the other poets of his era.

Although the *canções* and elegies show the poet's full powers, the *redondilhas* must not be underestimated. In the production of these elegant trifles Camões was inimitable. He rejuvenated the ancient art of glossing by the apparent spontaneity and simplicity, the delicate irony, and the piquant phraseology of his verses and so raised courtly grace in poetry to its highest level. These poems also show a Camões who could be happy and carefree.

The title of Camões' epic poem, *Os Lusíadas*, is taken from the word *Lusiads*, which means "Portuguese" and is in turn derived from the ancient Roman name for Portugal, *Lusitania*. The work extols the glorious deeds of the Portuguese and their victories over the enemies of Christianity: victories not only over their fellow man but also over the forces of nature as motivated by the inimical gods of classical mythology. The courage and enterprise of Portuguese explorers had inspired the idea of a national epic during the 15th century, but it was left to Camões in the 16th century to put it into execution. It is impossible to say for certain when he decided to do so or when he actually began to write his epic. *Os Lusíadas* describes the discovery of the sea route to India by Vasco da Gama. The

10 cantos of the poem are in ottava rima and amount to 1,102 stanzas in all. After an introduction, an invocation, and a dedication to King Sebastian, the action, on both the historical and the mythological levels, begins. Da Gama's ships are already under way in the Indian Ocean, sailing up the coast of East Africa, and the Olympian gods gather to discuss the fate of the expedition (which is favoured by Venus and attacked by Bacchus).

The voyagers spend several days in Melinde on the east coast of Africa, and at the king's request Vasco da Gama relates the entire history of Portugal from its origins to the inception of their great voyage (Cantos III, IV, and V). These cantos contain some of the most beautiful passages in the poem: the murder of Inês de Castro, who becomes a symbol of death for the sake of love; the battle of Aljubarrota; the vision of King Manuel I; the description of St. Elmo's fire and the waterspout; and the story of Adamastor, the giant of classical parentage who, as the Cape of Good Hope, tells da Gama he will lie in wait to destroy the fleets coming back from India.

When they re-embark the poet takes advantage of leisure hours on board to narrate the story of the Doze de Inglaterra (Canto VI, 43–69). In the meantime, Bacchus, ever ready to impede the progress of the Portuguese in the East, convokes a council of the sea gods and incites them to arrange the shipwreck of the Portuguese fleet. This is prevented by Venus (Canto VI, 85–91), and Vasco da Gama is able to reach Calicut (Kozhikode, now in Kerala state, southwestern India), the end of his voyage. There his brother, Paulo da Gama, receives the king's representative on board and explains the significance of the characters depicted on the banners that adorn the captain's ship (Cantos VII and VIII). On their homeward voyage the mariners chance upon the island that Venus has created for them, and the nymphs reward them for their labours. One of the nymphs sings of the future deeds of the Portuguese (Cantos IX and X), and the entertainment ends with a description of the universe given by Thetis and Vasco da Gama, after which the sailors embark once more and the nymphs accompany them on their homeward journey.

In *Os Lusíadas* Camões achieved an exquisite harmony between classical learning and practical experience, delicate perception and superb artistic skill, expressing through them the gravity of thought and the finest human emotions. The epic was his eulogy of the "dangerous life" (*vida perigosa*) and was a stern warning to the Christian monarchs, who, idling their time away in petty struggles, were failing to unite against the encroaching conquests of Islam in southeastern Europe. Realistic descriptions in the poem of sensual encounters, battles, and storms and other natural phenomena transcend the thrust of classical allusions that permeate the work and make for the high-flown yet fluent style of the poem. *Os Lusíadas* reveals an astonishing command of language and variety of styles and provides a fascinating portrait of an extraordinary man and poet.

In his dramatic works Camões tried to combine national and classical tendencies. In his comedy *Anfitriões* (*Enfatriões*; "The Two Amphitryons"), an adaptation of Plautus' *Amphitryon*, he accentuated the comic aspect of the myth of Amphitryon; in the comedy *El-rei Seleuco* ("King Seleucas"), he reduced the situation found in Plutarch (in which Seleucas' son wins his stepmother from his father) to pure farce; and in *Filodemo* he developed the *auto*, a kind of morality play, which Gil Vicente had earlier made popular. But Camões seems to have regarded comedy as unimportant, as a mere curiosity and a recreation to which he could give only transitory attention. Nevertheless, by imposing classical restraint on the Vicentian *auto*, by increasing the importance of the plot, by transferring the comic element from the characters to the action, and by refining the farce, Camões indicated a possible means of rejuvenating 16th-century comedy in Portugal. Later dramatists, unfortunately, were incapable of following the lead he had given. Drama, however, is the least important aspect of Camões' poetry. It was his epic and his lyrics, among which are some of the loveliest ever written, that made him one of the greatest poets of 16th-century Europe and have given him a lasting claim to fame.

JAN KOCHANOWSKI

(b. 1530, Sycyna, Poland—d. August 22, 1584, Lublin)

Jan Kochanowski was a humanist poet who dominated the culture of Renaissance Poland.

Born into the country nobility, Kochanowski studied at the Jagiellonian University in Kraków and later, between 1552 and 1559, at the University of Padua in Italy. On his return to Poland in 1559, he served as a secretary at the royal court in Kraków. He married in about 1575 and retired to his family estate at Czarnolas, in central Poland.

Kochanowski's first poems, mostly elegies, were written in Latin, but he soon turned to the vernacular. Since Polish was not fully developed at that time as a language of literary expression, he devised his own poetic syntax and patterns of versification, setting high standards for the centuries to come. His crowning achievement is the cycle *Treny* (1580; *Laments*), 19 poems inspired by the death of his beloved daughter, Urszula. Kochanowski was also the author of the first Polish Renaissance tragedy, *Odprawa posłów greckich* (1578; *The Dismissal of the Grecian Envoys*). With a plot from Homer's *Iliad* and written in blank verse, it was performed at the royal court in Ujazdów near

Warsaw in 1578 and was regarded as a political commentary on the contemporary situation in the country, which was getting ready for a war with Russia's Ivan the Terrible.

Kochanowski's role in developing Polish literary standards cannot be underestimated. Modeling his poetry on the best classical traditions, he was able to transpose them into his native tongue with a pertinence and elegance that had not hitherto been achieved. Besides his achievements in versification, he employed with great artistry a number of literary forms, such as hymns, lyrical songs, epigrams, satires, translations from the Bible, and others. Kochanowski's place was also unique in Slavic literature generally, and he is considered to have had no equals until the 19th century. A true humanist, he was the best representative of the Renaissance period in that region of Europe.

MICHEL DE MONTAIGNE

(b. February 28, 1533, Château de Montaigne, near Bordeaux, France—d. September 23, 1592, Château de Montaigne)

The French writer Michel Eyquem de Montaigne is best known for his *Essais* (*Essays*), which established a new literary form. In his *Essays* he wrote one of the most captivating and intimate self-portraits ever given.

Life

Born in the family domain of Château de Montaigne in southwestern France, Michel Eyquem spent most of his life at his château and in the city of Bordeaux, 30 miles (48 km) to the west. The family fortune had been founded in commerce by Montaigne's great-grandfather, who acquired the estate and the title of nobility. His grandfather and his father expanded their activities to the realm of public service and established the family in the *noblesse de robe*, the administrative nobility of France. Montaigne's father, Pierre Eyquem, served as mayor of Bordeaux.

As a young child Montaigne was tutored at home according to his father's ideas of pedagogy, which included the creation of a cosseted ambience of gentle encouragement and the exclusive use of Latin, still the international language of educated people. As a result the boy did not learn French until he was six years old. He continued his education at the College of Guyenne, where he found the strict discipline abhorrent and the instruction only moderately interesting, and eventually at the University of Toulouse, where he studied law. Following in the public-service tradition begun by his grandfather, he entered into the magistrature, becoming a member of the Board of Excise, the new tax court of Périgueux, and, when that body was dissolved in 1557, of the Parliament of Bordeaux, one of the eight regional parliaments that constituted the French Parliament, the highest national court of justice. There, at the age of 24, he made the acquaintance of Étienne de la Boétie, a meeting that was one of the most significant events in Montaigne's life. Between La Boétie (1530–63), an already distinguished civil servant, humanist scholar, and writer, and Montaigne an extraordinary friendship sprang up, based on a profound intellectual and emotional closeness and reciprocity. In his essay *On Friendship* Montaigne wrote in a very touching manner about his bond with La Boétie, which he called perfect and indivisible, vastly superior to all other human alliances. When La Boétie died of dysentery, he left a void in Montaigne's life that no other being was ever able to fill, and it is likely that Montaigne started on his writing career, six years after La Boétie's death, in order to fill the emptiness left by the loss of the irretrievable friend.

In 1565 Montaigne was married, acting less out of love than out of a sense of familial and social duty, to Françoise de la Chassaigne, the daughter of one of his colleagues at the Parliament of Bordeaux. He fathered six daughters, five of whom died in infancy, whereas the sixth, Léonore, survived him.

In 1569 Montaigne published his first book, a French translation of the 15th-century *Natural Theology* by the Spanish monk Raymond Sebond. He had undertaken the task at the request of his father, who, however, died in 1568, before its publication, leaving to his oldest son the title and the domain of Montaigne.

In 1570 Montaigne sold his seat in the Bordeaux Parliament, signifying his departure from public life. After taking care of the posthumous publication of La Boétie's works, together with his own dedicatory letters, he retired in 1571 to the castle of Montaigne in order to devote his time to reading, meditating, and writing. He spent the years from 1571 to 1580 composing the first two books of the *Essays*, which comprise respectively 57 and 37 chapters of greatly varying lengths; they were published in Bordeaux in 1580.

While in Italy, in the fall of 1581, Montaigne received the news that he had been elected to the office his father had held, that of mayor of Bordeaux. Reluctant to accept, because of the dismal political situation in France and because of ill health (he suffered from kidney stones, which had also plagued him on his trip), he nevertheless assumed the position at the request of Henry III and held it for two terms, until July 1585.

He spent the last years of his life at his château, continuing to read and to reflect and to work on the *Essays*, adding new passages, which signify not so much profound changes in his ideas as further explorations of his thought and experience. Different illnesses beset him during this period, and he died after an attack of quinsy, an inflammation of the tonsils, which had deprived him of speech. His death occurred while he was hearing mass in his room.

The Essays

Montaigne saw his age as one of dissimulation, corruption, violence, and hypocrisy, and it is therefore not surprising that the point of departure of the *Essays* is situated in negativity: the negativity of Montaigne's recognition of the rule of appearances and of the loss of connection with the truth of being. Montaigne's much-discussed skepticism results from that initial negativity, as he questions the possibility of all knowing and sees the human being as a creature of weakness and failure, of inconstancy and uncertainty, of incapacity and fragmentation, or, as he wrote in the first of the essays, as "a marvelously vain, diverse, and undulating thing." His skepticism is reflected in the French title of his work, *Essais*, or "Attempts," which implies not a transmission of proven knowledge or of confident opinion but a project of trial and error, of tentative exploration. Neither a reference to an established genre (for Montaigne's book inaugurated the term *essay* for the short prose composition treating a given subject in a rather informal and personal manner) nor an indication of a necessary internal unity and structure within the work, the title indicates an intellectual attitude of questioning and of continuous assessment.

Montaigne's skepticism does not, however, preclude a belief in the existence of truth but rather constitutes a defense against the danger of locating truth in false, unexamined, and externally imposed notions. His skepticism, combined with his desire for truth, drives him to the rejection of commonly accepted ideas and to a profound distrust of generalizations and abstractions; it also shows him the way to an exploration of the only realm that promises certainty: that of concrete phenomena and primarily the basic phenomenon of his own body-and-mind self. This self, with all its imperfections, constitutes the only possible site where the search for truth can start, and it is the reason Montaigne, from the beginning to the end of the *Essays*, does not cease to affirm that "I am myself the matter of my book." He finds that his identity, his "master form" as he calls it, cannot be defined in simple terms of a constant and stable self, since it is instead a changeable and fragmented thing, and that the valorization and acceptance of these traits is the only guarantee of authenticity and integrity, the only way of remaining faithful to the truth of one's being and one's nature rather than to alien semblances.

Yet, despite his insistence that the self guard its freedom toward outside influences and the tyranny of imposed customs and opinions, Montaigne believes in the value of reaching outside the self. Indeed, throughout his writings, as he did in his private and public life, he manifests the need to entertain ties with the world of other people and of events. For this necessary coming and going between the interiority of the self and the exteriority of the world, Montaigne uses the image of the back room: human beings have their front room, facing the street, where they meet and interact with others, but they need always to be able to retreat into the back room of the most private self, where they may reaffirm the freedom and strength of intimate identity and reflect upon the vagaries of experience. Given that always-available retreat, Montaigne encourages contact with others, from which one may learn much that is useful. In order to do so, he advocates travel, reading, especially of history books, and conversations with friends. These friends, for Montaigne, are necessarily men. While none can ever replace La Boétie, it is possible to have interesting and worthwhile exchanges with men of discernment and wit. As for his relations with women, Montaigne wrote about them with a frankness unusual for his time. The only uncomplicated bond is that of marriage, which reposes, for Montaigne, on reasons of family and posterity and in which one invests little of oneself. Love, on the other hand, with its emotional and erotic demands, comports the risk of enslavement and loss of freedom. Montaigne, often designated as a misogynist, does in fact recognize that men and women are fundamentally alike in their fears, desires, and attempts to find and affirm their own identity and that only custom and adherence to an antiquated status quo establish the apparent differences between the sexes, but he does not explore the possibility of overcoming that fundamental separation and of establishing an intellectual equality.

Montaigne applies and illustrates his ideas concerning the independence and freedom of the self and the importance of social and intellectual intercourse in all his writings and in particular in his essay on the education of children. There, as elsewhere, he advocates the value of concrete experience over abstract learning and of independent judgment over an accumulation of undigested notions uncritically accepted from others. He also stresses, throughout his work, the role of the body, as in his candid descriptions of his own bodily functions and in his extensive musings on the realities of illness, of aging, and of death. The presence of death pervades the *Essays*, as Montaigne wants to familiarize himself with the inevitability of dying and so to rid himself of the tyranny of fear, and he is able to accept death as part of nature's exigencies, inherent in life's expectations and limitations.

Montaigne seems to have been a loyal if not fervent Roman Catholic all his life, but he distrusted all human pretenses to knowledge of a spiritual experience which is not attached to a concretely lived reality. He declined to speculate on a transcendence that falls beyond human ken, believing in God but refusing to invoke him in necessarily presumptuous and reductive ways.

Although Montaigne certainly knew the classical philosophers, his ideas spring less out of their teaching than out of the completely original meditation on himself, which he extends to a description of the human being and to an ethics of authenticity, self-acceptance, and tolerance. The *Essays* are the record of his thoughts, presented not in artificially organized stages but as they occurred and reoccurred to him in different shapes throughout his thinking and writing activity. They are not the record of an intellectual evolution but of a continuous accretion, and he insists on the immediacy and the authenticity of their testimony. To denote their consubstantiality with his natural self, he describes them as his children, and, in an image of startling and completely nonpejorative earthiness, as the excrements of his mind. As he refuses to impose a false unity on the spontaneous workings of his thought, so he refuses to impose a false structure on his *Essays*. "As my mind roams, so does my style," he wrote, and the multiple digressions, the wandering developments, the savory, concrete vocabulary, all denote that fidelity to the freshness and the immediacy of the living thought.

Montaigne's *Essays* thus incorporate a profound skepticism concerning the human being's dangerously inflated claims to knowledge and certainty but also assert that there is no greater achievement than the ability to accept one's being without either contempt or illusion, in the full realization of its limitations and its richness.

ALONSO DE ERCILLA Y ZÚÑIGA

(b. August 7, 1533, Madrid, Spain—d. November 29, 1594, Madrid)

The Spanish poet Alonso de Ercilla y Zúñiga is the author of *La Araucana* (1569–89), the most celebrated Renaissance epic poem written in Castilian.

Ercilla received a rigorous literary education before going to the New World in 1555. He distinguished himself as a soldier in Chile during the wars against the Araucanian Indians, and he based *La Araucana* on his experiences. He composed the whole of the poem's first part and sections of the second and third while on the field of battle; a number of stanzas were written during breaks in the action on whatever he had at hand, including pieces of leather, some too small to contain more than six lines of poetry. He finished the poem after he returned to Spain in 1563.

La Araucana consists of 37 cantos that are distributed across the poem's three parts. The first part was published in 1569; the second part appeared in 1578, when it was published with the first part; the third part was published with the first and second parts in 1589. The poem shows Ercilla to be a master of the *octava real*, the complicated stanza in which many other Renaissance epics in Castilian were written. A difficult eight-line unit of 11-syllable verses that are linked by a tight rhyme scheme, the *octava real* was a challenge few poets met. It had been adapted from Italian only in the 16th century, and it produces resonant, serious-sounding verse that is appropriate to epic themes.

La Araucana describes Spanish conquests that were not comparable in importance to those of Hernán Cortés, who conquered the Aztec empire, and Francisco Pizarro, who overthrew the Inca empire. Contrary to the epic conventions of the time, however, Ercilla placed the lesser conquests of the Spanish in Chile at the core of his poem. *La Araucana*'s successes—and weaknesses—as a poem stem from the uneasy coexistence of characters and situations drawn from Classical sources (primarily Virgil) and Renaissance poets (Ludovico Ariosto and Torquato Tasso) with material derived from the actions of contemporary Spaniards and Araucanians.

The mixture of Classical and Araucanian motifs in *La Araucana* often strikes the modern reader as unusual, but Ercilla's turning native peoples into ancient Greeks, Romans, or Carthaginians was a common practice of his time. For Ercilla, the Araucanians were noble and brave—only lacking, as their Classical counterparts did, the Christian faith. Caupolicán, the Indian warrior and chieftain who is the protagonist of Ercilla's poem, has a panoply of Classical heroes behind him. His valour and nobility give *La Araucana* grandeur, as does the poem's exaltation of the vanquished: the defeated Araucanians are the champions in this poem, which was written by one of the victors, a Spaniard. Ercilla's depiction of Caupolicán elevates *La Araucana* above the poem's structural defects and prosaic moments, which occur toward the end when Ercilla follows Tasso too closely and the narrative strays from the author's lived experience. Ercilla, the poet-soldier, eventually emerges as the true hero of his own poem, and he is the figure that gives the poem unity and strength.

Ercilla embodied the Renaissance ideal of being at once a man of action and a man of letters. He was adept at blending personal, lived experience with literary tradition. He was widely acclaimed in Spain. In Miguel de Cervantes' 17th-century novel *Don Quixote*, Ercilla's *La Araucana* is proclaimed to be among the best poems in the heroic style ever written, good enough to compete with those of

Ariosto and Tasso. *La Araucana*'s more dramatic moments also became a source of plays. But the Renaissance epic is not a genre that has, as a whole, endured well, and today Ercilla is little known and *La Araucana* is rarely read except by specialists and students of Spanish and Latin American literatures.

GEORGE GASCOIGNE

(b. *c.* 1539, Cardington, Bedfordshire, England—d. October 7, 1577, Barnack, near Stamford, Lincolnshire)

George Gascoigne was an English poet and a major literary innovator.

Gascoigne attended the University of Cambridge, studied law at Gray's Inn in 1555, and thereafter pursued careers as a politician, country gentleman, courtier, soldier of fortune, and man of letters, all with moderate distinction. He was a member of Parliament (1557–59). Because of his extravagance and debts, he gained a reputation for disorderly living. He served with English troops in the Low Countries, ending his military career as a repatriated prisoner of war. In 1575 he helped to arrange the celebrated entertainments provided for Queen Elizabeth I at Kenilworth and Woodstock and in 1576 went to Holland as an agent in the royal service. Among his friends were many leading poets, notably George Whetstone, George Turberville, and Edmund Spenser.

Gascoigne was a skilled literary craftsman, memorable for versatility and vividness of expression and for his treatment of events based on his own experience. His chief importance, however, is as a pioneer of the English Renaissance who had a remarkable aptitude for domesticating foreign literary genres. He foreshadowed the English sonnet sequences with groups of linked sonnets in his first published work, *A Hundreth sundrie Flowres* (1573), a collection of verse and prose. In *The Posies of George Gascoigne* (1575), an authorized revision of the earlier work, which had been published anonymously, he included also "Certayne notes of Instruction," the first treatise on prosody in English. In *The Steele Glas* (1576), one of the earliest formal satires in English, he wrote the first original nondramatic English blank verse. In two amatory poems, the autobiographical "Dan Bartholomew of Bathe" (published in *A Hundreth sundrie Flowres*) and *The Complainte of Phylomene* (1576), Gascoigne developed Ovidian verse narrative, the form used by William Shakespeare in *Venus and Adonis* and *The Rape of Lucrece*.

"The Adventures of Master F.J.," published in *A Hundreth sundrie Flowres*, was the first original prose narrative of the English Renaissance. Another prose work, *The Spoyle of Antwerpe* (1576), is an early example of war journalism, characterized by objective and graphic reporting.

Gascoigne's *Jocasta* (performed in 1566) constituted the first Greek tragedy to be presented on the English stage. Translated into blank verse, with the collaboration of Francis Kinwelmersh, from Lodovico Dolce's *Giocasta*, the work derives ultimately from Euripides' *Phoenissae*. In comedy, Gascoigne's *Supposes* (1566?), a prose translation and adaptation of Ludovico Ariosto's *I Suppositi*, was the first prose comedy to be translated from Italian into English. A dramatically effective work, it provided the subplot for Shakespeare's *The Taming of the Shrew*. A third play, *The Glasse of Government* (1575), is a didactic drama on the Prodigal Son theme. It rounds out the picture of Gascoigne as a typical literary man of the early Renaissance.

SAINT JOHN OF THE CROSS

(b. June 24, 1542, Fontiveros, Spain—d. December 14, 1591, Ubeda; canonized 1726; feast day December 14)

Saint John of the Cross was one of the greatest Christian mystics and Spanish poets, doctor of the church, reformer of Spanish monasticism, and cofounder of the contemplative order of Discalced Carmelites.

Originally known as Juan de Yepes y Álvarez, John became a Carmelite monk at Medina del Campo, Spain, in 1563 and was ordained priest in 1567. St. Teresa of Ávila, the celebrated mystic, enlisted his help (1568) in her restoration of Carmelite life to its original observance of austerity. A year later, at Duruelo, he opened the first Discalced Carmelite monastery. Reform, however, caused friction within the order and led to his imprisonment, first in 1576 and again in 1577 at Toledo, where he wrote some of his finest poetry. Escaping in August 1578, he later won high office in the order, becoming vicar provincial of Andalusia from 1585 to 1587. Near the end of his life the Discalced Carmelites were again troubled by dissension, and he withdrew to absolute solitude.

John schematized the steps of mystical ascent—a self-communion that in quietude leads the individual from the inharmonious distractions of the world to the sublime peace of reunion between the soul and God. John's schematization combines a poetic sensitivity for the nuances of mystical experience with a theological and philosophical precision guided by his study of St. Thomas Aquinas. By virtue of his intense poems, "Cántico espiritual" ("The Spiritual Canticle"), "Noche obscura del alma" ("The Dark

Night of the Soul"), and "Llama de amor viva" ("The Living Flame of Love"), he achieves preeminence in Spanish mystical literature, expressing the experience of the mystical union between the soul and Christ.

In "Noche," perhaps his best-known work, he describes the process by which the soul sheds its attachment to everything and eventually passes through a personal experience of Christ's Crucifixion to his glory. The lyric consists of eight stanzas "in which the soul sings of the fortunate adventure that it had in passing through the dark night of faith . . . to union with the Beloved."

Though John reaches peaks of lyricism, he also presents the reader with considerable difficulties because his approach is rigorously intellectual. The same word may recur twice within four lines of a poem with a different symbolism on each occasion.

*T*ULSIDAS

(b. 1543?, probably Rajapur, India—d. 1623, Varanasi)

The Indian Vaishnavite (devotee of the deity Vishnu) poet Tulsidas is primarily known for his principal work, the *Ramcharitmanas* ("Sacred Lake of the Acts of Rama"), which is the greatest achievement of medieval Hindi literature and has exercised an abiding influence on northern Indian Hinduism.

The *Ramcharitmanas* expresses par excellence the religious sentiment of *bhakti* ("loving devotion") to Rama, a popular avatar (incarnation) of the deity Vishnu who is regarded as the chief means of salvation. Although Tulsidas was above all a devotee of Rama, he remained a Smarta Vaishnavite, following the more generally accepted traditions and customs of Hinduism rather than a strict sectarian outlook. His eclectic approach to doctrinal questions meant that he was able to rally wide support for the worship of Rama in northern India, and the success of the *Ramcharitmanas* has been a prime factor in the replacement of the cult of Krishna (another wildly popular avatar of Vishnu) with that of Rama as the dominant religious influence in that area.

Little is known about Tulsidas' life. He was probably born at Rajapur and lived most of his adult life at Varanasi. The *Ramcharitmanas* was written between 1574 and 1576 or 1577. A number of early manuscripts are extant—some fragmentary—and one is said to be an autograph. The oldest complete manuscript is dated 1647. The poem, written in Awadhi, an Eastern Hindi dialect, consists of seven cantos of unequal lengths. Although the ultimate source of the central narrative is the Sanskrit epic *Ramayana*, Tulsidas' principal immediate source was the *Adhyatma Ramayana*, a late medieval recasting of the epic that had sought to harmonize Advaita ("Nondual") Vedanta theology and the worship of Rama. The influence of the *Bhagavata-Purana*, the chief scripture of Krishna worshipers, is also discernible, as is that of a number of minor sources.

Eleven other works are attributed with some certainty to Tulsidas. These include *Krishna gitavali*, a series of 61 songs in honour of Krishna; *Vinay pattrika*, a series of 279 verse passages addressed to Hindu sacred places and deities (chiefly Rama and Sita); and *Kavitavali*, telling incidents from the story of Rama.

TORQUATO TASSO

(b. March 11, 1544, Sorrento, Kingdom of Naples [Italy]—d. April 25, 1595, Rome)

Lhe greatest Italian poet of the late Renaissance, Torquato Tasso is celebrated for his heroic epic poem *Gerusalemme liberata* (1581; "Jerusalem Liberated"), dealing with the capture of Jerusalem during the First Crusade.

Early Life and Works

Tasso was the son of Bernardo Tasso, a poet and courtier, and of Porzia de' Rossi. His childhood was overshadowed by family misfortunes: his father followed the prince of Salerno into exile in 1552; the family estates were confiscated; his mother died in 1556; and there was subsequent litigation about her dowry. Tasso joined his father in Rome in 1554 and two years later at the court of the Duke of Urbino, where he was educated with the duke's son. His imagination had already been fired by stories of the Crusades, and he was struck in 1558 by news of an attack by the Turks on Sorrento, where his sister Cornelia narrowly escaped the accompanying massacre.

While in Venice the following year, Tasso began to write an epic in ottava rima (an Italian stanza of eight 11-syllabled lines), *Gerusalemme*, about the First Crusade (which recovered Jerusalem from the Turks in 1099). He soon interrupted its composition, probably realizing that he was too inexperienced to write a historical epic, and turned to themes of chivalry. The resulting *Rinaldo* (1562) exhibited his technical ability but not as yet his poetic genius.

In 1560 he was sent to study law in Padua and there met the humanist and critic Sperone Speroni, under whose guidance he studied Aristotle's *Poetics*. It was probably then that he started writing his *Discorsi dell'arte poetica* (1587; "Treatise on the Art of Poetry"), explaining therein his qualified acceptance of the rules supposedly laid down by Aristotle in 4th-century-BCE Greece. (For instance, Tasso maintained that unity of action should not exclude a variety of episodes.)

In 1565 Tasso entered the service of Luigi, cardinal d'Este, and frequented the court of Duke Alfonso II d'Este at Ferrara, where he enjoyed the patronage of the duke's sisters, Lucrezia and Leonora, for whom he wrote some of his finest lyrical poems. In 1569 his father died; the following year Lucrezia left Ferrara, and Tasso followed the cardinal to Paris, where he met a fellow poet, the Frenchman Pierre Ronsard. Back in Ferrara in 1571, he became one of the duke's courtiers and devoted himself to intense poetic activity. In 1573 he wrote the pastoral drama *L'Aminta* (performed 1573; published 1581), which transcends the convention of artificial rusticity with the sensuous, lyrical inspiration of its picture of Arcadia. The tone of *L'Aminta* is lyrical rather than dramatic; the play presents with great delicacy of feeling a series of vignettes that culminate in the shepherd Aminta's long-sought attainment of his beloved, Silvia. The play reflects in its idealization of court life the ephemeral period of happiness Tasso had enjoyed at Ferrara.

Composition of the Gerusalemme Liberata

In 1575 Tasso completed his masterpiece, the *Gerusalemme liberata*, on which he had been working since his stay in Ferrara. In this epic poem Tasso narrates the actions of the Christian army led by Godfrey of Bouillon during the last months of the First Crusade, culminating in the conquest of Jerusalem and the Battle of Ascalon. To the poem's principal historical action Tasso added a number of imaginary episodes in which his lyrical and hedonistic imagination could find free expression. The most prominent of these episodes is the story of the Italian hero Rinaldo, including his rebellion, his love for the Saracen girl Armida, and his repentance and decisive participation in the final battle. Tasso also added the story of the Italian hero Tancred and his love for the beautiful Saracen Clorinda, whom Tancred unwittingly kills in battle; the secret passion of Erminia, princess of Antioch, for Tancred; and the intervention of supernatural forces in favour of Aladino, the king of Jerusalem.

In composing the *Liberata*, Tasso tried to establish a balance between the moral aspirations of his times and his own sensuous inspiration, and between the requirements of the formal rules laid down for the epic by Renaissance scholars and the impulse of his own lyrical fantasy. He succeeded in reconciling invention with historical truth by adding the aforementioned romantic and idyllic episodes to the firm groundwork of the principal historical action. These episodes contribute much of the lyrical charm that the poem possesses.

Aware of his epic's poetic novelty, Tasso went to Rome in order to arrange its revision by a group of critics. Back in Ferrara in 1576, he started revising his work in a contradictory mood, in which he felt the urge both to accept the criticism he himself had sought and yet to rebel against this kind of authority. He developed a persecution mania, accompanied by unwarranted scruples about his own religious orthodoxy, and the following years were characterized by sudden departures from Ferrara and by violent crises, the latter culminating in his incarceration in the hospital of Santa Anna (1579–86) by order of the Duke of Ferrara. During his confinement Tasso wrote a number of philosophical and moral dialogues that, together with his numerous letters, are among the best examples of 16th-century Italian prose. In 1581 the first editions of the *Gerusalemme liberata* and portions of the *Rime e prose* were published. A long controversy started among Italian critics on the respective merits of his epic and of its immediate predecessor, Ludovico Ariosto's chivalric poem *Orlando furioso*, Tasso himself taking part in the controversy with an *Apologia* (1585).

In July 1586 Tasso was released from Santa Anna, thanks to the intervention of Vincenzo Gonzaga, prince of Mantua, who received him at his court. After a revival of creative inspiration—at Mantua he completed his tragedy *Galealto*, retitled *Re Torrismondo* (1587)—he relapsed into his usual inquietude and fled from Mantua, wandering mainly between Rome and Naples, where he composed his religious poems *Monte oliveto* (1605; "Mount of Olives") and *Le sette giornate del mondo creato* (1607; "The Seven Days of Creation"). In May 1592 he was given hospitality in Rome by Cardinal Cinzio Aldobrandini, a nephew of Pope Clement VIII. To this patron he dedicated a new version of his epic (*Gerusalemme conquistata*, published 1593), a poetic failure that reveals the extent of Tasso's final submission to the moral and literary prejudices of the times. He wrote two more religious poems (*Lagrime di Maria Vergine* and *Lagrime di Gesù Cristo*), and in June 1594 he went again to Naples, where his *Discorsi del poema eroico* (1594; "Treatise on Epic Poetry") was published. In the *Discorsi* he tried to justify the new version of his epic according to his modified conception of poetic art. On Tasso's return to Rome in November 1594, the pope granted him an annual pension and promised to make him poet laureate. But Tasso fell ill in the following March, was moved to the convent of San Onofrio, and died within a few weeks.

Miguel de Cervantes

(b. September 29?, 1547, Alcalá de Henares, Spain—
d. April 22, 1616, Madrid)

Miguel de Cervantes Saavedra was a Spanish novelist, playwright, and poet, the creator of *Don Quixote* (1605, 1615) and the most important and celebrated figure in Spanish literature.

Cervantes was born some 20 miles (32 km) from Madrid, the fourth of seven children in a family whose origins were of the minor gentry but which had come down in the world. His father was a barber-surgeon who set bones, performed bloodlettings, and attended lesser medical needs. The family moved from town to town, and little is known of Cervantes' early education. The supposition, based on a passage in one of the *Exemplary Stories*, that he studied for a time under the Jesuits, though not unlikely, remains conjectural. Unlike most Spanish writers of his time, including some of humble origin, he apparently did not go to a university. What is certain is that at some stage he became an avid reader of books. The head of a municipal school in Madrid, a man with Erasmist intellectual leanings named Juan López de Hoyos, refers to a Miguel de Cervantes as his "beloved pupil." This was in 1569, when the future author was 21, so—if this was the same Cervantes—he must either have been a pupil-teacher at the school or have studied earlier under López de Hoyos. His first published poem, on the death of Philip II's young queen, Elizabeth of Valois, appeared at this time.

Soldier and Slave

That same year he left Spain for Italy. Whether this was because he was the "student" of the same name wanted by the law for involvement in a wounding incident is another mystery; the evidence is contradictory. In any event, in going to Italy Cervantes was doing what many young Spaniards of the time did to further their careers in one way or another. It seems that for a time he served as chamberlain in the household of Cardinal Giulio Acquaviva in Rome. However, by 1570 he had enlisted as a soldier in a Spanish infantry regiment stationed in Naples, then a possession of the Spanish crown. He was there for about a year before he saw active service.

Relations with the Ottoman Empire under Selim II were reaching a crisis, and the Turks occupied Cyprus in 1570. A confrontation between the Turkish fleet and the naval forces of Venice, the papacy, and Spain was inevitable. In mid-September 1571 Cervantes sailed on board the *Marquesa*, part of the large fleet under the command of Don Juan de Austria that engaged the enemy on October 7 in the Gulf of Lepanto near Corinth. The fierce battle ended in a crushing defeat for the Turks that was ultimately to break their control of the Mediterranean. There are independent accounts of Cervantes' conduct in the action, and they concur in testifying to his personal courage. Though stricken with a fever, he refused to stay below and joined the thick of the fighting. He received two gunshot wounds in the chest, and a third rendered his left hand useless for the rest of his life. He always looked back on his conduct in the battle with pride. From 1572 to 1575, based mainly in Naples, he continued his soldier's life; he was at Navarino and saw action in Tunis and La Goleta. Perhaps with a recommendation for promotion to the rank of captain, more likely just leaving the army, he set sail for Spain in September 1575 with letters of commendation to the king from the duque de Sessa and Don Juan himself.

On this voyage his ship was attacked and captured by Barbary corsairs, and Cervantes, together with his brother Rodrigo, was sold into slavery in Algiers, the centre of the Christian slave traffic in the Muslim world. The letters he carried magnified his importance in the eyes of his captors. This had the effect of raising his ransom price, and thus prolonging his captivity, while also, it appears, protecting his person from punishment by death, mutilation, or torture when his four daring bids to escape were frustrated. His masters treated him with considerable leniency in the circumstances, whatever the reason. At least two contemporary records of the life led by Christian captives in Algiers at this time mention Cervantes. He clearly made a name for himself for courage and leadership among the captive community. At long last, in September 1580, three years after Rodrigo had earned his freedom, Miguel's family, with the aid and intervention of the Trinitarian friars, raised the 500 gold escudos demanded for his release. Not surprisingly, this, the most adventurous period of Cervantes' life, supplied subject matter for several of his literary works, notably the Captive's tale in *Don Quixote* and the two Algiers plays, *El trato de Argel* ("The Traffic of Algiers") and *Los baños de Argel* ("The Bagnios [an obsolete word for "prisons"] of Algiers"), as well as episodes in a number of other writings, although never in straight autobiographical form.

Civil Servant and Writer

Back in Spain, Cervantes spent most of the rest of his life in a manner that contrasted entirely with his decade of action and danger. He would be constantly short of money and in tedious and exacting employment; it would be 25 years before he scored a major literary success with *Don Quixote*. On his return home he found that prices had risen and the standard of living for many, particularly those of the middle class, including his family, had fallen. Cervantes' war record did not now bring the recompense he expected. He applied unsuccessfully for several administrative posts in Spain's American empire. The most he succeeded in acquiring was a brief appointment as royal messenger to Oran, Algeria, in 1581. In vain he followed Philip II and the court to Lisbon in newly annexed Portugal.

About this time he had an affair with a young married woman named Ana de Villafranca (or Ana Franca de Rojas), the fruit of which was a daughter. Isabel de Saavedra, Cervantes' only child, was later brought up in her father's household. Late in 1584 he married Catalina de Salazar y Palacios, 18 years his junior. She had a small property in the village of Esquivias in La Mancha. Little is known about their emotional relationship. There is no reason to suppose that the marriage did not settle down into an adequate companionableness, despite Cervantes' enforced long absences from home. Neither is there any special reason to suppose that Catalina was an inspiration or a model for characters in the poetry Cervantes was now writing or in his first published fiction, *La Galatea* (1585; *Galatea: A Pastoral Romance*), in the newly fashionable genre of the pastoral romance. The publisher, Blas de Robles, paid him 1,336 reales for it, a good price for a first book. The dedication of the work to Ascanio Colonna, a friend of Acquaviva, was a bid for patronage that does not seem to have been productive. Doubtless helped by a small circle of literary friends, such as the poet Luis Gálvez de Montalvo, the book did bring Cervantes' name before a sophisticated reading public. But the only later editions in Spanish to appear in the author's lifetime were those of Lisbon, 1590, and Paris, 1611. *La Galatea* breaks off in mid-narrative; judging by his repeatedly expressed hopes of writing a sequel, Cervantes evidently maintained a lasting fondness for the work.

Cervantes also turned his hand to the writing of drama at this time, the early dawn of the Golden Age of the Spanish theatre. He contracted to write two plays for the theatrical manager Gaspar de Porras in 1585, one of which,

La confusa ("Confusion"), he later described as the best he ever wrote. Many years afterward he claimed to have written 20 or 30 plays in this period, which, he noted, were received by the public without being booed off the stage or having the actors pelted with vegetables. The number is vague; only two certainly survive from this time, the historical tragedy of *La Numancia* (1580s; *Numantia: A Tragedy*) and *El trato de Argel* (1580s; "The Traffic of Algiers"). He names nine plays, the titles of a few of which sound like the originals of plays reworked and published years later in the collection *Ocho comedias, y ocho entremeses nuevos* (1615; "Eight Plays and Eight New Interludes"). Fixed theatre sites were just becoming established in the major cities of Spain, and there was an expanding market geared to satisfying the demands of a public ever more hungry for entertainment. Lope de Vega was about to respond to the call, stamping his personal imprint on the Spanish comedia and rendering all earlier drama, including that of Cervantes, old-fashioned or inadequate by comparison. Though destined to be a disappointed dramatist, Cervantes went on trying to get managers to accept his stage works. By 1587 it was clear that he was not going to make a living from literature, and he was obliged to turn in a very different direction.

Cervantes became a commissary of provisions for the great Armada. It took him traveling all over Andalusia, an experience he was to put to good use in his writing. He was responsible for finances of labyrinthine complexity, and the failure to balance his books landed him in prolonged and repeated trouble with his superiors.

After the disastrous defeat of the Armada in 1588, Cervantes gravitated to Sevilla (Seville), the commercial capital of Spain and one of the largest cities in Europe. In 1590 he applied to the Council of the Indies for any one of four major crown posts vacant in Central and South

America. His petition was curtly rejected. Wrangles over his accounts and arrears of salary dragged on. He seems to have kept some contact with the literary world; there is a record of his buying certain books, and he must have managed to find time for reading. In 1592 he signed a contract to supply six plays to a theatrical manager, one Rodrigo Osorio. Nothing came of this. His commissary work continued, and the litigation came to a head; in September 1592 he was imprisoned for a few days in Castro del Río.

In 1594 Cervantes was in Madrid seeking a new post. He received an appointment that took him back to Andalusia to collect overdue taxes. Although it was in effect a promotion, the job was no more rewarding than the previous one and was similarly fraught with financial difficulties and confrontations. Cervantes was not by temperament a businessman. Probably by mutual agreement the appointment was terminated in 1596. The previous year he had won first prize (three silver spoons) in a poetry competition in Zaragoza. Back in Sevilla, he likely started seriously writing stories at about this time. Again he met with financial troubles. In the summer of 1597 discrepancies in his accounts of three years previous landed him in the Crown Jail of Sevilla. He was confined until the end of April 1598 and perhaps conceived there the idea of *Don Quixote*.

Information about Cervantes' life over the next four or five years is sparse. He had left Sevilla, and, perhaps for a while in Esquivias and Madrid, later for certain in Valladolid (where the royal court established itself from 1601 to 1606), he must have been writing the first part of *Don Quixote*. Early versions of two of his stories, *Rinconete y Cortadillo* ("Rinconete and Cortadillo") and *El celoso extremeño* ("The Jealous Extremaduran"), found their way into a miscellaneous compilation, unpublished, made by one Francisco Porras de la Cámara.

Bronze statues of Don Quixote and Sancho Panza in front of a stone sculpture of Miguel de Cervantes, Madrid, Spain. Hemera/ Thinkstock

Publication of Don Quixote

In July or August 1604 Cervantes sold the rights of *El ingenioso hidalgo don Quijote de la Mancha* ("The Ingenious Hidalgo Don Quixote of La Mancha," known as *Don Quixote*, Part I) to the publisher-bookseller Francisco de Robles for an unknown sum. License to publish was granted in September and the book came out in January 1605.

The novel was an immediate success. By August 1605 there were two Madrid editions, two published in Lisbon, and one in Valencia. Thomas Shelton's English translation of the first part appeared in 1612. The name of Cervantes was soon to be as well known in England, France, and Italy as in Spain.

The sale of the publishing rights, however, meant that Cervantes made no more financial profit on Part I of his novel. He had to do the best he could with patronage. The dedication to the young duque de Béjar had been a mistake. He had better fortune with two much more influential persons: the conde de Lemos, to whom he would dedicate Part II and no less than three other works, and Don Bernardo de Sandoval y Rojas, archbishop of Toledo. This eased his financial circumstances somewhat. However, it is apparent that he would have liked a securer place in the pantheon of the nation's writers than he ever achieved during his lifetime—he wanted a reputation comparable to that enjoyed by Lope de Vega or the poet Luis de Góngora, for example. His sense of his own marginal position may be deduced from his *Viage del Parnaso* (1614; *Voyage to Parnassus*), two or three of the later prefaces, and a few external sources. Nevertheless, relative success, still-unsatisfied ambition, and a tireless urge to experiment with the forms of fiction ensured that, at age 57, with less than a dozen years left to him, Cervantes was just entering the most productive period of his career.

In 1613 the 12 *Exemplary Stories* were published. Cervantes' claim in this prologue to be the first to write original novellas (short stories in the Italian manner) in Castilian is substantially justified. There is some variety in the collection, within the two general categories of romance-based stories and realistic ones. *El coloquio de los perros* ("Colloquy of the Dogs," Eng. trans. in *Three Exemplary Novels* [1952]), a quasi-picaresque novella, with its frame tale *El casamiento engañoso* ("The Deceitful Marriage"), is probably Cervantes' most profound and original creation next to *Don Quixote*. In the 17th century the romantic stories were the more popular; James Mabbe chose precisely these for the selective English version of 1640. Nineteenth- and 20th-century taste preferred the realistic ones, but by the turn of the 21st century the others were receiving again something like their critical due.

In 1614 Cervantes published *Viage del Parnaso*, a long allegorical poem in mock-mythological and satirical vein, with a postscript in prose. It was devoted to celebrating a host of contemporary poets and satirizing a few others. The author there admitted that writing poetry did not come easily to him. But he held poetry in the highest esteem as a pure art that should never be debased. Having lost all hope of seeing any more of his plays staged, he had eight of them published in 1615, together with eight short comic interludes, in *Ocho comedias, y ocho entremeses nuevos*. The plays show no shortage of inventiveness and originality but lack real control of the medium. The interludes, however, are reckoned among the very best of their kind.

Don Quixote, Part II, emerged from the same press as its predecessor late in 1615. The second part capitalizes on the potential of the first, developing and diversifying without sacrificing familiarity. Most people agree that it is richer and more profound.

The differences between Part I and Part II demonstrate Cervantes' awareness of the power of the printed word. Don Quixote's history began with his obsessive reading of chivalric romances; in Part II, he realizes that his adventures are eagerly read and discussed by others. The knight's visit in Part II to a Barcelona printing shop, where he finds a spurious Part II in press and denounces it as injurious to the innocent reader and to his own rightful authorship (since he stands to lose royalties from its sales), underscores the cultural and economic impact of books of fiction. His innovative reworkings of literary forms show just how well Cervantes understood not only the 17th-century marketplace but the social effect of literature.

In his last years Cervantes mentioned several works that apparently did not get as far as the printing press, if indeed he ever actually started writing them. There was *Bernardo* (the name of a legendary Spanish epic hero), the *Semanas del jardín* ("Weeks in the Garden"; a collection of tales, perhaps like Boccaccio's *Decameron*), and the continuation to his *Galatea*. The one that was published, posthumously in 1617, was his last romance, *Los trabaios de Persiles y Sigismunda, historia setentrional* ("The Labours of Persiles and Sigismunda: A Northern Story"). In it Cervantes sought to renovate the heroic romance of adventure and love in the manner of the *Aethiopica* of Heliodorus. It was an intellectually prestigious genre destined to be very successful in 17th-century France. Intended both to edify and to entertain, the *Persiles* is an ambitious work that exploits the mythic and symbolic potential of romance. It was very successful when it appeared; there were eight Spanish editions in two years and French and English translations in 1618 and 1619, respectively.

In the dedication, written three days before he died, Cervantes, "with a foot already in the stirrup," movingly bade farewell to the world. Clear-headed to the end, he seems to have achieved a final serenity of spirit. He died in 1616, almost certainly on April 22, not on the 23rd as had been traditionally thought. The burial certificate indicates that the latter was the day he was buried, in the convent of the Discalced Trinitarians in the Calle de Cantarranas (now the Calle de Lope de Vega). The exact spot is not marked. No will is known to have survived.

EDMUND SPENSER

(b. 1552/53, London, England—d. January 13, 1599, London)

Edmund Spenser was an English poet whose long allegorical poem *The Faerie Queene* is one of the greatest in the English language. It was written in what came to be called the Spenserian stanza.

Youth and Education

Little is certainly known about Spenser. He was related to a noble Midlands family of Spencer, whose fortunes had been made through sheep raising. His own immediate family was not wealthy. He was entered as a "poor boy" in the Merchant Taylors' grammar school, where he would have studied mainly Latin, with some Hebrew, Greek, and music.

In 1569, when Spenser was about 16 years old, his English versions of poems by the 16th-century French poet Joachim du Bellay and his translation of a French version of a poem by the Italian poet Petrarch appeared at the beginning of an anti-Catholic prose tract, *A Theatre for Voluptuous Worldlings*. From May 1569 Spenser was a student in Pembroke Hall (now Pembroke College) of the University of Cambridge, where, along with perhaps a quarter of the students, he was classed as a sizar—a student who, out of financial necessity, performed various menial or semi-menial duties. He received a Bachelor of Arts degree in 1573. Because of an epidemic, Spenser left Cambridge in 1574, but he received the Master of Arts degree in 1576.

Spenser's period at the University of Cambridge was undoubtedly important for the acquisition of his wide knowledge not only of the Latin and some of the Greek classics but also of the Italian, French, and English literature of his own and earlier times. His knowledge of the traditional forms and themes of lyrical and narrative poetry provided foundations for him to build his own highly original compositions. The patterns of meaning in Spenser's poetry are frequently woven out of the traditional interpretations—developed through classical times and his own—of pagan myth, divinities, and philosophies and out of an equally strong experience of the faith and doctrines of Christianity; these patterns he further enriched by the use of medieval and contemporary story, legend, and folklore.

Spenser's religious training was a most important part of his education. He could not have avoided some involvement in the bitter struggles that took place in his university over the path the new Church of England was to tread between Roman Catholicism and extreme Puritanism, and his own poetry repeatedly engages with the opposition between Protestantism and Catholicism and the need to protect the national and moral purity of the Elizabethan church. Contrary to a former view, there is little reason to believe that he inclined toward the Puritanical side. His first known appointment (after a blank of several years, when he may have been in the north of England) was in 1578 as secretary to Bishop John Young of Rochester, former master of Spenser's college at Cambridge. Spenser's first important publication, *The Shepheardes Calender* (1579 or 1580), is more concerned with the bishops and affairs of the English church than is any of his later work.

Early Works

The Shepheardes Calender can be called the first work of the English literary Renaissance. Following the example of Virgil and of many later poets, Spenser was beginning his career with a series of eclogues (literally "selections," usually short poems in the form of pastoral dialogues), in which various characters, in the guise of innocent and simple shepherds, converse about life and love in a variety of elegantly managed verse forms, formulating weighty— often satirical—opinions on questions of the day. The paradoxical combination in pastoral poetry of the simple, isolated life of shepherds with the sophisticated social ambitions of the figures symbolized or discussed by these shepherds (and of their probable readership) has been of some interest in literary criticism.

The *Calender* consists of 12 eclogues, one named after each month of the year. One of the shepherds, Colin Clout, who excels in poetry but is ruined by his hopeless love for one Rosalind, is Spenser himself. The eclogue "Aprill" is in praise of the shepherdess Elisa, really the queen (Elizabeth I) herself. "October" examines the various kinds of verse composition and suggests how discouraging it is for a modern poet to try for success in any of them. Most of the eclogues, however, concern good or bad shepherds— that is to say, pastors—of Christian congregations. The *Calender* was well received in its day, and it is still a revelation of what could be done poetically in English after a long period of much mediocrity and provinciality.

The years 1578–80 probably produced more changes in Spenser's life than did any other corresponding period.

He appears by 1580 to have been serving the fascinating, highly placed, and unscrupulous Robert Dudley, earl of Leicester and to have become a member of the literary circle led by Sir Philip Sidney, Leicester's nephew, to whom the *Calender* was dedicated and who praised it in his important critical work *The Defence of Poesie* (1595). Spenser remained permanently devoted to this brilliant writer and good nobleman, embodied him variously in his own poetry, and mourned his early death in an elegy. By 1580 Spenser had also started work on *The Faerie Queene*, and in the previous year he had apparently married one Machabyas Chylde. He was made secretary to the new lord deputy of Ireland, Arthur Lord Grey, who was a friend of the Sidney family, in 1580.

Career in Ireland

As Grey's secretary, Spenser accompanied the lord deputy on risky military campaigns as well as on more routine journeys. He may have witnessed the Smerwick massacre (1580), and his poetry is haunted by nightmare characters who embody a wild lawlessness. Spenser's *A View of the Present State of Ireland* (written 1595–96, published 1633), a later tract, argues lucidly for a typically 16th-century theory of rule: firm measures, ruthlessly applied, with gentleness only for completely submissive subject populations.

The fruits of his service in Ireland are plain. He was given a sinecure post and other favours, including the right to dispose of certain forfeited parcels of land (he no doubt indulged in profitable land speculation). In 1588 or 1589 Spenser took over the 3,000-acre (1,200-hectare) plantation of Kilcolman, about 25 miles (40 km) to the north and a little to the west of Cork. No doubt he took there his son and daughter and his wife, if she was still alive (she is known to have died by 1594, when Spenser married Elizabeth Boyle, a "kinswoman" of the earl of Cork, one of Ireland's wealthiest men). By acquiring this estate, Spenser made his choice for the future: to rise into the privileged class of what was, to all intents, a colonial land of opportunity rather than to seek power and position on the more crowded ground of the homeland, where he had made his poetic reputation. In his new situation he had much conflict with the local Anglo-Irish aristocracy. Nevertheless, it was under these conditions that Spenser brought his greatest poetry to completion.

The Faerie Queene *and Last Years*

In its present form, *The Faerie Queene* consists of six books and a fragment (known as the "Mutabilitie Cantos"). According to Spenser's introductory letter in the first edition (1590) of his great poem, it was to contain 12 books, each telling the adventure of one of Gloriana's knights. Like other poets, Spenser must have modified his general plan many times, yet this letter, inconsistent though it is with various plot details in the books that are extant, is probably a faithful mirror of his thinking at one stage. The stories actually published were those of Holiness (the Red Cross Knight), Temperance (Sir Guyon), Chastity (Britomart, a female knight), Friendship (ostensibly concerning Triamond and Cambello, although these play a small part), Justice (Artegall), and Courtesy (Calidore). As a setting Spenser invented the land of Faerie and its queen, Gloriana. To express himself he invented a nine-line stanza, the first eight of five stresses and the last of six, whose rhyme pattern is *ababbcbcc*.

What is most characteristic of Spenser in *The Faerie Queene* is his serious view of the capacity of the romance form to act as a paradigm of human experience: the moral life as quest, pilgrimage, aspiration; as eternal war with an enemy, still to be known; and as encounter, crisis, the moment of illumination—in short, as ethics, with the added dimensions of mystery, terror, love, and victory and with all the generous virtues exalted. In *The Faerie Queene* Spenser proves himself a master: picture, music, metre, story—all elements are at one with the deeper significance of his poem, providing a moral heraldry of colours, emblems, legends, folklore, and mythical allusion, all prompting deep, instinctive responses.

Arriving in London with the support of the queen's favourite, Sir Walter Raleigh (who helped publish *The Faerie Queen*), Spenser was well received—not least by Elizabeth herself. The first three books of *The Faerie Queene* were duly published in 1590, together with a dedication to her and commendatory sonnets to notables of the court. Spenser saw the book through the press, made a hurried visit to Ireland, and returned speedily to London—presumably in the hope of preferment. At this time he supervised the printing of certain other of his poems in a collection called *Complaints* (1591), many of which had probably been written earlier in his career and were now being published so as to profit from the great success of his new heroic poem. It is difficult to believe that the many titles of poems that have not survived but were mentioned earlier in his career were not published in revised form and under other titles in his known work, for *Complaints* suggests by its miscellaneous and uneven character that Spenser was hastily bringing to the light of day nearly every last shred that he had to offer; early translations, an elegy, and the delightful mock-heroic poem *Muiopotmos* are contained in it. Another item, the beast fable *Prosopopoia; or, Mother Hubberd's Tale,* apparently caused the authorities to withdraw unsold copies of the volume (perhaps in 1592) because it contained a covert attack on Lord Burghley, who was one of the most powerful figures of the court. Nevertheless, in 1591 Queen Elizabeth gave Spenser a small pension for life.

Back in Ireland, Spenser pressed on with his writing, in spite of the burdens of his estate. In early 1595 he published *Amoretti* and *Epithalamion*, a sonnet sequence and a marriage ode celebrating his marriage to Elizabeth Boyle after what appears to have been an impassioned courtship in 1594. This group of poems is unique among Renaissance sonnet sequences in that it celebrates a successful love affair culminating in marriage. The *Epithalamion* further idealizes the marriage by building into its structure the symbolic numbers 24 (the number of stanzas) and 365 (the total number of long lines), allowing the poem to allude to the structure of the day and of the year. The marriage is thus connected with the encompassing harmonies of the universe, and the cyclical processes of change and renewal are expressed in the procreation of the two mortal lovers. However, matters are less harmonious in Books IV, V, and VI of *The Faerie Queene*, which appeared in 1596 and are strikingly more ambiguous and ironic than the first three books. Book V includes much direct allegory of some of the most problematic political events of Queen Elizabeth's reign, and Book VI's Sir Calidore is a far less confident and effective fairy knight than his predecessors were. In the only surviving fragment of a projected seventh book (published posthumously in 1609), Spenser represents Elizabeth herself as subject to Mutability, the inexorable processes of aging and change.

This burst of publication was the last of his lifetime. His early death may have been precipitated by the penetration into Munster of the Irish uprising of 1598. The undertakers and other loyalists failed to make headway against this. Kilcolman was burned, and Spenser, probably in despair despite the Privy Council's having just recommended his appointment to the important post of sheriff of Cork, carried official letters about the desperate state of affairs from the president to London, where he died. He was buried with ceremony in Westminster Abbey close by the grave of Geoffrey Chaucer.

SIR PHILIP SIDNEY

(b. November 30, 1554, Penshurst, Kent, England—d. October 17, 1586, Arnhem, Netherlands)

An Elizabethan courtier, statesman, soldier, poet, and patron of scholars and poets, Sir Philip Sidney was considered the ideal gentleman of his day. After Shakespeare's sonnets, Sidney's *Astrophel and Stella* is considered the finest Elizabethan sonnet cycle. His *The Defence of Poesie* introduced the critical ideas of Renaissance theorists to England.

Philip Sidney was the eldest son of Sir Henry Sidney and his wife, Lady Mary Dudley, daughter of the duke of Northumberland, and godson of King Philip II of Spain. After Elizabeth I succeeded to the throne, his father was appointed lord president of Wales (and later served three times as lord deputy of Ireland), while his uncle, Robert Dudley, was created earl of Leicester and became the queen's most trusted adviser. In keeping with his family background, the young Sidney was intended for a career as a statesman and soldier. At age 10 he entered Shrewsbury School, where his classmate was Fulke Greville (later a court official under Elizabeth), who became his lifelong friend and was his early biographer. In February 1568 he began a three-year period of studies at Christ Church, Oxford, afterward traveling in Europe between May 1572 and June 1575, perfecting his knowledge of Latin,

French, and Italian. He also gained firsthand knowledge of European politics and became acquainted with many of Europe's leading statesmen.

His first court appointment came in the spring of 1576, when he succeeded his father as cupbearer to the queen, a ceremonial position. Then in February 1577, when he was only 22, he was sent as ambassador to the German emperor Rudolf II and the elector palatine Louis VI, carrying Queen Elizabeth's condolences on the deaths of their fathers. But along with this formal task, he also had secret instructions to sound out the German princes on their attitude toward the formation of a Protestant league—the chief political aim being to protect England by associating it with other Protestant states in Europe that would counterbalance the threatening power of Roman Catholic Spain. Sidney apparently brought back enthusiastic reports on the possibilities of forming such a league, but the cautious queen sent other emissaries to check on his reports, and they returned with less-optimistic accounts of the German princes' reliability as allies. He did not receive another major official appointment until eight years later.

He nevertheless continued to busy himself in the politics and diplomacy of his country. In 1579 he wrote privately to the queen, advising her against a proposal that she enter into a marriage with the duke of Anjou, the Roman Catholic heir to the French throne. Sidney, moreover, was a member of Parliament for Kent in 1581 and 1584–85. He corresponded with foreign statesmen and entertained important visitors—including the French Protestant envoy Philippe de Mornay in 1577, the German Calvinist prince Casimir in 1578, the Portuguese pretender Dom António in 1581, and, later, a number of Scottish lords. Sidney was among the few Englishmen of his time with any interest in the newly discovered Americas, and he supported maritime explorations by the navigator Sir Martin Frobisher. In 1582 Richard Hakluyt, who published accounts of English explorers' enterprises, dedicated his *Divers Voyages Touching the Discoverie of America* to him. Sidney later became interested in the project to establish the American colony of Virginia, sent out by Sir Walter Raleigh, and he intended to set out himself in an expedition with Sir Francis Drake against the Spaniards. He had wide-ranging intellectual and artistic interests, discussed art with the painter Nicholas Hilliard and chemistry with the scientist John Dee, and was a great patron of scholars and men of letters. More than 40 works by English and European authors were dedicated to him—works of divinity, ancient and modern history, geography, military affairs, law, logic, medicine, and poetry—indicating the breadth of his interests. Among the many poets and prose writers who sought his patronage were Edmund Spenser, Abraham Fraunce, and Thomas Lodge.

Sidney was an excellent horseman and became renowned for his participation in tournaments—elaborate entertainments, half athletic contest and half symbolic spectacle, that were a chief amusement of the court. He hankered after a life of heroic action, but his official activities were largely ceremonial—attending on the queen at court and accompanying her on her progresses about the country. In January 1583 he was knighted, not because of any outstanding accomplishment but in order to give him the qualifications needed to stand in for his friend Prince Casimir, who was to receive the honour of admittance to the Order of the Garter but was unable to attend the ceremony. In September he married Frances, daughter of Queen Elizabeth's secretary of state, Sir Francis Walsingham. They had one daughter, Elizabeth.

Because the queen would not give him an important post, he had turned to literature as an outlet for his energies. In 1578 he composed a pastoral playlet, *The Lady of May*, for the queen. By 1580 he had completed a version of his heroic prose romance, the *Arcadia*. It is typical of his gentlemanly air of assumed nonchalance that he should call it "a trifle, and that triflingly handled," whereas it is in fact an intricately plotted narrative of 180,000 words.

Early in 1581 his aunt, the countess of Huntington, had brought to court her ward, Penelope Devereux, who later that year married the young Lord Rich. Whether or not Sidney really did fall in love with her, during the summer of 1582 he composed a sonnet sequence, *Astrophel and Stella*, that recounts a courtier's passion in delicately fictionalized terms: its first stirrings, his struggles against it, and his final abandonment of his suit to give himself instead to the "great cause" of public service. These sonnets, witty and impassioned, brought Elizabethan poetry at once of age. About the same time, he wrote *The Defence of Poesie*, an urbane and eloquent plea for the social value of imaginative fiction, which remains the finest work of Elizabethan literary criticism. In 1584 he began a radical revision of his *Arcadia*, transforming its linear dramatic plot into a many-stranded, interlaced narrative. He left it half finished, but it remains the most important work of prose fiction in English of the 16th century. He also composed other poems and later began a paraphrase of the Psalms. He wrote for his own amusement and for that of his close friends; true to the gentlemanly code of avoiding commercialism, he did not allow his writings to be published in his lifetime.

The incomplete revised version of his *Arcadia* was not printed until 1590; in 1593 another edition completed the story by adding the last three books of his original version (the complete text of the original version remained in manuscript until 1926). His *Astrophel and Stella* was printed in 1591 in a corrupt text, his *Defence of Poesie* in 1595, and a collected edition of his works in 1598, reprinted in 1599 and nine times during the 17th century.

Although in July 1585 he finally received his eagerly awaited public appointment, his writings were to be his most lasting accomplishment. He was appointed, with his uncle, the earl of Warwick, as joint master of the ordnance, an office that administered the military supplies of the kingdom. In November the queen was finally persuaded to assist the struggle of the Dutch against their Spanish masters, sending them a force led by the earl of Leicester. Sidney was made governor of the town of Flushing (Dutch: Vlissingen) and was given command of a company of cavalry. But the following 11 months were spent in ineffective campaigns against the Spaniards, while Sidney was hard put to maintain the morale of his poorly paid troops. He wrote to his father-in-law that, if the queen did not pay her soldiers, she would lose her garrisons but that, for himself, the love of the cause would never make him weary of his resolution, because he thought "a wise and constant man ought never to grieve while he doth play his own part truly, though others be out."

On September 22, 1586, he volunteered to serve in an action to prevent the Spaniards from sending supplies into the town of Zutphen. The supply train was heavily guarded, and the English were outnumbered; but Sidney charged three times through the enemy lines, and, even though his thigh was shattered by a bullet, he rode his horse from the field. He was carried to Arnhem, where his wound became infected, and he prepared himself religiously for death. In his last hours he confessed:

> *There came to my remembrance a vanity wherein I had taken delight, whereof I had not rid myself. It was the Lady Rich. But I rid myself of it, and presently my joy and comfort returned.*

He was buried at St. Paul's Cathedral in London on February 16, 1587, with an elaborate funeral of a type usually reserved for great noblemen. The Universities of Oxford and Cambridge and scholars throughout Europe issued memorial volumes in his honour, while almost every English poet composed verses in his praise. He won this adulation even though he had accomplished no action of consequence; it would be possible to write a history of Elizabethan political and military affairs without so much as mentioning his name. It is not what he did but what he was that made him so widely admired: the embodiment of the Elizabethan ideal of gentlemanly virtue.

JOHN LYLY

(b. 1554?, Kent, England—d. November 1606, London)

The author considered to be the first English prose stylist to leave an enduring impression upon the language, John Lyly also contributed to the development of prose dialogue in English comedy through his plays.

Lyly was educated at Magdalen College, Oxford, and went to London about 1576. There he gained fame with the publication of two prose romances, *Euphues: The Anatomy of Wit* (1578) and *Euphues and His England* (1580), which together made him the most fashionable English writer of the 1580s. *Euphues* is a romantic intrigue told in letters interspersed with general discussions on such topics as religion, love, and epistolary style. Lyly's preoccupation with the exact arrangement and selection of words, his frequent use of similes drawn from classical mythology, and his artificial and excessively elegant prose inspired a short-lived Elizabethan literary style called "euphuism." The *Euphues* novels introduced a new concern with form into English prose.

After 1580 Lyly devoted himself almost entirely to writing comedies. In 1583 he gained control of the first Blackfriars Theatre, in which his earliest plays, *Campaspe* and *Sapho and Phao,* were produced. All of Lyly's comedies except *The Woman in the Moon* were presented by the Children of Paul's, a children's company that was periodically favoured by Queen Elizabeth. The performance dates of his plays are as follows: *Campaspe* and *Sapho and Phao*, 1583–84; *Gallathea*, 1585–88; *Endimion*, 1588; *Midas*, 1589; *Love's Metamorphosis*, 1590; *Mother Bombie*, 1590; and *The Woman in the Moon*, 1595. All but one of these are in prose. The finest is considered to be *Endimion*, which some critics hold a masterpiece.

Lyly's comedies mark an enormous advance upon those of his predecessors in English drama. Their plots are drawn from classical mythology and legend, and their characters engage in euphuistic speeches redolent of Renaissance pedantry; but the charm and wit of the dialogues and the light and skillful construction of the plots set standards that younger and more gifted dramatists could not ignore.

Lyly's popularity waned with the rise of Thomas Kyd, Christopher Marlowe, and William Shakespeare, and his appeals to Queen Elizabeth for financial relief went unheeded. He had hoped to succeed Edmund Tilney in the court post of Master of the Revels, but Tilney outlived him, and Lyly died a poor and bitter man.

THOMAS KYD

(baptized November 6, 1558, London, England—
d. *c.* December 1594, London)

Thomas Kyd was an English dramatist who, with his *The Spanish Tragedy* (sometimes called *Hieronimo,* or *Jeronimo*, after its protagonist), initiated the revenge tragedy of his day. Kyd anticipated the structure of many later plays, including the development of middle and final climaxes. In addition, he revealed an instinctive sense of tragic situation, while his characterization of Hieronimo in *The Spanish Tragedy* prepared the way for Shakespeare's psychological study of Hamlet.

The son of a scrivener, Kyd was educated at the Merchant Taylors School in London. There is no evidence that he attended the university before turning to literature. He seems to have been in service for some years with a lord (possibly Ferdinando, Lord Strange, the patron of Lord Strange's Men). *The Spanish Tragedy* was entered in the Stationers' Register in October 1592, and the undated

Frontispiece of a 1615 edition of Thomas Kyd's The Spanish Tragedy.
Universal Images Group/Getty Images

first quarto edition almost certainly appeared in that year. It is not known which company first played it, nor when; but Strange's company played *Hieronimo* 16 times in 1592, and the Admiral's Men revived it in 1597, as apparently did the Chamberlain's Men. It remained one of the most popular plays of the age and was often reprinted.

The only other play certainly by Kyd is *Cornelia* (1594), an essay in Senecan tragedy, translated from the French of Robert Garnier's academic *Cornélie*. He may also have written an earlier version of *Hamlet*, known to scholars as the *Ur-Hamlet*, and his hand has sometimes been detected in the anonymous *Arden of Feversham*, one of the first domestic tragedies, and in a number of other plays.

About 1591 Kyd was sharing lodgings with Christopher Marlowe, and on May 13, 1593, he was arrested and then tortured, being suspected of treasonable activity. His room had been searched and certain "atheistical" disputations denying the deity of Jesus Christ found there. He probably averred then and certainly confirmed later, in a letter, that these papers had belonged to Marlowe. That letter is the source for almost everything that is known about Kyd's life. He was dead by December 30, 1594, when his mother made a formal repudiation of her son's debt-ridden estate.

LUIS DE GÓNGORA Y ARGOTE

(b. July 11, 1561, Córdoba, Spain—d. May 23, 1627, Córdoba)

Luis de Góngora y Argote was one of the most influential Spanish poets of his era. His Baroque, convoluted style, known as Gongorism (*gongorismo*), was so exaggerated by less gifted imitators that his reputation suffered after his death until it underwent a revaluation in the 20th century.

The son of a judge, Góngora profited from his father's fine library and from relatives in positions to further his education. He attended the University of Salamanca and achieved fame quickly. He took religious orders so that he might receive an ecclesiastical benefice but was not ordained priest until he was 55 years old, when he was named chaplain to the royal court in Madrid. His letters, as well as some of his satirical verse, show an unhappy and financially distressed life vexed by the animosity that some of his writings had evoked. He had strong partisans—Lope de Vega was an admirer—and equally powerful enemies, none more so than his rival Francisco de Quevedo, who outdid even Góngora in mordant and unrelenting satire.

Góngora was always successful with his lighter poetry—the romances, *letrillas*, and sonnets—but his longer works, the *Fábula de Polifemo y Galatea* (circulated in manuscript in 1613; "Fable of Polyphemus and Galatea") and the *Soledades* (circulated in manuscript in 1613; "Solitudes"), written in an intensely difficult and purposely complex style, provoked the scorn and enmity of many. There has been a temptation to divide his work into the light-dark and easy-difficult, but 20th-century criticism has shown his compositions to have a unity that is perhaps clouded by the compactness and intensity of style in the longer ones. *Gongorismo* derives from a more general base, *culteranismo*, a Latinizing movement that had been an element in Spanish poetry since the 15th century. In the *Polifemo* and the *Soledades* Góngora elaborated his style by the introduction of numerous Latinisms of vocabulary and syntax and by exceedingly complex imagery and mythological allusions. In these long poems Góngora applied his full energies to enhancing and augmenting each device and decoration until the basically uncomplicated story was obscured. The same devices are found in his more popular lyrics.

The 19th century found little to like in the obscure and difficult Góngora, but his tercentenary in 1927 reestablished his importance. The cold beauty of his lines at last found an appreciative and receptive audience willing to see the value of verse that shunned intimate emotion but that created the purest poetry for its own sake. An English translation by R.O. Jones of selected poems was published in 1966.

LOPE DE VEGA

(b. November 25, 1562, Madrid, Spain—d. August 27, 1635, Madrid)

The outstanding dramatist of the Spanish Golden Age, Lope Félix de Vega Carpio is the author of as many as 1,800 plays and several hundred shorter dramatic pieces, of which 431 plays and 50 shorter pieces are extant.

Life

Lope de Vega was the second son and third child of Francisca Fernandez Flores and Félix de Vega, an embroiderer. He was taught Latin and Castilian in 1572–73 by the poet Vicente Espinel, and the following year he entered the Jesuit Imperial College, where he learned the rudiments of the humanities. Captivated by his talent and grace, the bishop of Ávila took him to the Alcalá de Henares (Universidad Complutense) in 1577 to study for the priesthood, but Vega soon left the Alcalá on the heels of a married woman.

On his father's death in 1578, the embroidery shop passed to the husband of one of the poet's sisters, Isabel del Carpio. Vega later adopted the noble name of Carpio in order to give an aristocratic tone to his own. He acquired a humanistic education from his abundant though haphazard readings in erudite anthologies. In 1583 he took part in the Spanish expedition against the Azores.

By this time Vega had established himself as a playwright in Madrid and was living from his comedias (tragicomic social dramas). He also exercised an undefined role as gentleman attendant or secretary to various nobles, adapting his role as servant or panderer according to the situation. By this time, also, the poet's life was already launched on a course of tempestuous passion. The "remote beauty" who took him from the Alcalá was followed by Elena Osorio, an actress of exceptional beauty and maturity. His romantic involvement with her was intense, violent, and marred by Vega's jealousy over Elena's liaison with the powerful gallant Don Francisco Perrenot de Granvelle, nephew of the cardinal de Granvelle. Finally, when Elena abandoned the poet, he wrote such fierce libels against her and her family that he landed in prison. The libel continued in a court case in 1588, which sent him into exile from Castile for eight years. In the middle of this incredible court scandal, Vega abducted Isabel de Urbina (the "Belisa" of many of his poems), the beautiful 16-year-old sister of Philip II's earl marshal. They were forced to marry, and the new husband immediately departed with the Spanish Armada against England. On his return, he passed the remainder of his exile in Valencia, at that time a centre of considerable dramatic activity, and took to the serious writing of plays. Here, too, he engaged in writing *romanceros*, or ballad poetry, which had become fashionable. In 1590 he was appointed secretary to the duke of Alba, whom he followed to Toledo and then to the ducal estate at Alba de Tormes, where his wife died in childbirth in 1595. He auctioned off everything he owned and left for Madrid, where his public concubinage with the widow Antonia Trillo de Armenta caused him another lawsuit (1596).

He had left the duke's service in 1595, and in 1598 he went to the home of the marqués de Sarriá, with whom he remained until 1600. Sometime around 1595 he also met the illiterate and singularly beautiful actress Micaela de Luján, who was to be for nearly 20 years the poet's most peaceful love; she was the "Camila Lucinda" of numerous magnificent verses composed for her by Vega. He took a second wife, Juana de Guardo, the daughter of a wealthy pork butcher, by whom he had two children, Carlos Félix and Feliciana. He was mercilessly pilloried by his literary enemies for such an opportunistic union.

Height of Literary Productivity

From 1605 until his death he remained a confidential secretary and counselor to the duke of Sessa, with whom he maintained a voluminous and revealing correspondence. In 1608 he was also named to a sinecure position as a familiar of the Inquisition and then prosecutor (*promotor fiscal*) of the Apostolic Chamber. By this time, Vega had become a famous poet and was already regarded as the "phoenix of Spanish wits." In 1609 he published *Arte nuevo de hacer comedias en este tiempo* ("New Art of Writing Plays in This Time"), a poetic treatise in which he defended his own plays with more wit than effectiveness.

In 1610, in the midst of full literary production—on the road to his 500 comedias—Vega moved his household definitively from Toledo to Madrid. In Madrid, Vega was afflicted by painful circumstances that complicated his life in a period when he was still very creative. Juana became ill, miscarried, and lived in precarious health under Vega's constant care; Carlos Félix, his favourite son, also became ill and died, in 1612. Juana died in childbirth with Feliciana, and Micaela de Luján must also have died during that time, since Vega took into his own home the children remaining from this relationship, Marcela and Lope Félix, or Lopito.

These heartbreaks moved the poet to a deep religious crisis. In 1609 he entered the first of several religious orders. From this time on he wrote almost exclusively religious works, though he also continued his theatrical work, which was financially indispensable. In 1614 he entered the priesthood, but his continued service as secretary and panderer to his patron, the duke of Sessa, hindered him from obtaining the ecclesiastical benefits he sought. The duke, fearful of losing Vega's services, succeeded in having one of the poet's former lovers, the actress Lucia de Salcedo, seduce Vega. The duke thus permanently recovered his secretary. Vega thereafter became involved in new and scandalous romantic relationships. In 1627 his verse epic on the life and execution of Mary, queen of Scots, *La corona trágica*, which was dedicated to Pope Urban VIII, brought in reward a doctorate in theology of the Collegium Sapientiae and the cross of the Order of Malta, out of which came his proud use of the title *Frey* ("Brother"). His closing years were full of gloom. His last lover, Marta de Nevares, who shared his life from 1619 until her death in 1632, lost first her sight and then her sanity in the 1620s. The death at sea of his son Lope Félix del Carpio y Luján and the abduction and abandonment of his youngest daughter, Antonia Clara, both in 1634, were blows that rent his soul. His own death in Madrid in August 1635 evoked national mourning.

Works

Vega became identified as a playwright with the comedia, a comprehensive term for the new drama of Spain's Golden Age. Vega's productivity for the stage, however exaggerated by report, remains phenomenal. He claimed to have written an average of 20 sheets a day throughout his life and left untouched scarcely a vein of writing then current. Cervantes called him "the prodigy of nature." Juan Pérez de Montalván, his first biographer, in his *Fama póstuma* (1636), attributed to Vega a total of 1,800 plays, as well as more than 400 *autos sacramentales* (short allegorical plays on sacramental subjects). The dramatist's own first figure of 230 plays in 1603 rises to 1,500 in 1632; more than 100, he boasts, were composed and staged in 24 hours. The titles are known of 723 plays and 44 *autos*, and the texts survive of 426 and 42, respectively.

The earliest firm date for a play written by Vega is 1593. His 18 months in Valencia in 1589–90, during which he was writing for a living, seem to have been decisive in shaping his vocation and his talent. The influence in particular of the Valencian playwright Cristóbal de Virués (1550–1609) was obviously profound. Toward the end of his life, in *El laurel de Apolo*, Vega credits Virués with having, in his "famous tragedies," laid the very foundations of the comedia.

There can be no claiming that Vega learned his whole art from Virués. Bartolomé de Torres Naharro at the beginning of the 16th century had already foreshadowed the cloak and sword (*cape y espada*) play of middle-class manners. A decade before Virués, Juan de la Cueva had discovered the dramatic interest latent in earlier Spanish history and its potential appeal to a public acutely responsive to national greatness. In the formation of the comedia this proved another decisive factor on which Vega fastened instinctively.

It was at this point that Vega picked up the inheritance and, by sheer force of creative genius and fertility of invention, gave the comedia its basic formula and raised it to a peak of splendour. The comedia's manual was Vega's own poetic treatise, *El arte nuevo de hacer comedias en este tiempo* ("The new art of making comedies in this time"), in which he firmly rejected the Classical and Neoclassical "rules," opted for a blend of comedy and tragedy and for metrical variety, and made public opinion the ultimate arbiter of taste.

The comedia was essentially, therefore, a social drama, ringing a thousand changes on the accepted foundations of society: respect for crown, for church, and for the human personality, the latter being symbolized in the "point of honour" (*pundonor*) that Vega commended as the best theme of all "since there are none but are strongly moved thereby." This "point of honour" was a matter largely of convention, "honour" being equivalent, in a very limited and brittle sense, to social reputation; men were expected to be brave and proud and not to put up with an insult, while "honour" for women basically meant maintaining their chastity (if unmarried) or their fidelity (if married). It followed that this was a drama less of character than of action and intrigue that rarely, if ever, grasped the true essence of tragedy.

Few of the plays that Vega wrote were perfect, but he had an unerring sense for the theme and detail that could move an audience conscious of being on the crest of its country's greatness to respond to a mirroring on the stage of some of the basic ingredients of that greatness. Because of him the comedia became a vast sounding board for every chord in the Spanish consciousness, a "national" drama in the truest sense.

In theme Vega's plays range over a vast horizon. Traditionally his plays have been grouped as religious, mythological, classical, historical (foreign and national), pastoral, chivalric, fantastic, and of contemporary manners. In essence the categories come down to two, both

Spanish in setting: the heroic, historical play based on some national story or legend, and the cloak and sword drama of contemporary manners and intrigue.

For his historical plays Vega ransacked the medieval chronicle, the *romancero*, and popular legend and song for heroic themes, chosen for the most part as throwing into relief some aspect either of the national character or of that social solidarity on which contemporary Spain's greatness rested. The conception of the crown as fount of justice and bulwark of the humble against oppression inspires some of his finest plays. In *Fuente Ovejuna* the entire eponymous village assumes responsibility before the king for the slaying of its overlord and wins his exoneration. This experiment in mass psychology, the best known outside Spain of all his plays, evoked a particular response from audiences in tsarist Russia.

Vega's cloak and sword plays are all compounded of the same ingredients and feature the same basic situations: gallants and ladies falling endlessly in and out of love, the "point of honour" being sometimes engaged, but very rarely the heart, while servants imitate or parody the main action and one, the *gracioso*, exercises his wit and common sense in commenting on the follies of his social superiors.

Vega's nondramatic works in verse and prose filled 21 volumes in 1776–79. Much of this vast output has withered, but its variety remains impressive. Vega wrote pastoral romances, verse histories of recent events, verse biographies of Spanish saints, long epic poems and burlesques upon such works, and prose tales, imitating or adapting works by Ariosto and Cervantes in the process. His lyric compositions—ballads, elegies, epistles, sonnets (there are 1,587 of these)—are myriad. Formally they rely much on the conceit, and in content they provide a running commentary on the poet's whole emotional life.

CHRISTOPHER MARLOWE

(baptized February 26, 1564, Canterbury, Kent, England—d. May 30, 1593, Deptford, near London)

A n Elizabethan poet and Shakespeare's most important predecessor in English drama, Christopher Marlowe is noted especially for his establishment of dramatic blank verse.

Education and Government Service

Marlowe was the second child and eldest son of John Marlowe, a Canterbury shoemaker. Nothing is known of his first schooling, but on January 14, 1579, he entered the King's School, Canterbury, as a scholar. A year later he went to Corpus Christi College, Cambridge. Obtaining his bachelor of arts degree in 1584, he continued in residence at Cambridge—which may imply that he was intending to take Anglican orders. In 1587, however, the university hesitated about granting him the master's degree; its doubts (arising from his frequent absences from the university) were apparently set at rest when the Privy Council sent a letter declaring that he had been employed "on matters touching the benefit of his country"—apparently in Elizabeth I's secret service.

After 1587 Marlowe was in London, writing for the theatres, occasionally getting into trouble with the authorities because of his violent and disreputable behaviour, and probably also engaging himself from time to time in government service. Marlowe won a dangerous reputation for

Detail of a portrait thought to be of Christopher Marlowe, dated 1585, artist unknown; in the collection of Corpus Christi College, Cambridge, England. Keystone/Hulton Archive/Getty Images

"atheism," but this could, in Elizabeth I's time, indicate merely unorthodox religious opinions. In Robert Greene's deathbed tract, *Greenes groats-worth of witte*, Marlowe is referred to as a "famous gracer of Tragedians" and is reproved for having said, like Greene himself, "There is no god" and for having studied "pestilent Machiuilian pollicie." There is further evidence of his unorthodoxy, notably in the denunciation of him written by the spy Richard Baines and in the letter of Thomas Kyd to the lord keeper in 1593 after Marlowe's death. Kyd alleged that certain papers "denying the deity of Jesus Christ" that were found in his room belonged to Marlowe, who had shared the room two years before. Both Baines and Kyd suggested on Marlowe's part atheism in the stricter sense and a persistent delight in blasphemy.

Whatever the case may be, on May 18, 1593, the Privy Council issued an order for Marlowe's arrest; two days later the poet was ordered to give daily attendance on their lordships "until he shall be licensed to the contrary." On May 30, however, Marlowe was killed by Ingram Frizer, in the dubious company of Nicholas Skeres and Robert Poley, at a lodging house in Deptford, where they had spent most of the day and where, it was alleged, a fight broke out between them over the bill.

Literary Career

In a playwriting career that spanned little more than six years, Marlowe's achievements were diverse and splendid. Perhaps before leaving Cambridge he had already written *Tamburlaine the Great* (in two parts, both performed by the end of 1587; published 1590). Almost certainly during his later Cambridge years, Marlowe had translated Ovid's *Amores* (*The Loves*) and the first book of Lucan's *Pharsalia* from the Latin. About this time he also wrote the play

Dido, Queen of Carthage (published in 1594 as the joint work of Marlowe and Thomas Nashe). With the production of *Tamburlaine* he received recognition and acclaim, and playwriting became his major concern in the few years that lay ahead. Both parts of *Tamburlaine* were published anonymously in 1590, and the publisher omitted certain passages that he found incongruous with the play's serious concern with history; even so, the extant *Tamburlaine* text can be regarded as substantially Marlowe's. No other of his plays or poems or translations was published during his life. His unfinished but splendid poem *Hero and Leander*—which is almost certainly the finest nondramatic Elizabethan poem apart from those produced by Edmund Spenser—appeared in 1598.

There is argument among scholars concerning the order in which the plays subsequent to *Tamburlaine* were written. It is not uncommonly held that *Faustus* quickly followed *Tamburlaine* and that then Marlowe turned to a more neutral, more "social" kind of writing in *Edward II* and *The Massacre at Paris*. His last play may have been *The Jew of Malta*, in which he signally broke new ground. It is known that *Tamburlaine*, *Faustus*, and *The Jew of Malta* were performed by the Admiral's Men, a company whose outstanding actor was Edward Alleyn, who most certainly played Tamburlaine, Faustus, and Barabas the Jew.

Works

In the earliest of Marlowe's plays, the two-part *Tamburlaine the Great* (c. 1587; published 1590), Marlowe's characteristic "mighty line" (as Ben Jonson called it) established blank verse as the staple medium for later Elizabethan and Jacobean dramatic writing. It appears that originally Marlowe intended to write only the first part, concluding with Tamburlaine's marriage to Zenocrate and his making "truce with all the world." But the popularity of the first part encouraged Marlowe to continue the story to Tamburlaine's death. This gave him some difficulty, as he had almost exhausted his historical sources in part I; consequently the sequel has, at first glance, an appearance of padding. Yet the effort demanded in writing the continuation made the young playwright look more coldly and searchingly at the hero he had chosen, and thus part II makes explicit certain notions that were below the surface and insufficiently recognized by the dramatist in part I.

The play is based on the life and achievements of Timur (Timurlenk), the bloody 14th-century conqueror of Central Asia and India. Tamburlaine is a man avid for power and luxury and the possession of beauty: at the beginning of part I he is only an obscure Scythian shepherd, but he wins the crown of Persia by eloquence and bravery and a readiness to discard loyalty. He then conquers Bajazeth, emperor of Turkey, he puts the town of Damascus to the sword, and he conquers the sultan of Egypt; but, at the pleas of the sultan's daughter Zenocrate, the captive whom he loves, he spares him and makes truce. In part II Tamburlaine's conquests are further extended; whenever he fights a battle, he must win, even when his last illness is upon him. But Zenocrate dies, and their three sons provide a manifestly imperfect means for ensuring the preservation of his wide dominions; he kills Calyphas, one of these sons, when he refuses to follow his father into battle. Always, too, there are more battles to fight: when for a moment he has no immediate opponent on earth, he dreams of leading his army against the powers of heaven, though at other times he glories in seeing himself as "the scourge of God"; he burns the Qur'ān, for he will have no intermediary between God and himself, and there is a hint of doubt whether even God is to be granted recognition. Certainly Marlowe feels sympathy with his hero, giving him magnificent verse to speak, delighting in his dreams of power and of the possession of beauty.

But, especially in part II, there are other strains: the hero can be absurd in his continual striving for more demonstrations of his power; his cruelty, which is extreme, becomes sickening; his human weakness is increasingly underlined, most notably in the onset of his fatal illness immediately after his arrogant burning of the Qur'ān. In this early play Marlowe already shows the ability to view a tragic hero from more than one angle, achieving a simultaneous vision of grandeur and impotence.

Marlowe's most famous play is *The Tragicall History of Dr. Faustus;* but it has survived only in a corrupt form, and its date of composition has been much-disputed. It was first published in 1604, and another version appeared in 1616. *Faustus* takes over the dramatic framework of the morality plays in its presentation of a story of temptation, fall, and damnation and its free use of morality figures such as the good angel and the bad angel and the seven deadly sins, along with the devils Lucifer and Mephistopheles. In *Faustus* Marlowe tells the story of the doctor-turned-necromancer Faustus, who sells his soul to the devil in exchange for knowledge and power. The devil's intermediary in the play, Mephistopheles, achieves tragic grandeur in his own right as a fallen angel torn between satanic pride and dark despair. The play gives eloquent expression to this idea of damnation in the lament of Mephistopheles for a lost heaven and in Faustus' final despairing entreaties to be saved by Christ before his soul is claimed by the devil.

Just as in *Tamburlaine* Marlowe had seen the cruelty and absurdity of his hero as well as his magnificence, so here he can enter into Faustus' grandiose intellectual ambition, simultaneously viewing those ambitions as futile, self-destructive, and absurd. The text is problematic in the low comic scenes spuriously introduced by later hack writers, but its more sober and consistent moments are certainly the uncorrupted work of Marlowe.

In *The Famous Tragedy of the Rich Jew of Malta*, Marlowe portrays another power-hungry figure in the Jew Barabas, who in the villainous society of Christian Malta shows no scruple in self-advancement. But this figure is more closely incorporated within his society than either Tamburlaine, the supreme conqueror, or Faustus, the lonely adventurer against God. In the end Barabas is overcome, not by a divine stroke but by the concerted action of his human enemies. There is a difficulty in deciding how fully the extant text of *The Jew of Malta* represents Marlowe's original play, for it was not published until 1633. But *The Jew* can be closely associated with *The Massacre at Paris* (1593), a dramatic presentation of incidents from contemporary French history, including the Massacre of St. Bartholomew's Day, and with *The Troublesome Raigne and Lamentable Death of Edward the Second* (published 1594), Marlowe's great contribution to the Elizabethan plays on historical themes.

As *The Massacre* introduces in the duke of Guise a figure unscrupulously avid for power, so in the younger Mortimer of *Edward II* Marlowe shows a man developing an appetite for power and increasingly corrupted as power comes to him. In each instance the dramatist shares in the excitement of the pursuit of glory, but all three plays present such figures within a social framework: the notion of social responsibility, the notion of corruption through power, and the notion of the suffering that the exercise of power entails are all prominently the dramatist's concern. Apart from *Tamburlaine* and the minor work *Dido, Queen of Carthage* (of uncertain date, published 1594 and written in collaboration with Thomas Nashe), *Edward II* is the only one of Marlowe's plays whose extant text can be relied on as adequately representing the author's manuscript. And certainly *Edward II* is a major work, not merely one of the first Elizabethan plays on an English historical theme. The relationships linking the king, his neglected queen, the king's favourite, Gaveston, and the ambitious Mortimer are studied with detached sympathy and remarkable understanding: no character here is lightly disposed of, and the abdication and the brutal murder of Edward show the same dark and violent imagination as appeared in Marlowe's presentation of Faustus' last hour. Though this play, along with *The Jew* and *The Massacre*, shows Marlowe's fascinated response to the distorted Elizabethan idea of Machiavelli, it more importantly shows Marlowe's deeply suggestive awareness of the nature of disaster, the power of society, and the dark extent of an individual's suffering.

WILLIAM SHAKESPEARE

(baptized April 26, 1564, Stratford-upon-Avon, Warwickshire, England—d. April 23, 1616, Stratford-upon-Avon)

William Shakespeare was an English poet, dramatist, and actor, often called the English national poet and considered by many to be the greatest dramatist of all time.

Shakespeare occupies a position unique in world literature. Other poets, such as Homer and Dante, and novelists, such as Leo Tolstoy and Charles Dickens, have transcended national barriers; but no writer's living reputation can compare to that of Shakespeare, whose plays, written in the late 16th and early 17th centuries for a small repertory theatre, are now performed and read more often and in more countries than ever before. The prophecy of his great contemporary, the poet and dramatist Ben Jonson, that Shakespeare "was not of an age, but for all time," has been fulfilled.

Life

Although the amount of factual knowledge available about Shakespeare is surprisingly large for one of his station in life, many find it a little disappointing, for it is mostly gleaned from documents of an official character. Dates of baptisms, marriages, deaths, and burials; wills, conveyances, legal processes, and payments by the court— these are the dusty details. There are, however, many contemporary allusions to him as a writer, and these add a reasonable amount of flesh and blood to the biographical skeleton.

The parish register of Holy Trinity Church in Stratford-upon-Avon, Warwickshire, shows that he was baptized there on April 26, 1564; his birthday is traditionally celebrated on April 23. His father, John Shakespeare, was a burgess of the borough. His mother, Mary Arden, of Wilmcote, Warwickshire, came from an ancient family and was the heiress to some land.

William Shakespeare. Oli Scarff/Getty Images

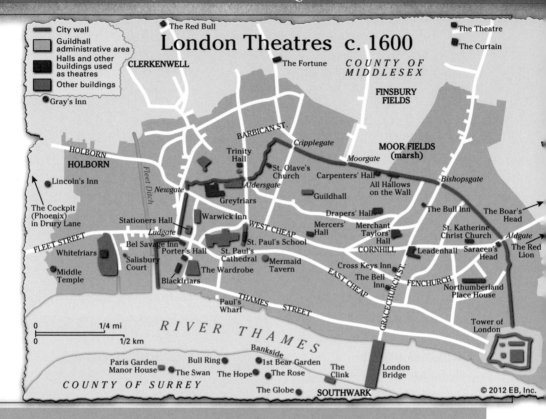

London theatres, c. 1600. Encyclopædia Britannica, Inc.

Stratford enjoyed a grammar school of good quality, and the education there was free, the schoolmaster's salary being paid by the borough. No lists of the pupils who were at the school in the 16th century have survived, but it would be absurd to suppose the bailiff of the town did not send his son there. The boy's education would consist mostly of Latin studies—learning to read, write, and speak the language fairly well and studying some of the Classical historians, moralists, and poets. Shakespeare did not go on to the university, and indeed it is unlikely that the scholarly round of logic, rhetoric, and other studies then followed there would have interested him.

Instead, at age 18 he married. Where and exactly when are not known, but the episcopal registry at Worcester preserves a bond dated November 28, 1582, and executed by two yeomen of Stratford, named Sandells and Richardson, as a security to the bishop for the issue of a license for the marriage of William Shakespeare and "Anne Hathaway of Stratford," upon the consent of her friends and upon once asking of the banns (a public announcement of a proposed marriage that gives others the chance to state any known objection to the union). The next date of interest is found in the records of the Stratford church, where a daughter, named Susanna, born to William Shakespeare, was baptized on May 26, 1583. On February 2, 1585, twins were baptized, Hamnet and Judith. (Hamnet, Shakespeare's only son, died 11 years later.)

The first reference to Shakespeare in the literary world of London comes in 1592, when a fellow dramatist, Robert Greene, insulted him in a pamphlet written on his deathbed. How Shakespeare's career in the theatre began is unclear, but from roughly 1594 onward he was an important member of the Lord Chamberlain's company of players (called the King's Men after the accession of James I in 1603). They had the best actor, Richard Burbage; they had the best theatre, the Globe (finished by the autumn of 1599); they had the best dramatist, Shakespeare. It is no wonder that the company prospered. Shakespeare became a full-time professional man of his own theatre, sharing in a cooperative enterprise and intimately concerned with the financial success of the plays he wrote.

Unfortunately, written records give little indication of the way in which Shakespeare's professional life molded his marvelous artistry. All that can be deduced is that for 20 years Shakespeare devoted himself assiduously to his art, writing more than a million words of poetic drama of the highest quality.

Shakespeare's Plays and Poems

The Early Plays

Shakespeare arrived in London probably sometime in the late 1580s. He was in his mid-20s. It is not known how he got started in the theatre or for what acting companies he wrote his early plays, which are not easy to date. Indicating a time of apprenticeship, these plays show a more direct debt to London dramatists of the 1580s and to Classical examples than do his later works. He learned a great deal about writing plays by imitating the successes of the London theatre, as any young poet and budding dramatist might do. *Titus Andronicus* (c. 1589–92) is a case in point. As Shakespeare's first full-length tragedy, it owes much of its theme, structure, and language to Thomas Kyd's *The Spanish Tragedy*, a revenge tragedy that was a huge success in the late 1580s. Shakespeare's most violent play, *Titus* relates the story of the titular Roman general who bloodily avenges his butchered sons and mutilated daughter.

Other than *Titus*, however, Shakespeare did not experiment with formal tragedy in his early years. The young playwright was drawn more quickly into comedy, and with more immediate success. Shakespeare's early comedies revel in stories of amorous courtship in which a plucky and admirable young woman (played by a boy actor) is paired off against her male wooer. Julia, one of two young heroines in *The Two Gentlemen of Verona* (c. 1590–94), disguises herself as a man in order to follow her lover, Proteus, when he is sent from Verona to Milan. Proteus (appropriately named for the changeable Proteus of Greek myth), she discovers, is paying far too much attention to Sylvia, the beloved of Proteus's best friend, Valentine. Love and friendship thus do battle for the divided loyalties of the erring male until the generosity of his friend and, most of all, the enduring chaste loyalty of the two women bring Proteus to his senses.

Shakespeare's most classically inspired early comedy is *The Comedy of Errors* (c. 1589–94). Here he turned particularly to Plautus' farcical play called the *Menaechmi* (*Twins*). The story of one twin (Antipholus) looking for his lost brother, accompanied by a clever servant (Dromio) whose twin has also disappeared, results in a farce of mistaken identities that also thoughtfully explores issues of identity and self-knowing.

Shakespeare's early romantic comedy most indebted to John Lyly is *Love's Labour's Lost* (c. 1588–97), a confection set in the never-never land of Navarre where the King and his companions are visited by the Princess of France and her ladies-in-waiting on a diplomatic mission that soon devolves into a game of courtship. As is often the case in Shakespearean romantic comedy, the young women are sure of who they are and whom they intend to marry. The young men, conversely, fall all over themselves in their comically futile attempts to eschew romantic love in favour of more serious pursuits. They perjure themselves, are shamed and put down, and are finally forgiven their follies by the women. Shakespeare brilliantly portrays male discomfiture and female self-assurance as he explores the treacherous but desirable world of sexual attraction, while the verbal gymnastics of the play emphasize the wonder and the delicious foolishness of falling in love.

In *The Taming of the Shrew* (c. 1590–94), Shakespeare employs a device of multiple plotting that is to become a standard feature of his romantic comedies. In one plot, a young woman (Bianca) carries on a risky courtship with a young man who appears to be a tutor, much to the dismay of her father, who hopes to marry her to a wealthy suitor of his own choosing. Simultaneously, Bianca's shrewish sister Kate denounces (and terrorizes) all men. Bianca's suitors commission the self-assured Petruchio to pursue Kate so that Bianca, the younger sister, will be free to wed. The wife-taming plot is itself based on folktale and ballad tradition in which men assure their ascendancy in the marriage relationship by beating their wives into submission. Shakespeare transforms this raw, antifeminist material into a study of the struggle for dominance in the marriage relationship.

Unlike the rich tradition of classical drama on which he was able to draw for his comedies, Shakespeare in 1590 or thereabouts had really only one viable model for the English history play, an anonymous and sprawling drama called *The Famous Victories of Henry the Fifth* (1583–88) that told the saga of Henry IV's son, Prince Hal, from the days of his adolescent rebellion down through his victory over the French at the Battle of Agincourt in 1415—in other words, the material that Shakespeare would later use in writing three major plays, *Henry IV, Part 1*; *Henry IV, Part 2*; and *Henry V*. Shakespeare chose to start not with Prince Hal but with more recent history in the reign of Henry V's son Henry VI and with the civil wars that saw the overthrow of Henry VI by Edward IV and then the accession to power in 1483 of Richard III. This material proved to be so rich in themes and dramatic conflicts that he wrote four plays on it, a "tetralogy" extending from *Henry VI* in three parts (c. 1589–93) to *Richard III* (c. 1592–94).

These plays were immediately successful. Contemporary references indicate that audiences of the early 1590s thrilled to the story (in *Henry VI, Part 1*) of the brave Lord Talbot doing battle in France against the witch Joan of Arc and her lover, the French dauphin, but being undermined in his heroic effort by effeminacy and corruption at home. Henry VI himself is, as Shakespeare portrays him, a weak king, raised to the kingship by the early death of his father, incapable of controlling factionalism in his court, and enervated personally by his infatuation with a dangerous Frenchwoman, Margaret of Anjou. Henry VI is cuckolded by his wife and her lover, the Duke of Suffolk, and (in *Henry VI, Part 2*) proves unable to defend his virtuous uncle, the Duke of Gloucester, against opportunistic enemies. The result is civil unrest, lower-class rebellion, and eventually all-out civil war between the Lancastrian faction, nominally headed by Henry VI, and the Yorkist claimants under the leadership of Edward IV and his brothers. *Richard III* completes the saga with its account of the baleful rise of Richard of Gloucester through the murdering of his brother the Duke of Clarence and of Edward IV's two sons, who were also Richard's nephews. Richard's tyrannical reign yields eventually and inevitably to the newest and most successful claimant of the throne, Henry Tudor, earl of Richmond. This is the man who becomes Henry VII, scion of the Tudor dynasty and grandfather of Queen Elizabeth I, who reigned from 1558 to 1603 and hence during the entire first decade and more of Shakespeare's productive career.

The Poems

Shakespeare seems to have wanted to be a poet as much as he sought to succeed in the theatre. His plays are wonderfully and poetically written, often in blank verse. And when he experienced a pause in his theatrical career about 1592–94, the plague having closed down much theatrical activity, he wrote poems. *Venus and Adonis* (1593) and *The Rape of Lucrece* (1594) are the only works that Shakespeare seems to have shepherded through the printing process. Both owe a good deal to Ovid, the Classical poet whose writings Shakespeare encountered repeatedly in school. These two poems are the only works for which he wrote dedicatory prefaces. Both are to Henry Wriothesley, earl of Southampton. This young man, a favourite at court, seems to have encouraged Shakespeare and to have served for a brief time at least as his sponsor.

Shakespeare may also have written at least some of his sonnets to Southampton, beginning in these same years of 1593–94 and continuing on through the decade and later. The question of autobiographical basis in the sonnets is much debated, but Southampton at least fits the portrait of a young gentleman who is being urged to marry and produce a family. As a narrative, the sonnet sequence tells of strong attachment, of jealousy, of grief at separation, of joy at being together and sharing beautiful experiences. The emphasis on the importance of poetry as a way of eternizing human achievement and of creating a lasting memory for the poet himself is appropriate to a friendship between a poet of modest social station and a friend who is better-born. When the sonnet sequence introduces the so-called "Dark Lady," the narrative becomes one of painful and destructive jealousy. Scholars do not know the order in which the sonnets were composed—Shakespeare seems to have had no part in publishing them—but no order other than the order of publication has been proposed, and, as the sonnets stand, they tell a coherent and disturbing tale. The poet experiences sex as something that fills him with revulsion and remorse, at least in the lustful circumstances in which he encounters it. His attachment to the young man is a love relationship that sustains him at times more than the love of the Dark Lady can do, and yet this loving friendship also dooms the poet to disappointment and self-hatred. Whether the sequence reflects any circumstances in Shakespeare's personal life, it certainly is told with an immediacy and dramatic power that bespeak an extraordinary gift for seeing into the human heart and its sorrows.

Plays of the Middle and Late Years

ROMANTIC COMEDIES

In the second half of the 1590s, Shakespeare brought to perfection the genre of romantic comedy that he had helped to invent. *A Midsummer Night's Dream* (*c.* 1595–96), is one of the most successful of all his plays. The overarching plot is of Duke Theseus of Athens and his impending marriage to an Amazonian warrior, Hippolyta, whom Theseus has recently conquered and brought back to Athens to be his bride. Their marriage ends the play. They share this concluding ceremony with four young lovers who have fled into an enchanted forest nearby to escape the Athenian law and to pursue one another, whereupon they are subjected to a complicated series of mix-ups. Eventually all is righted by fairy magic. Thus four separate strands or plots interact with one another. Despite the play's brevity, it is a masterpiece of artful construction.

The Merchant of Venice (*c.* 1596–97) uses a double plot structure to contrast a tale of romantic wooing with one that comes close to tragedy. Portia is a fine example of a romantic heroine in Shakespeare's mature comedies: she is witty, rich, exacting in what she expects of men, and adept at putting herself in a male disguise to make her presence felt. She is loyally obedient to her father's will and yet determined that she shall have Bassanio. She triumphantly resolves the murky legal affairs of Venice when the men have all failed. Shylock, the Jewish moneylender, is at the point of exacting a pound of flesh from Bassanio's friend Antonio as payment for a forfeited loan. Portia foils him in his attempt in a way that is both clever and shystering. Sympathy is uneasily balanced in Shakespeare's portrayal of Shylock, who is both persecuted by his

Christian opponents and all too ready to demand an eye for an eye according to ancient law. Ultimately Portia triumphs, not only with Shylock in the court of law but in her marriage with Bassanio.

Much Ado About Nothing (c. 1598–99) revisits the issue of power struggles in courtship, again in a revealingly double plot. The more conventional story of a young heroine being wooed is overshadowed by the back-and-forth repartee between Beatrice and Benedick, who are both skeptical about romance. In what could be regarded as a brilliant rewriting of *The Taming of the Shrew*, the witty battle of the sexes is no less amusing and complicated, but the eventual accommodation finds something much closer to mutual respect and equality between men and women.

Rosalind, in *As You Like It* (c. 1598–1600), makes use of the by-now familiar device of disguise as a young man in order to pursue the ends of promoting a rich and substantial relationship between the sexes. As in other of these plays, Rosalind is more emotionally stable and mature than her young man, Orlando. Although Rosalind's male disguise is at first a means of survival in a seemingly inhospitable forest, it soon serves a more interesting function. As "Ganymede," Rosalind befriends Orlando, offering him counseling in the affairs of love. Orlando, much in need of such advice, readily accepts and proceeds to woo his "Rosalind" ("Ganymede" playing her own self) as though she were indeed a woman. Her wryly amusing perspectives on the follies of young love helpfully puncture Orlando's inflated and unrealistic "Petrarchan" stance as the young lover who writes poems to his mistress and sticks them up on trees. Once he has learned that love is not a fantasy of invented attitudes, Orlando is ready to be the husband of the real young woman who is presented to him as the transformed Ganymede-Rosalind.

Twelfth Night (c. 1600–02) pursues a similar motif of female disguise. Viola, cast ashore in Illyria by a shipwreck and obliged to disguise herself as a young man in order to gain a place in the court of Duke Orsino, falls in love with the duke and uses her disguise as a cover for an educational process not unlike that given by Rosalind to Orlando. Orsino is as unrealistic a lover as one could hope to imagine; he pays fruitless court to the Countess Olivia and seems content with the unproductive love melancholy in which he wallows. Only Viola, as "Cesario," is able to awaken in him a genuine feeling for friendship and love. They become inseparable companions and then seeming rivals for the hand of Olivia until the presto change of Shakespeare's stage magic is able to restore "Cesario" to her woman's garments and thus present to Orsino the flesh-and-blood woman whom he has only distantly imagined.

The Merry Wives of Windsor (c. 1597–1601) is an interesting deviation from the usual Shakespearean romantic comedy in that it is set not in some imagined far-off place such as Illyria or Belmont or the forest of Athens but in Windsor, a solidly bourgeois village near Windsor Castle in the heart of England. Uncertain tradition has it that Queen Elizabeth wanted to see Falstaff (a popular character in Shakespeare's second tetralogy of history plays) in love. There is little, however, in the way of romantic wooing (the story of Anne Page and her suitor Fenton is rather buried in the midst of so many other goings-on), but the play's portrayal of women, and especially of the two "merry wives," Mistress Alice Ford and Mistress Margaret Page, reaffirms what is so often true of women in these early plays, that they are good-hearted, chastely loyal, and wittily self-possessed. Falstaff, a suitable butt for their cleverness, is a scapegoat figure who must be publicly humiliated as a way of transferring onto him the human frailties that Windsor society wishes to expunge.

HISTORIES AND THE "PROBLEM" PLAYS

Concurrent with his writing of these fine romantic comedies, Shakespeare also brought to completion (for the time being, at least) his project of writing 15th-century English history. After having finished in 1589–94 the tetralogy about Henry VI, Edward IV, and Richard III, bringing the story down to 1485, and then circa 1594–96 a play about John that deals with a chronological period (the 13th century) that sets it quite apart from his other history plays, Shakespeare turned to the late 14th and early 15th centuries and to the chronicle of Richard II, Henry IV, and Henry's legendary son Henry V. This inversion of historical order in the two tetralogies allowed Shakespeare to finish his sweep of late medieval English history with Henry V, a hero king in a way that Richard III could never pretend to be.

Richard II (*c.* 1595–96), written throughout in blank verse, is a sombre play about political impasse. It contains almost no humour, other than a wry scene in which the new king, Henry IV, must adjudicate the competing claims of the Duke of York and his Duchess, the first of whom wishes to see his son Aumerle executed for treason and the second of whom begs for mercy. Henry is able to be merciful on this occasion, since he has now won the kingship, and thus gives to this scene an upbeat movement. Earlier, however, the mood is grim. Richard, installed at an early age into the kingship, proves irresponsible as a ruler. He unfairly banishes his own first cousin, Henry Bolingbroke (later to be Henry IV), whereas the king himself appears to be guilty of ordering the murder of an uncle. When Richard keeps the dukedom of Lancaster from Bolingbroke without proper legal authority, he manages to alienate many nobles and to encourage Bolingbroke's return from exile. That return, too, is illegal, but it is a fact, and, when several of the nobles (including York) come over to Bolingbroke's side, Richard is forced to abdicate. The rights and wrongs of this power struggle are masterfully ambiguous. History proceeds without any sense of moral imperative. Henry IV is a more capable ruler, but his authority is tarnished by his crimes (including his seeming assent to the execution of Richard), and his own rebellion appears to teach the barons to rebel against him in turn. Henry eventually dies a disappointed man.

The dying king Henry IV must turn royal authority over to young Hal, or Henry, now Henry V. The prospect is dismal both to the dying king and to the members of his court, for Prince Hal has distinguished himself to this point mainly by his penchant for keeping company with the disreputable if engaging Falstaff. The son's attempts at reconciliation with the father succeed temporarily, especially when Hal saves his father's life at the battle of Shrewsbury, but (especially in *Henry IV, Part 2*) his reputation as wastrel will not leave him. Everyone expects from him a reign of irresponsible license, with Falstaff in an influential position. It is for these reasons that the young king must publicly repudiate his old companion of the tavern and the highway, however much that repudiation tugs at his heart and the audience's. Falstaff, for all his debauchery and irresponsibility, is infectiously amusing and delightful; he represents in Hal a spirit of youthful vitality that is left behind only with the greatest of regret as the young man assumes manhood and the role of crown prince. Hal manages all this with aplomb and goes on to defeat the French mightily at the Battle of Agincourt. Even his high jinks are a part of what is so attractive in him. Maturity and position come at a great personal cost: Hal becomes less a frail human being and more the figure of royal authority.

Apart from the early *Titus Andronicus*, the only other play that Shakespeare wrote prior to 1599 that is classified as a tragedy is *Romeo and Juliet* (*c.* 1594–96), which is quite untypical of the tragedies that are to follow. Written more or less at the time when Shakespeare was writing *A Midsummer Night's Dream*, *Romeo and Juliet* shares many of the characteristics of romantic comedy. Romeo and Juliet are character types more suited to Classical comedy in that they do not derive from the upper class. Their wealthy families are essentially bourgeois. The eagerness with which Capulet and his wife court Count Paris as their prospective son-in-law bespeaks their desire for social advancement.

Accordingly, the first half of *Romeo and Juliet* is very funny, while its delight in verse forms reminds us of *A Midsummer Night's Dream*. The play is ultimately a tragedy, of course, and indeed warns its audience at the start that the lovers are "star-crossed." Yet the tragic vision is not remotely that of *Hamlet* or *King Lear*. Romeo and Juliet are unremarkable, nice young people doomed by a host of considerations outside themselves: the enmity of their two families, the misunderstandings that prevent Juliet from being able to tell her parents whom it is that she has married, and even unfortunate coincidence. Yet there is the element of personal responsibility upon which most mature tragedy rests when Romeo chooses to avenge the death of Mercutio by killing Tybalt, knowing that this deed will undo the soft graces of forbearance that Juliet has taught him. Romeo succumbs to the macho peer pressure of his male companions, and tragedy results in part from this choice. Yet so much is at work that the reader ultimately sees *Romeo and Juliet* as a love tragedy—celebrating the exquisite brevity of young love, regretting an unfeeling world, and evoking an emotional response that differs from that produced by the other tragedies.

Whatever his reasons, about 1599–1600 Shakespeare turned with unsparing intensity to the exploration of darker issues such as revenge, sexual jealousy, aging, midlife crisis, and death. Perhaps he saw that his own life was moving into a new phase of more complex and vexing experiences. Perhaps he felt, or sensed, that he had worked through the romantic comedy and history play and the emotional trajectories of maturation that they encompassed. In any event, he began writing not only his great tragedies but a group of plays that are hard to classify in terms of genre. They are sometimes grouped today as "problem" plays or "problem" comedies. An examination of these plays is crucial to understanding this period of transition from 1599 to 1605.

The three problem plays dating from these years are *All's Well That Ends Well*, *Measure for Measure*, and *Troilus and Cressida*. *All's Well* is a comedy ending in acceptance of marriage, but in a way that poses thorny ethical issues. Count Bertram cannot initially accept his marriage to Helena, a woman of lower social station who has grown up in his noble household and has won Bertram as her husband by her seemingly miraculous cure of the French king. Bertram's reluctance to face the responsibilities of marriage is all the more dismaying when he turns his amorous intentions to a Florentine maiden, Diana, whom he wishes to seduce without marriage. Helena's stratagem to resolve this difficulty is the so-called bed trick, substituting herself in Bertram's bed for the arranged assignation and then calling her wayward husband to account when she is pregnant with his child. Her ends are achieved by such morally ambiguous means that marriage seems at best a precarious institution on which to base the presumed reassurances of romantic comedy. The pathway toward resolution and emotional maturity is not easy; Helena is a more ambiguous heroine than Rosalind or Viola.

Measure for Measure (c. 1603–04) similarly employs the bed trick, and for a similar purpose, though in even murkier circumstances. Isabella, on the verge of becoming a nun, learns that she has attracted the sexual desire of Lord Angelo, the deputy ruler of Vienna serving in the mysterious absence of the Duke. Her plea to Angelo for her brother's life, when that brother (Claudio) has been sentenced to die for fornication with his fiancée, is met with a demand that she sleep with Angelo or forfeit Claudio's life. This ethical dilemma is resolved by a trick (devised by the Duke, in disguise) to substitute for Isabella a woman (Mariana) whom Angelo was supposed to marry but refused when she could produce no dowry. The Duke's motivations in manipulating these substitutions and false appearances are unclear, though arguably his wish is to see what the various characters of this play will do when faced with seemingly impossible choices. Angelo is revealed as a morally fallen man, a would-be seducer and murderer who is nonetheless remorseful and ultimately glad to have been prevented from carrying out his intended crimes; Claudio learns that he is coward enough to wish to live by any means, including the emotional and physical blackmail of his sister; and Isabella learns that she is capable of bitterness and hatred, even if, crucially, she finally discovers that she can and must forgive her enemy.

Troilus and Cressida (c. 1601–02) is the most experimental and puzzling of these three plays. Simply in terms of genre, it is virtually unclassifiable. It can hardly be a comedy, ending as it does in the deaths of Patroclus and Hector and the looming defeat of the Trojans. Nor is the ending normative in terms of romantic comedy: the lovers, Troilus and Cressida, are separated from one another and embittered by the failure of their relationship. The play is a history play in a sense, dealing as it does with the great Trojan War celebrated in Homer's *Iliad*, and yet its purpose is hardly that of telling the story of the war. As a tragedy, it is perplexing in that the chief figures of the play (apart from Hector) do not die at the end, and the mood is one of desolation and even disgust rather than tragic catharsis. Perhaps the play should be thought of as a satire; the choric observations of Thersites and Pandarus serve throughout as a mordant commentary on the interconnectedness of war and lechery. With fitting ambiguity, the play was placed in the Folio of 1623 between the histories and the tragedies, in a category all by itself. Clearly, in these problem plays Shakespeare was opening up for himself a host of new problems in terms of genre and human sexuality.

THE TRAGEDIES

Written in 1599 or 1600, *Julius Caesar* illustrates similarly the transition in Shakespeare's writing toward darker themes and tragedy. It, too, is a history play in a sense, dealing with a non-Christian civilization existing 16 centuries before Shakespeare wrote his plays. Roman history opened up for Shakespeare a world in which divine purpose could not be easily ascertained. The characters of *Julius Caesar* variously interpret the great event of the assassination of Caesar as one in which the gods are angry or disinterested or capricious or simply not there. The wise Cicero observes, "Men may construe things after their fashion, / Clean from the purpose of the things themselves" (Act I, scene 3, lines 34–35).

In form, *Hamlet* (c. 1599–1601) is a revenge tragedy. It features characteristics found in *Titus* as well: a protagonist charged with the responsibility of avenging a heinous crime against the protagonist's family, a cunning antagonist, the appearance of the ghost of the murdered person, the feigning of madness to throw off the villain's suspicions, the play within the play as a means of testing the villain, and still more.

Yet to search out these comparisons is to highlight what is so extraordinary about *Hamlet*, for it refuses to be merely a revenge tragedy. Shakespeare's protagonist is unique in the genre in his moral qualms, and most of all in his finding a way to carry out his dread command without becoming a cold-blooded murderer. Hamlet does act bloodily, especially when he kills Polonius, thinking that the old man hidden in Gertrude's chambers must be the King whom Hamlet is commissioned to kill. The act seems plausible and strongly motivated, and yet Hamlet sees at once that he has erred. He has killed the wrong man, even if Polonius has brought this on himself with his incessant spying. Hamlet sees that he has offended heaven and that he will have to pay for his act. When, at the play's end, Hamlet encounters his fate in a duel with Polonius' son, Laertes, Hamlet interprets his own tragic story as one that Providence has made meaningful. By placing himself in the hands of Providence and believing devoutly that "There's a divinity that shapes our ends, / Rough-hew them how we will" (Act V, scene 2, lines 10–11), Hamlet finds himself ready for a death that he has longed for. He also finds an opportunity for killing Claudius almost unpremeditatedly, spontaneously, as an act of reprisal for all that Claudius has done.

These plays are deeply concerned with domestic and family relationships. In *Othello* (c. 1603–04) Desdemona is the only daughter of Brabantio, an aging senator of Venice, who dies heartbroken because his daughter has eloped with a dark-skinned man who is her senior by many years and is of another culture. With Othello, Desdemona is briefly happy, despite her filial disobedience, until a terrible sexual jealousy is awakened in him, quite without cause other than his own fears and susceptibility to Iago's insinuations that it is only "natural" for Desdemona to seek erotic pleasure with a young man who shares her background. As a tragedy, the play adroitly exemplifies the traditional Classical model of a good man brought to misfortune by hamartia, or tragic flaw; as Othello grieves, he is one who has "loved not wisely, but too well" (Act V, scene 2, line 354).

Daughters and fathers are also at the heart of the major dilemma in *King Lear* (*c.* 1605–06). In this configuration, Shakespeare does what he often does in his late plays: erase the wife from the picture, so that father and daughter(s) are left to deal with one another. Lear's banishing of his favourite daughter, Cordelia, because of her laconic refusal to proclaim a love for him as the essence of her being, brings upon this aging king the terrible punishment of being belittled and rejected by his ungrateful daughters, Goneril and Regan. Concurrently, in the play's second plot, the Earl of Gloucester makes a similar mistake with his good-hearted son, Edgar, and thereby delivers himself into the hands of his scheming bastard son, Edmund. Both these erring elderly fathers are ultimately nurtured by the loyal children they have banished, but not before the play has tested to its absolute limit the proposition that evil can flourish in a bad world.

The gods seem indifferent, perhaps absent entirely; pleas to them for assistance go unheeded while the storm of fortune rains down on the heads of those who have trusted in conventional pieties. Part of what is so great in this play is that its testing of the major characters requires them to seek out philosophical answers that can arm the resolute heart against ingratitude and misfortune by constantly pointing out that life owes one nothing. The consolations of philosophy preciously found out by Edgar and Cordelia are those that rely not on the suppositious gods but on an inner moral strength demanding that one be charitable and honest because life is otherwise monstrous and subhuman. The play exacts terrible prices of those who persevere in goodness, but it leaves them and the reader, or audience, with the reassurance that it is simply better to be a Cordelia than to be a Goneril, to be an Edgar than to be an Edmund.

Macbeth (c. 1606–07) is in some ways Shakespeare's most unsettling tragedy, because it invites the intense examination of the heart of a man who is well-intentioned in most ways but who discovers that he cannot resist the temptation to achieve power at any cost. Macbeth is a sensitive, even poetic person, and as such he understands with frightening clarity the stakes that are involved in his contemplated deed of murder. Duncan is a virtuous king and his guest. The deed is regicide and murder and a violation of the sacred obligations of hospitality. Macbeth knows that Duncan's virtues, like angels, "trumpet-tongued," will plead against "the deep damnation of his taking-off" (Act I, scene 7, lines 19–20). The only factor weighing on the other side is personal ambition, which Macbeth understands to be a moral failing. The question of why he proceeds to murder is partly answered by the insidious temptations of the three Weird Sisters, who sense Macbeth's vulnerability to their prophecies, and the terrifying strength of his wife, who drives him on to the murder by describing his reluctance as unmanliness. Ultimately, though, the responsibility lies with Macbeth. His collapse of moral integrity confronts the audience and perhaps implicates it. The loyalty and decency of such characters as Macduff hardly offset what is so painfully weak in the play's protagonist.

Antony and Cleopatra (c. 1606–07) approaches human frailty in terms that are less spiritually terrifying. The story of the lovers is certainly one of worldly failure. Plutarch's *Lives* gave to Shakespeare the object lesson of a brave general who lost his reputation and sense of self-worth through his infatuation with an admittedly attractive but nonetheless dangerous woman. Shakespeare changes none of the circumstances: Antony hates himself for dallying in Egypt with Cleopatra, agrees to marry with Octavius Caesar's sister Octavia as a way of recovering his status in the Roman triumvirate, cheats on Octavia eventually, loses the battle of Actium because of his fatal attraction for Cleopatra, and dies in Egypt a defeated, aging warrior. Shakespeare adds to this narrative a compelling portrait of midlife crisis. Antony is deeply anxious about his loss of sexual potency and position in the world of affairs. His amorous life in Egypt is manifestly an attempt to affirm and recover his dwindling male power.

Two late tragedies also choose the ancient Classical world as their setting but do so in a deeply dispiriting way. Shakespeare appears to have been much preoccupied with ingratitude and human greed in these years. *Timon of Athens* (c. 1605–08), probably an unfinished play and possibly never produced, initially shows us a prosperous man fabled for his generosity. When he discovers that he has exceeded his means, he turns to his seeming friends for the kinds of assistance he has given them, only to discover that their memories are short. Retiring to a bitter isolation, Timon rails against all humanity and refuses every sort of consolation, even that of well-meant companionship and sympathy from a former servant. He dies in isolation. Seldom has a more unrelievedly embittered play been written.

Coriolanus (c. 1608) similarly portrays the ungrateful responses of a city toward its military hero. The problem is complicated by the fact that Coriolanus, egged on by his mother and his conservative allies, undertakes a political role in Rome for which he is not temperamentally fitted. Yet his fury only makes matters worse and leads to an exile from which he returns to conquer his own city, in league with his old enemy and friend, Aufidius. When his mother comes out for the city to plead for her life and that of other Romans, he relents and thereupon falls into defeat as a kind of mother's boy, unable to assert his own sense of self. As a tragedy, *Coriolanus* is again bitter, satirical, ending in defeat and humiliation. It is an immensely powerful play, and it captures a philosophical mood of nihilism and bitterness that hovers over Shakespeare's writings throughout these years in the first decade of the 1600s.

THE ROMANCES

Concurrently, nonetheless, and then in the years that followed, Shakespeare turned again to the writing of comedy. The late comedies are usually called romances or tragicomedies because they tell stories of wandering and separation leading eventually to tearful and joyous reunion. They are suffused with a bittersweet mood that seems eloquently appropriate to a writer who has explored with such unsparing honesty the depths of human suffering and degradation in the great tragedies.

Pericles, written perhaps in 1606–08 employs a chorus figure, John Gower (author of an earlier version of this story), to guide the reader or viewer around the Mediterranean on Pericles' various travels, as he avoids marriage with the daughter of the incestuous King Antiochus of Antioch; marries Thaisa, the daughter of King Simonides of Pentapolis; has a child by her; believes his wife to have died in childbirth during a storm at sea and has her body thrown overboard to quiet the superstitious fears of the sailors; puts his daughter Marina in the care of Cleon of Tarsus and his wicked wife, Dionyza; and is eventually restored to his wife and child after many years.

The Winter's Tale (c. 1609–11) is in some ways a replaying of this same story, in that King Leontes of Sicilia, smitten by an irrational jealousy of his wife, Hermione, brings about the seeming death of that wife and the real death of their son. The resulting guilt is unbearable for Leontes and yet ultimately curative over a period of many years that are required for his only daughter, Perdita (whom he has nearly killed also), to grow to maturity in distant Bohemia. The reunion with daughter and then wife is deeply touching as in *Pericles*, with the added magical touch that the audience does not know that Hermione is alive and in fact has been told that she is dead. Her wonderfully staged appearance as a statue coming to life is one of the great theatrical coups in Shakespeare, playing as it does with favourite Shakespearean themes in these late plays of the ministering daughter, the guilt-ridden husband, and the miraculously recovered wife.

In *Cymbeline* (c. 1608–10) King Cymbeline drives his virtuous daughter Imogen into exile by his opposition to her marriage with Posthumus Leonatus. The wife in this case is Cymbeline's baleful Queen, a stereotypical wicked stepmother whose witless and lecherous son Cloten (Imogen's half brother) is the embodiment of everything that threatens and postpones the eventual happy ending of this tale. Posthumus, too, fails Imogen by being irrationally jealous of her, but he is eventually recovered to a belief in her goodness.

The Tempest (c. 1611) sums up much of what Shakespeare's mature art was all about. Once again we find a wifeless father with a daughter, in this case on a deserted island where the father, Prospero, is entirely responsible for his daughter's education. He behaves like a dramatist in charge of the whole play as well, arranging her life and that of the other characters. *The Tempest* seems to have been intended as Shakespeare's farewell to the theatre. It contains moving passages of reflection on what his powers as artist have been able to accomplish, and valedictory themes of closure. As a comedy, it demonstrates perfectly the way that Shakespeare was able to combine precise artistic construction (the play chooses on this farewell occasion to observe the Classical unities of time, place, and action) with his special flair for stories that transcend the merely human and physical: *The Tempest* is peopled with spirits, monsters, and drolleries. This, it seems, is Shakespeare's summation of his art as comic dramatist.

But *The Tempest* proved not to be Shakespeare's last play after all. Perhaps he discovered, as many people do, that he was bored in retirement. In 1613 or thereabouts, he wrote a history play titled *Henry VIII* (1613), which is extraordinary in a number of ways: it relates historical events substantially later chronologically than those of the 15th century that had been his subject in his earlier historical plays; it is separated from the last of those plays by perhaps 14 years; and, perhaps most significant, it is as much romance as history play. History in this instance is really about the birth of Elizabeth I, who was to become England's great queen. The circumstances of Henry VIII's troubled marital affairs, his meeting with Anne Boleyn, his confrontation with the papacy, and all the rest turn out to be the humanly unpredictable ways by which Providence engineers the miracle of Elizabeth's birth. Thus history yields its providential meaning in the shape of a play that is both history and romance.

THOMAS NASHE

(b. 1567, Lowestoft, Suffolk, England—
d. *c.* 1601, Yarmouth, Norfolk?)

Thomas Nashe (also spelled Nash) was a pamphleteer, poet, dramatist, and author of *The Unfortunate Traveller; or, The Life of Jacke Wilton* (1594), the first picaresque novel in English.

Nashe was educated at the University of Cambridge, and about 1588 he went to London, where he became associated with Robert Greene and other professional writers. In 1589 he wrote *The Anatomie of Absurditie* and the preface to Greene's *Menaphon*. Both works are bold, opinionated surveys of the contemporary state of writing; occasionally obscure, they arc euphuistic in style and range freely over a great variety of topics.

In 1589 and 1590 he evidently became a paid hack of the episcopacy in the Marprelate controversy, matching wits with the unidentified Puritan "Martin," the author of the anti-Anglican Church pamphlets. Almost all the Anglican replies to Martin have variously been assigned to Nashe, but only *An Almond for a Parrat* (1590) has been convincingly attributed to him. He wrote the preface to Thomas Newman's unauthorized edition of Sir Philip Sidney's *Astrophel and Stella* (1591). Though Nashe penned an extravagant dedication to Sidney's sister, the countess of Pembroke, the book was withdrawn and reissued in the same year without Nashe's foreword.

Pierce Penilesse His Supplication to the Divell (1592), a satire focused on the seven deadly sins, was Nashe's first distinctive work. Using a free and extemporaneous prose style, full of colloquialisms, newly coined words, and fantastic idiosyncrasies, Nashe buttonholes the reader with a story in which a need for immediate entertainment seems to predominate over any narrative structure or controlling objective. Having become involved in his friend Greene's feud with the writer Gabriel Harvey, Nashe satirized Harvey and his brothers in *Pierce* and then joined the combat in an exchange of pamphlets with Harvey, *Strange Newes* (1592) and *Have with You to Saffron-Walden* (1596). If Harvey is to be credited, Nashe was a hack for the printer John Danter in 1593. The controversy was terminated in 1599, when the archbishop of

Thomas Nashe, engraving from the pamphlet The Trimming of Thomas Nashe Gentleman *by Gabriel Harvey, 1597.* Hulton Archive/Getty Images

Canterbury ordered that "all Nasshes bookes and Doctor Harveyes bookes be taken wheresoever they maye be found and that none of theire bookes bee ever printed hereafter."

Apparently Nashe wrote *Strange Newes* while he was living at the home of Sir George Carey, who momentarily relieved his oppressive poverty. In *Christs Teares over Jerusalem* (1593), Nashe warned his countrymen during one of the country's worst outbreaks of bubonic plague that, unless they reformed, London would suffer the fate of Jerusalem. *The Terrors of the Night* (1594) is a discursive, sometimes bewildering, attack on demonology.

Pierce Penilesse excepted, Nashe's most successful works were his entertainment *Summers Last Will and Testament* (1592, published 1600); his picaresque novel *The Unfortunate Traveller; or, The Life of Jacke Wilton*; *Dido, Queen of Carthage* (1594; with Christopher Marlowe); and *Nashes Lenten Stuffe* (1599). *The Unfortunate Traveller* is a brutal and realistic tale of adventure narrated with speed and economy. The book describes the travels through Germany and Italy of its rogue hero, Jacke Wilton, who lives by his wits and witnesses all sorts of historic events before he is converted to a better way of life. *Lenten Stuffe*, in praise of herrings, contains a charming description of the town of Yarmouth, Norfolk, a herring fishery. Nashe retreated to Yarmouth when he and Ben Jonson were prosecuted as a result of their satirical play *The Isle of Dogs* (1597).

Nashe was the first of the English prose eccentrics, an extraordinary inventor of verbal hybrids. *The Works* were edited by R.B. McKerrow, 5 vol. (1904–10; reprinted and reedited by F.P. Wilson, 1958).

GIAMBATTISTA MARINO

(b. October 18, 1569, Naples — d. March 25, 1625, Naples)

The Italian poet Giambattista Marino (also spelled Marini) was the founder of the school of Marinism (later Secentismo), which dominated 17th-century Italian poetry. Marino's own work, praised throughout Europe, far surpassed that of his imitators, who carried his complicated word play and elaborate conceits and metaphors to such extremes that Marinism became a pejorative term. His work was translated all over Europe.

Marino trained for the law because of parental pressure but refused to practice his profession. His life after 1590 consisted of wild living, wandering between Italian and French courts, frequent money problems, brushes with the law, and immense success with the poetry that he managed to get published despite censorship. Much of his early work was circulated, with great acclaim, in manuscript and published later in his life. In 1596 he wrote *La sampogna* ("The Syrinx"), a series of sensual idylls using mythological and pastoral subjects, but he was unable to publish it until 1620.

After serving for a while as secretary to a Neapolitan prince, Marino was arrested in 1598 and 1600 for immorality, each time obtaining release through powerful admirers. He went to Rome and attached himself to Cardinal Pietro Aldobrandini, a nephew of the pope. Together they visited several Italian cities. Marino tried to publish some of his voluptuous poems in Parma but was halted by the Inquisition. Finally he was able to publish his early poetry as *Le rime* (1602; "The Rhymes") and under the title *La lira*, 2 vol. (1608 and 1614; "The Lyre").

At Torino (Turin) from 1608 to 1615 he enjoyed the patronage of the duke of Savoy but was resented for his satirical poems against a rival poet, Gaspare Murtola (*La Murtoleide*, 1619; "The Murtoliad"). Murtola had him imprisoned for this offense and others; and, though his friends secured his release, Marino left Torino for Paris in 1615, where he staycd until 1623 under the patronage of Marie de Médicis and Louis XIII.

Before leaving Paris Marino published his most important work, a labour of 20 years, *Adone* (1623; definitive ed. by R. Balsamo-Crivelli, 1922; *Adonis* [selections]). *Adone*, an enormous poem (45,000 lines), relates, with many digressions, the love story of Venus and Adonis and shows the best and worst of Marino's style. The best is found in brilliant passages, written in a masterly style; the worst, in excessive conceits and metaphors, word play, and hyperbole. On returning to Italy in 1623, Marino encountered new difficulties with censorship, but he stayed in Naples until his death.

Other works for which Marino is remembered are *La galeria* (1620; "The Gallery"), an attempt to recreate works of art poetically, and *La strage degli innocenti* (1632; *The Slaughter of the Innocents*). His correspondence was published as *Lettere* ("Letters") in 1627.

JOHN DONNE

(b. sometime between January 24 and June 19, 1572, London,
England—d. March 31, 1631, London)

The leading English poet of the Metaphysical school and dean of St. Paul's Cathedral, London (1621–31), John Donne is often considered the greatest love poet in the English language. He is also noted for his religious verse and treatises and for his sermons, which rank among the best of the 17th century.

Life and Career

Donne was born of Roman Catholic parents. Donne was four when his father died, and shortly thereafter his mother married Dr. John Syminges, who raised the Donne children. At age 12 Donne matriculated at the University of Oxford, where he studied for three years, and he then most likely continued his education at the University of Cambridge, though he took no degree from either university because as a Roman Catholic he could not swear the required oath of allegiance to the Protestant queen, Elizabeth. Following his studies Donne probably traveled in Spain and Italy and then returned to London to read law. There he turned to a comparative examination of Roman Catholic and Protestant theology and perhaps even toyed with religious skepticism. In 1596 he enlisted as a gentleman with the earl of Essex's successful privateering expedition against Cádiz, and the following year he sailed with Sir Walter Raleigh and Essex in the near-disastrous Islands expedition, hunting for Spanish treasure ships in the Azores.

After his return to London in 1597, Donne became secretary to Sir Thomas Egerton, lord keeper of the great seal, in whose employ Donne remained for almost five years. The appointment itself makes it probable that Donne had become an Anglican by this time. While in Egerton's service, Donne met and fell in love with Anne More, niece of Egerton's second wife and the daughter of Sir George More, who was chancellor of the garter. Knowing there was no chance of obtaining Sir George's blessing on their union, the two married secretly, probably in December 1601. For this offense Sir George had Donne briefly imprisoned and dismissed from his post with Egerton as well. He also denied Anne's dowry to Donne. Because of the marriage, moreover, all possibilities of a career in public service were dashed, and Donne found himself at age 30 with neither prospects for employment nor adequate funds with which to support his household.

During the next 10 years Donne lived in poverty and humiliating dependence, first on the charity of Anne's cousin at Pyrford, Surrey, then at a house in Mitcham, about 7 miles (11 km) from London, and sometimes in a London apartment, where he relied on the support of noble patrons. All the while he repeatedly tried (and failed) to secure employment, and in the meantime his family was growing; Anne ultimately bore 12 children, 5 of whom died before they reached maturity.

In spite of his misery during these years, Donne wrote and studied assiduously, producing prose works on theology, canon law, and anti-Catholic polemics and composing love lyrics, religious poetry, and complimentary and funerary verse for his patrons. As early as 1607 friends had begun urging him to take holy orders in the Church of England, but he felt unworthy and continued to seek secular employment.

John Donne. Kean Collection/Archive Photos/Getty Images

In 1614 King James I refused Donne's final attempt to secure a post at court and said that he would appoint him to nothing outside the church. By this time Donne himself had come to believe he had a religious vocation, and he finally agreed to take holy orders. He was ordained deacon and priest on January 23, 1615, and preferment soon followed. He was made a royal chaplain and received, at the king's command, the degree of doctor of divinity from Cambridge. On November 22, 1621, Donne was installed as dean of St. Paul's Cathedral, at which he carried out his duties with efficiency and integrity. But this turnabout in Donne's professional life was accompanied by searing personal grief. Two years after his ordination, in 1617, Anne Donne died at age 33 after giving birth to a stillborn child. Donne's bereavement turned him fully to his vocation as an Anglican divine. The power and eloquence of his sermons soon secured for him a reputation as the foremost preacher in the England of his day, and he became a favourite of both Kings James I and Charles I.

In 1623 Donne fell seriously ill with either typhus or relapsing fever, and during his sickness he reflected on the parallels between his physical and spiritual illnesses—reflections that culminated during his recovery in the prose *Devotions upon Emergent Occasions,* published in 1624. On February 25, 1631, Donne, who was fatally ill with stomach cancer, left his sickbed to preach a final sermon at court; this was published posthumously as *Death's Duell* and is sometimes considered to be his own funeral sermon.

Poetry

Donne's poetry is marked by strikingly original departures from the conventions of 16th-century English verse, particularly that of Sir Philip Sidney and Edmund Spenser.

Even his early satires and elegies, which derive from classical Latin models, contain versions of his experiments with genre, form, and imagery. His poems contain few descriptive passages like those in Spenser, nor do his lines follow the smooth metrics and euphonious sounds of his predecessors. Donne replaced their mellifluous lines with a speaking voice whose vocabulary and syntax reflect the emotional intensity of a confrontation and whose metrics and verbal music conform to the needs of a particular dramatic situation. One consequence of this is a directness of language that electrifies his mature poetry. "For Godsake hold your tongue, and let me love," begins his love poem *The Canonization,* plunging the reader into the midst of an encounter between the speaker and an unidentified listener. Holy Sonnet XI opens with an imaginative confrontation wherein Donne, not Jesus, suffers indignities on the cross: "Spit in my face yee Jewes, and pierce my side...."

From these explosive beginnings, the poems develop as closely reasoned arguments or propositions that rely heavily on the use of the conceit—i.e., an extended metaphor that draws an ingenious parallel between apparently dissimilar situations or objects. Donne, however, transformed the conceit into a vehicle for transmitting multiple, sometimes even contradictory, feelings and ideas. And, changing again the practice of earlier poets, he drew his imagery from such diverse fields as alchemy, astronomy, medicine, politics, global exploration, and philosophical disputation. Donne's famous analogy of parting lovers to a drawing compass affords a prime example.

The presence of a listener is another of Donne's modifications of the Renaissance love lyric, in which the lovers lament, hope, and dissect their feelings without facing their ladies. Donne, by contrast, speaks directly to the lady or some other listener. The latter may even determine the course of the poem, as in *The Flea,* in which the speaker changes his tack once the woman crushes the insect on which he has built his argument about the innocence of lovemaking. But for all their dramatic intensity, Donne's poems still maintain the verbal music and introspective approach that define lyric poetry. His speakers may fashion an imaginary figure to whom they utter their lyric outburst, or, conversely, they may lapse into reflection in the midst of an address to a listener. "But O, selfe traytor," the forlorn lover cries in *Twickham Garden* as he transforms part of his own psyche into a listener. Donne also departs from earlier lyrics by adapting the syntax and rhythms of living speech to his poetry, as in "I wonder by my troth, what thou, and I/Did, till we lov'd?"

Donne also radically adapted some of the standard materials of love lyrics. For example, even though he continued to use such Petrarchan conceits as "parting from one's beloved is death," a staple of Renaissance love poetry, he either turned the comparisons into comedy, as when the man in *The Apparition* envisions himself as a ghost haunting his unfaithful lady, or he subsumed them into the texture of his poem, as the title *A Valediction: Forbidding Mourning* exemplifies. Donne's love lyrics provide keen psychological insights about a broad range of lovers and a wide spectrum of amorous feelings. His speakers range from lustful men so sated by their numerous affairs that they denounce love as a fiction and women as objects—food, birds of prey, mummies—to platonic lovers who celebrate both the magnificence of their ladies and their own miraculous abstention from consummating their love. In the poems of mutual love, however, Donne's lovers rejoice in the compatibility of their sexual and spiritual love and seek immortality for an emotion that they elevate to an almost religious plane.

Donne's devotional lyrics, especially the "Holy Sonnets," *Good Friday 1613, Riding Westward,* and the hymns, passionately explore his love for God, sometimes through sexual metaphors, and depict his doubts, fears, and sense of spiritual unworthiness. None of them shows him spiritually at peace.

The most sustained of Donne's poems, the *Anniversaries*, were written to commemorate the death of Elizabeth Drury, the 14-year-old daughter of his patron, Sir Robert Drury. These poems subsume their ostensible subject into a philosophical meditation on the decay of the world. Elizabeth Drury becomes, as Donne noted, "the Idea of a woman," and a lost pattern of virtue. Through this idealized feminine figure, Donne in *The First Anniversarie: An Anatomie of the World* laments humanity's spiritual death, beginning with the loss of Eden and continuing in the decay of the contemporary world, in which men have lost the wisdom that connects them to God. In *The Second Anniversarie: Of the Progres of the Soule*, Donne, partly through a eulogy on Elizabeth Drury, ultimately regains the wisdom that directs him toward eternal life.

Prose

Donne's earliest prose works, *Paradoxes and Problems,* probably were begun during his days as a student at Lincoln's Inn. These witty and insouciant paradoxes defend such topics as women's inconstancy and pursue such questions as "Why do women delight much in feathers?" and "Why are Courtiers sooner Atheists than men of other conditions?" While living in despair at Mitcham in 1608, Donne wrote a casuistic defense of suicide entitled *Biathanatos*. His own contemplation of suicide, he states, prompted in him "a charitable interpretation of theyr Action, who dye so." Donne's *Pseudo-Martyr*, published in 1610, attacks the recusants' unwillingness to swear the oath of allegiance to the king, which Roman Catholics were required to do after the Gunpowder Plot (1605). (The Gunpowder Plot being a conspiracy of a group of Englishmen to blow up Parliament and King James I in retaliation for the increasing oppression of Roman Catholics in England.)

In 1611 Donne completed his *Essays in Divinity*, the first of his theological works. Upon recovering from a life-threatening illness, Donne in 1623 wrote *Devotions upon Emergent Occasions,* the most enduring of his prose works. Each of its 23 devotions consists of a meditation, an expostulation, and a prayer, all occasioned by some event in Donne's illness, such as the arrival of the king's personal physician or the application of pigeons to draw vapours from Donne's head. The *Devotions* correlate Donne's physical decline with spiritual sickness, until both reach a climax when Donne hears the tolling of a passing bell (16, 17, 18) and questions whether the bell is ringing for him. Like Donne's poetry, the *Devotions* are notable for their dramatic immediacy and their numerous Metaphysical conceits, such as the well-known "No man is an *Iland*," by which Donne illustrates the unity of all Christians in the mystical body of Christ.

It is Donne's sermons, however, that most powerfully illustrate his mastery of prose. One-hundred and fifty-six of them were published by his son in three great folio editions (1640, 1649, and 1661). Though composed during a time of religious controversy, Donne's sermons—intellectual, witty, and deeply moving—explore the basic tenets of Christianity rather than engage in theological disputes. Donne brilliantly analyzed Biblical texts and applied them to contemporary events, such as the outbreak of plague that devastated London in 1625. The power of his sermons derives from their dramatic intensity, candid personal revelations, poetic rhythms, and striking conceits.

BEN JONSON

(b. June 11?, 1572, London, England—d. August 6, 1637, London)

B enjamin Jonson was an English Stuart dramatist, lyric poet, and literary critic. He is generally regarded as the second most important English dramatist, after William Shakespeare, during the reign of James I.

Theatrical Career

Jonson was born two months after his father died. His stepfather was a bricklayer, but by good fortune the boy was able to attend Westminster School. His formal education, however, ended early, and he at first followed his stepfather's trade, then fought with some success with the English forces in the Netherlands. On returning to England, he became an actor and playwright, experiencing the life of a strolling player. By 1597 he was writing plays for Philip Henslowe, the leading impresario for the public theatre. With one exception (*The Case Is Altered*), these early plays are known, if at all, only by their titles. Jonson apparently wrote tragedies as well as comedies in these years, but his extant writings include only two tragedies, *Sejanus* (1603) and *Catiline* (1611).

The year 1598 marked an abrupt change in Jonson's status, when *Every Man in His Humour* was successfully presented by the Lord Chamberlain's theatrical company, and his reputation was established. In this play Jonson tried to bring the spirit and manner of Latin comedy to

Ben Jonson. Hulton Archive/Getty Images

the English popular stage by presenting the story of a young man with an eye for a girl, who has difficulty with a phlegmatic father, is dependent on a clever servant, and is ultimately successful. But at the same time Jonson sought to embody in four of the main characters the four "humours" of medieval and Renaissance medicine—choler, melancholy, phlegm, and blood--which were thought to determine human physical and mental makeup.

That same year Jonson killed a fellow actor in a duel, and, though he escaped capital punishment by pleading "benefit of clergy" (the ability to read from the Latin Bible), he could not escape branding. During his brief imprisonment over the affair he became a Roman Catholic.

Following the success of *Every Man in His Humour*, the same theatrical company acted Jonson's *Every Man Out of His Humour* (1599), which was even more ambitious. It was the longest play ever written for the Elizabethan public theatre, and it strove to provide an equivalent of the Greek comedy of Aristophanes; "induction," or "prelude," and regular between-act comment explicated the author's views on what the drama should be.

The play, however, proved a disaster, and Jonson had to look elsewhere for a theatre to present his work. The obvious place was the "private" theatres, in which only young boys acted. The high price of admission they charged meant a select audience, and they were willing to try strong satire and formal experiment; for them Jonson wrote *Cynthia's Revels* (c. 1600) and *Poetaster* (1601). Even in these, however, there is the paradox of contempt for human behaviour hand in hand with a longing for human order.

From 1605 to 1634 he regularly contributed masques for the courts of James I and Charles I, collaborating with the architect and designer Inigo Jones. This marked his favour with the court and led to his post as poet laureate.

Court Masques

It appears that Jonson won royal attention by his *Entertainment at Althorpe*, given before James I's queen as she journeyed down from Scotland in 1603, and in 1605 *The Masque of Blackness* was presented at court. The "masque" was a quasi-dramatic entertainment, primarily providing a pretense for a group of strangers to dance and sing before an audience of guests and attendants in a royal court or nobleman's house. This elementary pattern was much elaborated during the reign of James I, when Jones provided increasingly magnificent costumes and scenic effects for masques at court. The few spoken words that the masque had demanded in Elizabethan days expanded into a "text" of a few hundred lines and a number of set songs. Thus the author became important as well as the designer: he was to provide not only the necessary words but also a special "allegorical" meaning underlying the whole entertainment. It was Jonson, in collaboration with Jones, who gave the Jacobean masque its characteristic shape and style. He did this primarily by introducing the suggestion of a "dramatic" action. It was thus the poet who provided the informing idea and dictated the fashion of the whole night's assembly. Jonson's early masques were clearly successful, for during the following years he was repeatedly called upon to function as poet at court. Among his masques were *Hymenaei* (1606), *Hue and Cry After Cupid* (1608), *The Masque of Beauty* (1608), and *The Masque of Queens* (1609). In his masques Jonson was fertile in inventing new motives for the arrival of the strangers. But this was not enough: he also invented the "antimasque," which preceded the masque proper and which featured grotesques or comics who were primarily actors rather than dancers or musicians.

Jonson's Prime and Later Life

In 1606 Jonson and his wife (whom he had married in 1594) were brought before the consistory court in London to explain their lack of participation in the Anglican church. He denied that his wife was guilty but admitted that his own religious opinions held him aloof from attendance. The matter was patched up through his agreement to confer with learned men, who might persuade him if they could. Apparently it took six years for him to decide to conform. For some time before this he and his wife had lived apart, Jonson taking refuge in turn with his patrons Sir Robert Townshend and Esmé Stuart, Lord Aubigny.

During this period, nevertheless, he made a mark second only to Shakespeare's in the public theatre. His comedies *Volpone; or, the Foxe* (1606) and *The Alchemist* (1610) were among the most popular and esteemed plays of the time. Each exhibited man's folly in the pursuit of gold. Set respectively in Italy and London, they demonstrate Jonson's enthusiasm both for the typical Renaissance setting and for his own town on Europe's fringe. Both plays are eloquent and compact, sharp-tongued and controlled. The comedies *Epicoene* (1609) and *Bartholomew Fair* (1614) were also successful.

Jonson embarked on a walking tour in 1618–19, which took him to Scotland. On his return to England he received an honorary Master of Arts degree from Oxford University, a most signal honour in his time. Jonson's life was a life of talk as well as of writing. He engaged in "wit-combats" with Shakespeare and reigned supreme. It was a young man's ultimate honour to be regarded as a "son of Ben."

In 1628 he suffered what was apparently a stroke and, as a result, was confined to his room and chair, ultimately to his bed. That same year he was made city chronologer (thus theoretically responsible for the city's pageants), though in 1634 his salary for the post was made into a pension. Jonson died in 1637 and was buried in Westminster Abbey.

The first folio edition of his works had appeared in 1616; posthumously, in a second Jonson folio (1640), appeared *Timber: or, Discoveries*, a series of observations on life and letters. Here Jonson held forth on the nature of poetry and drama and paid his final tribute to Shakespeare: in spite of acknowledging a belief that his great contemporary was, on occasion, "full of wind"—*sufflaminandus erat*—he declared that "I loved the man, and do honour his memory, on this side idolatry, as much as any."

Plays and Achievement

Ben Jonson occupies by common consent the second place among English dramatists of the reigns of Elizabeth I and James I. He was a man of contraries. For "twelve years a papist," he was also—in fact though not in title—Protestant England's first poet laureate. His major comedies express a strong distaste for the world in which he lived and a delight in exposing its follies and vices. A gifted lyric poet, he wrote two of his most successful plays entirely in prose, an unusual mode of composition in his time. Though often an angry and stubborn man, no one had more disciples than he. He was easily the most learned dramatist of his time, and he was also a master of theatrical plot, language, and characterization. It is a measure of his reputation that his dramatic works were the first to be published in folio (the term, in effect, means the "collected works") and that his plays held their place on the stage until the period of the Restoration. Later they fell into neglect, though *The Alchemist* was revived during the 18th century, and in the mid-20th century several came back into favour: *Volpone, The Alchemist*, and *Bartholomew Fair* especially have been staged with striking success.

Jonson's chief plays are still very good theatre. His insistence on putting classical theory into practice in them has reinforced rather than weakened the effect of his gift of lively dialogue, robust characterization, and intricate, controlled plotting. In each of them he maneuvers a large cast of vital personages, all consistently differentiated from one another. Jonson's plots are skillfully put together; incident develops out of incident in a consistent chain of cause and effect, taking into account the respective natures of the personages involved and proceeding confidently through a twisting, turning action that is full of surprises without relying on coincidence or chance. Sometimes Jonson's comedy derives from the dialogue, especially when it is based on his observation of contemporary tricks of speech. But there are also superbly ludicrous situations, often hardly removed from practical joke.

Jonson is renowned for his method of concentrating on a selected side, or on selected sides, of a character, showing how they dominate the personality. This is to some extent a natural outcome of his classical conception of art, but it also stems from his clear, shrewd observation of people. In Jonson's plays both eccentricity and normal behaviour are derived from a dominating characteristic, so that the result is a live, truthfully conceived personage in whom the ruling passion traces itself plainly. The later plays, for example, have characters whose behaviour is dominated by one psychological idiosyncrasy. But Jonson did not deal exclusively in "humours." In some of his plays (notably *Every Man in His Humour*), the stock types of Latin comedy contributed as much as the humours theory did. What the theory provided for him and for his contemporaries was a convenient mode of distinguishing among human beings. The distinctions so made could be based on the "humours," on Latin comic types, or, as in *Volpone*, in the assimilation of humans to different members of the animal kingdom. The characters Volpone, Mosca, Sir Epicure Mammon, Face, Subtle, Dol Common, Overdo, and Ursula are not simply "humours"; they are glorious type figures, so vitally rendered as to take on a being that transcends the type. This method was one of simplification, of typification, and yet also of vitalization.

The Restoration dramatists' use of type names for their characters (Cockwood, Witwoud, Petulant, Pinchwife, and so on) was a harking back to Jonson. He thus exerted a great influence on the playwrights who immediately followed him. In the late Jacobean and Caroline years, it was he, Shakespeare, and Francis Beaumont and John Fletcher who provided all the models. But it was he, and he alone, who gave the essential impulse to dramatic characterization in comedy of the Restoration and also in the 18th and 19th centuries.

Nef'i

(b. *c.* 1572, Hasankale, Ottoman Empire [now Pasinier, Turkey]—d. 1635, Constantinople [now Istanbul])

Nef'i (a pseudonym of Ömer) was one of the greatest classical Ottoman poets and one of the most famous satirists and panegyrists in Ottoman Turkish literature.

Little is known of Nef'i's early life; he served as a minor government official in the reign of the sultan Ahmed I (1603–17). Not until the time of Sultan Murad IV (1623–40), himself a poet, did Nef'i gain court favour. He became famous as a court panegyrist and as a powerful satirist. Except for his patron, the sultan, Nef'i attacked the highest public figures with his vituperative pen. These sketches, often obscene and vulgar, reveal his most candid opinions of those in power. He often satirized a figure he had eulogized earlier in his career. Nef'i's biting invective earned him many enemies at the court; Bayram Pasa, deputy prime minister and brother-in-law of the sultan, finally secured his execution in 1635.

Nef'i is considered one of the finest *qaṣīdah* ("ode") writers of Ottoman literature. His famous divan, or collection of poems, contains many examples of his eloquent poetic style. Though his *qaṣīdahs*, mainly eulogies, are considered to be extremely tasteful and proper, his satiric works are held to be calumnious and abusive. Nef'i also left a Persian divan praised by his patron, Murad IV, who was a great admirer of Persian letters. Some examples of his work have been published in the anthology *Ottoman Lyric Poetry* (1997), edited and translated by Walter G. Andrews, Najaat Black, and Mehmet Kalpakli.

GIAMBATTISTA BASILE

(b. *c.* 1575, Naples—d. February 23, 1632, Giugliano, Campania)

The Neapolitan soldier, public official, poet, and short-story writer Giambattista Basile is the author of *Lo cunto de li cunti*, 50 zestful tales written in Neapolitan, which was one of the earliest such collections based on folktales and served as an important source both for the later fairy-tale writers Charles Perrault in France in the 17th century and the brothers Grimm in Germany in the 19th century, and for the Italian commedia dell'arte dramatist Carlo Gozzi in the 18th century.

Basile was a soldier as a young man and began a career in government after moving to Naples in 1608. He later was part of the Mantuan court of Ferdinando Gonzaga, and then moved on to become governor, successively, of several small Italian states.

Basile was most at home in Naples, and during his career he became fascinated with the folklore, customs, literature, music, and dialect of the Neapolitan people. He began serious study of things Neapolitan and began to collect fairy tales and folktales, setting them down in a lively Neapolitan style with much local flavour and all the ornament and flamboyance of his influential contemporary Giambattista Marino.

Basile's collection, *Lo cunto de li cunti* (1634; "The Story of Stories"; best Italian translation B. Croce, 1925; best English translation N.B. Penzer, *The Pentamerone*, 2 vol., 1932), was published posthumously under the anagrammatic pseudonym Gian Alesio Abbattutis and referred to by its first editor as *Il pentamerone* because of the similarity of its framework to that of Boccaccio's *Decameron*.

In *Lo cunto de li cunti*, a prince and his wife, a slave who has been posing as a princess, are entertained for 5 days by 10 women, who tell them 50 stories, among which are the familiar tales of Puss in Boots, Rapunzel, Cinderella, Snow White and Rose Red, the Three Oranges, and Beauty and the Beast. On the last day of storytelling, the real princess appears, tells her story, and ousts the deceptive slave.

Basile also wrote Italian and Spanish verse. *Le muse napolitane* (1635) was a series of satirical verse dialogues on Neapolitan mores.

ROBERT BURTON

(b. February 8, 1577, Lindley, Leicestershire, England—d. January 25, 1640, Oxford)

Robert Burton was an English scholar, writer, and Anglican clergyman whose *Anatomy of Melancholy* is a masterpiece of style and a valuable index to the philosophical and psychological ideas of the time.

Burton was educated at Oxford, elected a student (life fellow) of Christ Church (one of the colleges of the university) in 1599, and lived there the rest of his life, becoming a bachelor of divinity in 1614 and vicar of St. Thomas's Church, Oxford, in 1616. He also held livings in Lincolnshire (1624–31) and Leicestershire, the latter bestowed by his patron, Lord Berkeley. His "silent, sedentary, solitary" life, as he himself described it, lent his view of mankind an ironic detachment, but it certainly did not make it that of a scholar remote from reality: he is as informative on the pastimes of his day as on the ideas of the ancients, and as keen to recommend a rational diet as to relate human disorders to his own essentially Christian view of the universe.

Burton's first work was the Latin comedy *Philosophaster* (1606; edited with an English translation by P. Jordan-Smith, 1931), a vivacious exposure of charlatanism that has affinities with Ben Jonson's *The Alchemist*. It was acted at Christ Church in 1618.

The *Anatomy of Melancholy, What it is; with all the Kindes, Causes, Symptomes, Prognostickes and Several Cures of it: In Three Maine Partitions With Their Several Sections, Members, and Subsections, Philosophically, Medicinally, Historically Opened and Cut up, by Democritus Junior* appeared in 1621, and five subsequent editions (1624, 1628, 1632, 1638, and 1651) incorporated Burton's revisions and alterations. In the treatise, Burton sets himself in the first part to define melancholy, discuss its causes, and set down the symptoms. The second part is devoted to its cure. Love melancholy is the subject of the lively first three sections of the third part. A master of narrative, Burton includes as examples most of the world's great love stories, again showing a modern approach to psychological problems. The fourth section deals with religious melancholy, and on the cure of despair he rises to heights of wisdom and of meditation.

Burton's colloquial style is as individual as his matter. It is imaginative and eloquent, full of classical allusions and Latin tags that testify to his love of curious and out-of-the-way information as well as to his erudition. He is a master of lists and catalogs, but their sonorous roll is often broken by his humorous asides.

The *Anatomy*, widely read in the 17th century, lapsed for a time into obscurity, but in the 18th it was admired by Samuel Johnson, and Laurence Sterne's borrowings from it are notorious. In the 19th century the devotion of Charles Lamb helped to bring the *Anatomy* into favour with the Romantics. The standard modern edition is *The Anatomy of Melancholy*, 6 vol., edited by Thomas C. Faulkner, Nicolas K. Kiessling, and Rhonda L. Blair (1989–2000).

JOHN FLETCHER

(baptized December 20, 1579, Rye, Sussex, England—d. August 29, 1625, London)

The English Jacobean dramatist John Fletcher collaborated with Francis Beaumont and other dramatists on comedies and tragedies between about 1606 and 1625.

His father, Richard Fletcher, was minister of the parish in which John was born and became afterward queen's chaplain, dean of Peterborough, and bishop successively of Bristol, Worcester, and London, gaining a measure of fame as an accuser in the trial of Mary, Queen of Scots, and as the chaplain sternly officiating at her execution. When not quite 12, John was apparently admitted pensioner of Corpus Christi College, Cambridge, and two years later became a Bible clerk. From the time of his father's death (1596) until 1607 nothing is known of him. His name is first linked with Beaumont's in Ben Jonson's *Volpone* (1607), to which both men contributed encomiums.

Fletcher began to work with Beaumont probably about 1607, at first for the Children of the Queen's Revels and its successor and then (from *c.* 1609 until Beaumont's retirement in 1613) mainly for the King's Men at the Globe and Blackfriars theatres. After 1613 he often collaborated with or had his plays revised by Philip Massinger, who actually succeeded him in 1625 as chief playwright of the King's Men; other collaborators included Nathan Field and William Rowley. Throughout his career he also wrote plays unaided. He died in the London plague of 1625 that killed some 40,000 others; the antiquarian John Aubrey claimed that he had lingered in the city to be measured for a suit of clothes instead of making his escape to the country.

The canon of the Beaumont and Fletcher plays is approximately represented by the 52 plays in the folio *Fifty Comedies and Tragedies...* (1679); but any consideration of the canon must omit one play from the 1679 folio (James Shirley's *Coronation*) and add three not to be found in it (*Henry VIII, Sir John van Olden Barnavelt, A Very Woman*). Of these 54 plays not more than 12 are by Beaumont or by Beaumont and Fletcher in collaboration. Another 3 were probably collaborations with Beaumont and Massinger. The others represent Fletcher either unaided or in collaboration with dramatists other than Beaumont, principally Massinger.

The masterpieces of the Beaumont and Fletcher collaboration—*Philaster*, *The Maides Tragedy*, and *A King and No King*—show, most clearly in the last, the emergence of most of the features that distinguish the Fletcherian mode from that of Shakespeare, George Chapman, or John Webster: the remote, often pseudohistorical, fairy-tale setting; the clear, smooth speech rising to great emotional arias of declamatory rhetoric; the basically sensational or bizarre plot that faces the characters with wild "either–or" choices between extremes and that can be manipulated toward a sad or a happy ending as the playwrights choose; the sacrifice of consistency and plausibility in character-ization so that patterns can be made out of constantly shifting emotional states and piquant situations can be prolonged.

Of Fletcher's unaided plays, *The Faithfull Shepheardesse*, *The Mad Lover*, *The Loyall Subject*, *The Humorous Lieutenant*, *Women Pleas'd*, *The Island Princesse*, and *A Wife for a Moneth* (all between *c.* 1608 and *c.* 1624) are perhaps the best. Each of these is a series of extraordinary situations and extreme attitudes, displayed through intense declamations. The best of these are perhaps *The Loyall Subject* and *A Wife for a Moneth*, the latter a florid and loquacious play, in which a bizarre sexual situation is handled with cunning piquancy, and the personages illustrate clearly Fletcher's tendency to make his men and women personifications of vices and virtues rather than individuals. The best of Fletcher's comedies, for urbanity and consistency of tone, is prob-ably *The Wild-Goose Chase*, a play of episodes rather than of intricate intrigue, but alive with irony and easy wit.

Lastly, there are the Fletcherian plays in which others besides Beaumont had a hand. *Wit at Several Weapons* is a comedy that might have been written wholly by Thomas Middleton; and *The Captaine* (to which Beaumont may, however, have contributed) is a lively, complex play of sexual intrigue, with tragic dilemmas too. Notable among the numerous plays in this group are *The False One* and *The Beggars Bush*. The former is an original, incisive, and moderately subtle treatment of the story of Caesar and Cleopatra, which may well have aided John Dryden to compose *All for Love* and for which the greater credit goes to Massinger. The latter is worth reading for its "version of pastoral," which genially persuades the audience that it is better to be a country beggar than a tyrannical king.

PIETER CORNELISZOON HOOFT

(b. March 16, 1581, Amsterdam, Netherlands —
d. May 21, 1647, The Hague)

The Dutch dramatist and poet Pieter Corneliszoon Hooft is regarded by many as the most brilliant representative of Dutch Renaissance literature. Hooft's prose style continued to provide a model into the 19th century.

During three years spent in France and Italy, Hooft came completely under the spell of the new learning and art; the impact of that experience is shown by the contrast between his letter in pre-Renaissance verse sent from Florence to his friends in Amsterdam and the first poetry he wrote after his return: love lyrics and the pastoral play *Grandida* (1605). That play is noted for the delicacy of its poetry and the simplicity of its moral—that individuals and nations can be at peace only when rulers and subjects alike shun ambition and seek only to serve.

Hooft's personal and pragmatic ethic is more explicit in the *Sticht-rijmen* (1618 or 1619; "Edifying Verses") and two Senecan tragedies. *Geeraert van Velsen* (1613) is a quasi-historical dramatization of the murder of Count Floris V, and *Baeto* (1617) portrays an Aeneas-type hero who goes into exile rather than cause civil war. Both plays reveal Hooft's pacifist hatred of tyranny.

In *Nederlandse historiën* (20 vol., published 1642, a continuation in 1654), the glory of the epic hero, the prince of Orange, is reflected in Hooft's affection for the commoners who fought for the new democracy in Holland (now part of the Netherlands). Tacitus was his model for this monumental work, on which he spent 19 years chronicling only the period from 1555 to 1585.

The Muiderslot (the castle that he restored) became, after his second marriage in 1627, the centre of the Muiderkring, a circle of accomplished and cultured friends including Constantijn Huygens and Joost van den Vondel.

PHILIP MASSINGER

(b. 1583, near Salisbury, Wiltshire, England—
d. March 1639/40, London)

Philip Massinger was an English Jacobean and Caroline playwright noted for his gifts of comedy, plot construction, social realism, and satirical power.

Besides the documentation of his baptism at St. Thomas's Church, Salisbury, it is known that Massinger attended St. Alban Hall, Oxford, in 1602, but nothing certain is known about his life from then until 1613, when he was in prison for debt. Bailed out by the theatrical impresario Philip Henslowe, he spent a period working as the junior partner in coauthored plays, collaborating with established dramatists such as Thomas Dekker and John Fletcher, and eventually graduated to his own independent productions. In 1625 he succeeded Fletcher, some of whose plays he revised, as the chief playwright of the King's Men (formerly Lord Chamberlain's Men). Though apparently not as successful as Fletcher, he remained with the King's Men until his death, producing plays marked by a high moral tone and elevated philosophic character.

Among the plays Massinger collaborated on with Fletcher is *The False One* (*c.* 1620), a treatment of the story of Caesar and Cleopatra. Two other important plays written in collaboration are *The Fatal Dowry* (1616–19, with Nathan Field), a domestic tragedy in a French setting, and *The Virgin Martyr* (1620?, with Thomas Dekker), a historical play about the persecution of Christians under the Roman emperor Diocletian. Fifteen plays written solely by Massinger have survived, but many of their dates can only be conjectured. The four tragedies are *The Duke of Milan* (1621–22) and *The Unnatural Combat* (1624?)—both skillfully told mystery stories of a melodramatic type—and *The Roman Actor* (1626) and *Believe As You List* (1631)—each a historical tragedy in a classical setting. *The Roman Actor* is considered his best serious play.

The Bondman (1623), about a slave revolt in the Greek city of Syracuse, is one of Massinger's seven tragicomedies and shows his concern for state affairs. *The Renegado* (1624), a tragicomedy with a heroic Jesuit character, gave rise to the still-disputed theory that he became a Roman Catholic. Another tragicomedy, *The Maid of Honour* (1621?), combines political realism with the courtly refinement of later Caroline drama. The tendency of his serious plays to conform to Caroline fashion, however, is contradicted by the mordant realism and satirical force of his two great comedies—*A New Way to Pay Old Debts*, his most popular and influential play, in which he expresses genuine indignation at economic oppression and social disorder, and *The City Madam* (1632?), dealing with similar evils but within a more starkly contrived plot that curiously combines naturalistic and symbolic modes. One of his last plays, *The King and the Subject*

(1638), had politically objectionable lines cut from it by King Charles himself.

TIRSO DE MOLINA

(b. March 9?, 1584, Madrid, Spain—d. March 12, 1648, Soria)

Tirso de Molina (a pseudonym of Gabriel Téllez) was one of the outstanding dramatists of the Golden Age of Spanish literature.

Tirso studied at the University of Alcalá and in 1601 was professed in the Mercedarian Order. As the order's official historian he wrote *Historia general de la orden de la Merced* in 1637. He was also a theologian of repute. Guided to drama by an inborn sense of the theatrical and inspired by the achievements of Lope de Vega, creator of the Spanish *comedia*, Tirso built on the "free-and-easy" prescriptions that Lope had propounded for dramatic construction. In his plays he sometimes accentuated the religious and philosophical aspects that attracted his theological interest; at other times he drew on his own topographical and historical knowledge, gained while traveling for his order through Spain, Portugal, and the West Indies. Sometimes he borrowed from the vast common stock of Spanish stage material, and at other times he relied on his own powerful imagination.

Three of his dramas appeared in his *Cigarrales de Toledo* (1621; "Weekend Retreats of Toledo"), a set of verses, tales, plays, and critical observations that, arranged after the Italian fashion in a picturesque framework, affect to provide a series of summer recreations for a group of friends. Otherwise his extant output of about 80 dramas—a fragment of the whole—was published chiefly in five *Partes* between 1627 and 1636. The second part presents apparently insoluble problems of authenticity, and the authorship of certain other of his plays outside this part has also been disputed.

The most powerful dramas associated with his name are two tragedies, *El burlador de Sevilla* ("The Seducer of Seville") and *El condenado por desconfiado* (1635; *The Doubted Damned*). The first introduced into literature the hero-villain Don Juan, a libertine whom Tirso derived from popular legends but recreated with originality. The figure of Don Juan subsequently became one of the most famous in all literature through Wolfgang Amadeus Mozart's opera *Don Giovanni* (1787). *El burlador* rises to a majestic climax of nervous tension when Don Juan is confronted with the statue-ghost of the man he has killed, and deliberately chooses to defy this emanation of his diseased conscience. *El condenado por desconfiado* dramatizes a theological paradox: the case of a notorious evildoer who has kept and developed the little faith he had, and who is granted salvation by an act of divine grace, contrasted with the example of a hitherto good-living hermit, eternally damned for allowing his one-time faith to shrivel. Tirso was at his best when portraying the psychological conflicts and contradictions involved in these master characters. At times he reaches Shakespearean standards of insight, tragic sublimity, and irony. The same qualities are found in isolated scenes of his historical dramas, for example in *Antona García* (1635), which is notable for its objective analysis of mob emotion; in *La prudencia en la mujer* (1634; "Prudence in Woman"), with its modern interpretation of ancient regional strife; and in the biblical *La venganza de Tamar* (1634), with its violently realistic scenes.

When inspired, Tirso could dramatize personality and make his best characters memorable as individuals. He is more stark and daring than Lope but less ingenious, more spiritually independent than Pedro Calderón de la Barca but less poetic. His plays of social types and manners, such as *El vergonzoso en palacio* (written 1611, published 1621; "The Bashful Man in the Palace"), are animated, varied in mood, and usually lyrical. At the same time, however, Tirso's style is erratic and sometimes trite. In pure comedy he excels in cloak-and-sword situations; and in, for example, *Don Gil de las calzas verdes* (1635; "Don Gil of the Green Stockings"), he manipulates a complex, rapidly moving plot with exhilarating vitality. His tragedies and comedies are both famous for their clowns, whose wit has a tonic air of spontaneity. Naturalness in diction suited his dramatic purpose better than the ornamental rhetoric then coming into vogue, and generally he avoided affectations, remaining in this respect nearer to Lope than to Calderón. Tirso was not as consistently brilliant as these great contemporaries, but his finest comedies rival theirs, and his best tragedies surpass them.

FRANCIS BEAUMONT

(b. *c.* 1585, Grace-Dieu, Leicestershire, England —
d. March 6, 1616, London)

The English Jacobean poet and playwright Francis Beaumont collaborated with John Fletcher on comedies and tragedies between about 1606 and 1613.

The son of Francis Beaumont, justice of common pleas of Grace-Dieu priory, Charnwood Forest, Leicestershire, Beaumont entered Broadgates Hall (later Pembroke College), Oxford, in 1597. His father dying the following year, he abruptly left the university without a degree and later (November 1600) entered London's Inner Temple, where he evidently became more involved in London's lively literary culture than in legal studies.

In 1602 there appeared the poem *Salmacis and Hermaphroditus*, generally attributed to Beaumont, a voluptuous and voluminous expansion of the Ovidian legend that expanded the story humour and added a fantastic array of episodes and conceits. At age 23 he prefixed to Ben Jonson's *Volpone* (1607) some verses in honour of his "dear friend" the author. John Fletcher contributed verses to the same volume, and, by about this time, the

Francis Beaumont, engraving. © Photos.com/Thinkstock

two were collaborating on plays for the Children of the Queen's Revels. According to John Aubrey, a 17th-century memorialist, in *Brief Lives*,

> *They lived together on the Banke side, not far from the Play-house, both batchelors; lay together...; had one wench in the house between them...; the same cloathes and cloake, &c., betweene them.*

Their collaboration as playwrights was to last for some seven years. In 1613 Beaumont married an heiress, Ursula Isley of Sundridge in Kent, and retired from the theatre. He died in London in 1616 and was buried in Westminster Abbey.

It is difficult to disentangle Beaumont's share in the 35 plays published in 1647 as by "Beaumont and Fletcher" (to which another 18 were added in the 1679 collection). Scholars now believe that only 10 of these were by the two friends, while Beaumont's hand also appears in 3 plays substantially written by Fletcher and Philip Massinger. The rest are plays written by Fletcher alone or in collaboration with other dramatists, except for *The Knight of the Burning Pestle*, which is Beaumont's unaided work. Attempts to separate the shares of Beaumont and Fletcher in any given work are complicated by the fact that Beaumont sometimes revised scenes by Fletcher and Fletcher edited some of Beaumont's work. *The Knight of the Burning Pestle* parodies a then popular kind of play—sprawling, episodic, with sentimental lovers and chivalric adventures. It opens with The Citizen and his Wife taking their places on the stage to watch "The London Merchant"—itself a satire on the work of a contemporary playwright, Thomas Dekker. Citizen and Wife interrupt, advise, and insist that the play should be more romantic and their apprentice should take a leading part. Thereafter these two contradictory plots go forward side by side, allowing Beaumont to have fun with bourgeois naïveté about art.

JOOST VAN DEN VONDEL

(b. November 17, 1587, Cologne—d. February 5, 1679, Amsterdam)

T he Dutch poet and dramatist Joost van den Vondel produced some of the greatest works of Dutch literature.

Van den Vondel's Mennonite parents had fled from Antwerp to Cologne and ended up in Amsterdam. The young van den Vondel was largely self-educated. He taught himself French, and he also studied Latin and eventually translated works by Virgil and Seneca. He early showed a preference for using Christian mythology as a subject matter for the plays he wrote. By treating classical themes as representations of Christian truths, he was able to reconcile Renaissance learning with his own personal religious faith. *Het Pascha* (1612; "The Passover"), a dramatization of the Exodus of the Jews from Egypt, was his most important early work, in which the power and splendour of his verse is already apparent. This play was an allegory for the Calvinists who had fled from Spanish tyranny in the southern Netherlands.

The execution of Holland's lord advocate, Johan van Oldenbarnevelt, in 1619, provoked Vondel to write a flood of spirited lampoons and satirical poems against the Dutch church and government. His play *Palamedes* (1625), which dramatized the political trial in a classical setting, incurred his prosecution by the government. Around this time he also translated the great jurist Hugo Grotius' drama *Sophompaneas* into Dutch. Grotius influenced van den Vondel to turn from the emulation of ancient Latin to that of ancient Greek drama. Van den Vondel's *Gijsbrecht van Aemstel* (1637), written during this transitional period, provides a hero for the capital of the new Dutch Republic who was modeled on Virgil's Aeneas. In 1639 van den Vondel completed his first translation of a Greek tragedy, Sophocles' *Electra*. His original play *Gebroeders*, a Hebrew Bible tragedy of the same year, is the first of his plays on the Greek model; they include *Jeptha* (1659) and his greatest achievements, the trilogy comprising *Lucifer* (1654), *Adam in ballingschap* (1664; *Adam in Exile*, 1952), and *Noah* (1667). *Lucifer*, which is generally regarded as van den Vondel's masterpiece, treats the same theme as had John Milton: the inexplicable revolt of the angels against God. Meanwhile, van den Vondel's religious liberalism had gradually led him from Calvinism to Remonstrant views and eventually, at the age of 54, to the Roman Catholic Church, in which he found the peace of mind he sought in a universal faith.

Van den Vondel was more than 60 years old before he reached his literary maturity. He had shown himself to be a master of the lyric, the ode and sonnet, the epic, the long religious poem, and the essay, but his dramatic tragedies, with their powerful and lyrical language and the grandeur of their conception, remain his most important literary achievement.

IVAN GUNDULIĆ

(b. January 8, 1589, Dubrovnik, republic of Venice [now in Croatia]—d. December 8, 1638, Dubrovnik)

Ivan Franov Gundulić was a Croatian poet and dramatist whose epic poem *Osman* (the oldest existing copy is dated approximately 1651; it was first published in 1826;

Eng. trans. *Osman*) was the outstanding achievement of the Renaissance and Baroque flowering of art and literature that gave Dubrovnik the name of the "South Slav Athens."

Son of a five-time *knez* (the highest government post, held for only one month) of the Dubrovnik city-republic, Gundulić himself occupied various public positions, serving as a captain of the night, supervisor of the armament magazine, member of the Senate, and judge. He was a pupil of the Croatian priest Petar Palikuća, who did translations from the Italian, and of Siena's Camilo Camilli (a great connoisseur of Torquato Tasso's *Gerusalemme liberata*), and in his youth Gundulić wrote 10 plays, which were performed with musical accompaniment. Some parts of them may have been sung. These plays were based on motifs from either classical mythology or Tasso's epic; they had fantastic elements and happy endings, and they were popular with Dubrovnik's audiences. The four plays that have survived are mostly variations on or translations of Italian works.

Gundulić later changed the tenor of his work toward a more solemn Baroque Catholic religiosity, and he wrote spiritual poetry. His poem *Suze sina razmetnoga* (1622; "The Tears of the Prodigal Son") is the monologue of a repentant man who reflects on his sin and the futility of human existence and then turns to God. Divided into three laments ("sin," "comprehension," and "humility"), the poem is marked by genuine religious feeling. Although its plot involves obstacles in the way of true love between young shepherds Dubravka (whose name is also that of a nymph symbolizing freedom) and Miljenko, Gundulić's original pastoral play *Dubravka* (1628) is primarily concerned with patriotic and ethical issues and with celebrating the long-standing autonomy of Dubrovnik.

Gundulić's most ambitious work is the epic *Osman*, whose creation was prompted by the Ottoman sultan

Osman II's defeat by the Poles at Chocim (Khotin, now in Ukraine) in Bessarabia in 1621, subsequent attempts by the young sultan to restructure his army, and the resulting rebellion against him, which led to his violent death in 1622. Though basing his plot on contemporary events of great political importance and giving realistic descriptions of Turkish and Polish settings, Gundulić nevertheless follows the conventions of the chivalrous epic by incorporating supernatural forces, love interests related to women warriors, and pastoral episodes. He uses the unfortunate fate of the young sultan as a springboard for more general reflections on the transience of human glory. The work comprises 20 cantos, but Gundulić died before finishing cantos 14 and 15; the poet Ivan Mažuranić (a member of the so-called Illyrian movement that sought to unite South Slavs) successfully wrote two substitute cantos, and *Osman* thus completed was published in Zagreb in 1844.

ROBERT HERRICK

(baptized August 24, 1591, London, England—d. October 1674, Dean Prior, Devonshire)

An English cleric and poet, Robert Herrick revived the spirit of the ancient classic lyric. The most original of the "sons of Ben [Jonson]," he is best remembered for the line "Gather ye rosebuds while ye may."

As a boy, Herrick was apprenticed to his uncle, Sir William Herrick, a prosperous and influential goldsmith. In 1613 he went to the University of Cambridge, graduating in 1617. He took his M.A. in 1620 and was ordained in 1623. He then lived for a time in London, cultivating the society of the city's wits, enlarging his acquaintance with writers (Ben Jonson being the most prominent) and musicians, and enjoying the round of court society. In 1627 he went as a chaplain to the Duke of Buckingham on the military expedition to the Île de Ré to relieve La Rochelle from the French Protestants. He was presented with the living of Dean Prior (1629), where he remained for the rest of his life, except when, because of his Royalist sympathies, he was deprived of his post from 1646 until after the Restoration (1660).

Herrick became well known as a poet about 1620–30; many manuscript commonplace books from that time contain his poems. The only book that Herrick published was *Hesperides* (1648), which included *His Noble Numbers*, a collection of poems on religious subjects with its own title page dated 1647 but not previously printed. *Hesperides* contained about 1,400 poems, mostly very short, many of them being brief epigrams. His work appeared after that in miscellanies and songbooks; the 17th-century English composer Henry Lawes and others set some of his songs.

Herrick wrote elegies, satires, epigrams, love songs to imaginary mistresses, marriage songs, complimentary verse to friends and patrons, and celebrations of rustic and ecclesiastical festivals. The appeal of his poetry lies in its truth to human sentiments and its perfection of form and style. Frequently light, worldly, and hedonistic, and making few pretensions to intellectual profundity, it yet covers a wide range of subjects and emotions, ranging from lyrics inspired by rural life to wistful evocations of life and love's evanescence and fleeting beauty. Herrick's lyrics are notable for their technical mastery and the interplay of thought, rhythm, and imagery that they display. As a poet Herrick was steeped in the classical tradition; he was also influenced by English folklore and lyrics, by Italian madrigals, by the Bible and patristic literature, and by contemporary English writers, notably Jonson and Robert Burton.

GEORGE HERBERT

(b. April 3, 1593, Montgomery Castle, Wales—d. March 1, 1633,
Bemerton, Wiltshire, England)

George Herbert was an English religious poet, a major metaphysical poet, notable for the purity and effectiveness of his choice of words.

A younger brother of Edward Herbert, 1st Baron Herbert of Cherbury, a notable secular metaphysical poet, in honor of the New Year in 1610 George sent his mother two sonnets on the theme that the love of God is a fitter subject for verse than the love of woman, a foreshadowing of his poetic and vocational bent.

Educated at home, at Westminster School, and at Trinity College, Cambridge, he was in 1620 elected orator of the university, a position that he described as "the finest place in the university." His two immediate predecessors in the office had risen to high positions in the state, and Herbert was much involved with the court. During Herbert's academic career, his only published verse was that written for special occasions in Greek and Latin. By 1625 Herbert's sponsors at court were dead or out of favour, and he turned to the church, being ordained deacon. He resigned as orator in 1627 and in 1630 was ordained priest and became rector at Bemerton. He became friends with Nicholas Ferrar, who had founded a religious community at nearby Little Gidding, and devoted himself to his rural parish and the reconstruction of his church. Throughout his life he wrote poems, and from his deathbed he sent a manuscript volume to Ferrar, asking him to decide whether to publish or destroy them. Ferrar published them with the title *The Temple: Sacred Poems and Private Ejaculations* in 1633.

George Herbert. Hulton Archive/Getty Images

Herbert described his poems as "a picture of the many spiritual conflicts that have passed between God and my soul, before I could subject mine to the will of Jesus, my Master, in whose service I have now found perfect freedom." Herbert shares his conflicts with John Donne, the archetypal metaphysical poet and a family friend. As well as personal poems, *The Temple* includes doctrinal poems, notably "The Church Porch," the first in the volume, and the last, "The Church Militant." Other poems are concerned with church ritual.

The main resemblance of Herbert's poems to Donne's is in the use of common language in the rhythms of speech. Some of his poems, such as "The Altar" and "Easter Wings," are "pattern" poems, the lines forming the shape of the subject, a practice Joseph Addison in the 18th century called "false wit." Samuel Taylor Coleridge in the 19th century wrote of Herbert's diction, "Nothing can be more pure, manly, and unaffected." Herbert was a versatile master of metrical form and all aspects of the craft of verse. Though he shared the critical disapproval given the metaphysical poets until the 20th century, he was still popular with readers. Herbert also wrote at Bemerton *A Priest to the Temple: Or The Country Parson, his Character and Rule of Life* (1652). Herbert's *Works* (1941; corrected, 1945), edited by F. Hutchinson, is the standard text.

IZAAK WALTON

(b. August 9, 1593, Stafford, Staffordshire, England—d. December 15, 1683, Winchester, Hampshire)

The English biographer Izaak Walton is the author of *The Compleat Angler* (1653), a pastoral discourse on the joys and stratagems of fishing that has been one of the most frequently reprinted books in English literature.

After a few years of schooling, Walton was apprenticed to a kinsman in the linendrapers' trade in London, where he acquired a small shop of his own and began to prosper. Despite his modest education he read widely, developed scholarly tastes, and associated with men of learning. Walton lived and worked close to St. Dunstan's Church, and he became active in parish affairs and a friend and fishing companion of the vicar, John Donne. Donne died in 1631, and, when his poems were published two years later, Walton composed "An Elegie" for the volume. In 1640 he wrote *The Life and Death of Dr. Donne* to accompany a collection of Donne's sermons. The *Life* was revised and enlarged in 1658.

During the Civil Wars, Walton, a staunch Royalist, quit London for the relative security of his native Staffordshire. After the Royalist defeat at Worcester in 1651, he took part in a successful adventure to preserve a jewel belonging to Charles II. He spent the remainder of his life reading, writing and editing, fishing, and visiting among the eminent clergymen who were his friends.

The second of Walton's biographies, *The Life of Sir Henry Wotton* (provost of Eton), appeared in 1651. Two years later the work that made Walton immortal, *The Compleat Angler, or, the Contemplative Man's Recreation*, was published. Walton enlarged and improved the work through four subsequent editions, a quest for perfection also evident in repeated revisions of the biographies. He wrote *The Life of Mr. Richard Hooker*, the Elizabethan bishop, in 1665 and revised it the next year. In 1670 he issued *The Life of Mr. George Herbert*, the poet, and in the same year he brought out an edition containing all four lives.

Upon the Restoration, one of Walton's Royalist friends, George Morley, was made bishop of Winchester and offered Walton residence in the bishop's palace, where he stayed for the rest of his life. His final personal revision (the fifth edition) of *The Compleat Angler* appeared in 1676 and included additional material written by his friend Charles Cotton. Walton published a biography of Bishop Sanderson in 1678.

Since the late 18th century, more than 300 editions of *The Compleat Angler* have appeared, and the unpretentious treatise, of which Walton did not even claim authorship on its first appearance, became a household word. Many of its devotees have been fishermen, but Walton's attractive style in dialogue and description, his enthusiasm for innocent outdoor recreation, and his genial partiality for the past have lifted *The Compleat Angler* out of the category of handbooks into that of the pastoral. The book opens on the first day of May, as three sportsmen—Auceps the fowler, Venator the hunter, and Piscator the fisherman—compare their favoured pastimes while traveling through the English countryside along the River Lea. The discourse is enlivened by songs and poems, country folklore, recipes, anecdotes, moral meditations, quotes from the Bible and from classic literature, and lore about fishing and waterways. The central character, Piscator, is not simply a champion and expositor of the art of angling but a man of tranquil, contented temper, pious and sententious, with a relish for the pleasures of friendship, verse and song, good food, and drink.

MARTIN OPITZ

(b. December 23, 1597, Bunzlau, Silesia [now Bolesławiec, Poland]—d. August 20, 1639, Danzig [now Gdansk, Poland])

The German poet and literary theorist Martin Opitz von Boberfeld introduced foreign literary models into German poetry and was a pioneer in establishing a national German literature.

Opitz studied at universities in Frankfurt an der Oder, Heidelberg, and Leiden, where he met the Dutch poet Daniël Heinsius. He led a wandering life in the service of various territorial nobles. In 1625, as a reward for a requiem poem on the death of Charles Joséph of Austria, he was crowned laureate by the Holy Roman emperor Ferdinand II, who later ennobled him. In 1629 he was elected to the Fruchtbringende Gesellschaft, the most important of the literary societies that aimed to reform the German language. He went to Paris in 1630, where he made the acquaintance of the Dutch jurist Hugo Grotius. He lived from 1635 until his death at Danzig (Gdansk), where Władysław IV of Poland made him his historian and secretary.

Opitz was the head of the so-called First Silesian school of poets and during his life was regarded as the greatest German poet. He was the "father of German poetry," at least in respect to its form. His *Aristarchus sive de Contemptu Linguae Teutonicae* (1617) asserted the suitability of the German language for poetry. His influential *Buch von der deutschen Poeterey*, written in 1624, established long-standing rules for the "purity" of language, style, verse, and rhyme. It insisted upon word stress rather than syllable counting as the basis of German verse and recommended the alexandrine. The scholarly, stilted, and courtly style introduced by Opitz dominated German poetry until the middle of the 18th century. Opitz's poems follow his own rigorous rules and are mostly didactic and descriptive—formal elaborations of carefully considered themes.

In retrospect, Opitz's activities as an aesthetic educator and translator have assumed much importance. He translated from Heinsius, Grotius, Seneca, and Sophocles; he partly translated from the text by O. Rinuccini the libretto of *Dafne*, the first opera in German; he introduced the political novel (John Barclay's *Argenis*) into Germany; and he edited (1638) the German version of Sir Philip Sidney's prose romance *Arcadia* and the 11th-century poem *Annolied*. Opitz's *Opera Poetica* appeared in 1646.

GEORG STIERNHIELM

(b. August 7, 1598, Vika, Sweden—d. April 22, 1672, Stockholm)

The poet and scholar Georg Stiernhielm (also known as Georgius Olai or Göran Lilia) is often called "the father of Swedish poetry."

Originally named Jöran Olofsson and the son of a miner, he studied at Uppsala and spent several years at the German universities of Greifswald, Wittenberg, and Helmstedt. He returned to Sweden in 1626 and soon obtained a judicial position in Dorpat. In 1631 he was raised to the nobility. From *c.* 1640 he was occasionally in Stockholm as poet in attendance at the court of Queen Christina, although his home was in Estonia until 1656, when he fled before the Russian invaders. Thereafter he lived in Stockholm in straitened circumstances. In 1661 he was appointed councillor of war and in 1667 director of the college of antiquities.

Stiernhielm's first poetic works in Swedish appeared during the 1640s. They included verses in celebration of the queen and three court masques adapted from the French. His most important work is the allegorical, didactic epic, *Hercules* (written about 1647; published 1658), a fine example of late Renaissance classicism. It is a sermon on virtue and honour and is imbued with the spirit of humanism. The theme is developed with power and originality; the imagery is exuberant; the construction, faultless. It had great influence on the development of Swedish poetry. Stiernhielm's poems were collected in *Musae Suethizantes* (1668).

Stiernhielm's scholarship was encyclopaedic, and in numerous writings, many unpublished, he dealt with philological, historical, and philosophical problems. An earnest patriot, he claimed that Swedish was man's original language. He sought to purify it by eliminating words borrowed from other languages and enlarging its stock from the popular dialect and from Swedish words that had become obsolete. In his fragmentary works of natural philosophy, he expounded a theory of the universe's origins based on the platonic, mystical tradition of such thinkers as Paracelsus, Robert Fludd, and Comenius.

PEDRO CALDERÓN DE LA BARCA

(b. January 17, 1600, Madrid, Spain—d. May 25, 1681, Madrid)

The dramatist and poet Pedro Calderón de la Barca succeeded Lope de Vega as the greatest Spanish playwright of the Golden Age.

Early Life

Calderón's father, a fairly well-to-do government official who died in 1615, was a man of harsh and dictatorial temper. Strained family relations apparently had a profound effect on the youthful Calderón, for several of his plays show a preoccupation with the psychological and moral effects of unnatural family life, presenting anarchical behaviour directly traced to the abuse of paternal authority.

Destined for the church, Calderón matriculated at the University of Alcalá in 1614 but transferred a year later to Salamanca, where he continued his studies in arts, law, and probably theology until 1619 or 1620. Abandoning an ecclesiastical career, he entered the service of the constable of Castile and in 1623 began to write plays for the court, rapidly becoming the leading member of the small group of dramatic poets whom King Philip IV gathered around him. In 1636 the king made him a Knight of the Military Order of St. James. Calderón's popularity was not confined to the court, for these early plays were also acclaimed in the public theatres, and on the death of Lope de Vega (1635) Calderón became the master of the Spanish stage. On the outbreak of the Catalan rebellion, he enlisted in 1640 in a cavalry company of knights of the military orders and served with distinction until 1642, when he was invalided out of the army. In 1645 he entered the service of the Duke de Alba, probably as secretary. A few years later an illegitimate son was born to him; nothing is known about the mother, and the idea that sorrow at her death led him to return to his first vocation, the priesthood, is pure surmise. He was ordained in 1651 and announced that he would write no more for the stage. This intention he kept as regards the public theatres, but at the king's command he continued to write regularly for the court theatre. Appointed a prebendary of Toledo Cathedral, he took up residence in 1653. The fine meditative religious poem *Psalle et sile* ("Sing Psalms and Keep Silent") is of this period. Receiving permission to hold his prebend without residence, he returned to Madrid in 1657 and was appointed honorary chaplain to the king in 1663.

Aesthetic Milieu and Achievement

The court patronage that Calderón enjoyed constitutes the most important single influence in the development of his art.

The court drama grew out of the popular drama, and at first there was no distinction in themes and style between the two. The construction, however, of a special theatre in the new palace, the Buen Retiro, completed in 1633, made possible spectacular productions beyond the resources of the public stage. The court plays became a distinctive Baroque genre, combining drama with dancing, music, and the visual arts and departing from contemporary life into the world of classical mythology and ancient history. Thus Calderón, as court dramatist, became associated with the rise of opera in Spain. In 1648 he wrote *El jardín de Falerina* ("The Garden of Falerina"), the first of his zarzuelas, plays in two acts with alternating spoken and sung dialogue. In 1660 he wrote his first opera, the one-act *La púrpura de la rosa* ("The Purple of the Rose"), with all of the dialogue set to music. This was followed by *Celos, aun del aire matan* (1660; "Jealousy Even of the Air Can Kill"), an opera in three acts with music by Juan Hidalgo.

Calderón's drama must be placed within the context of the court theatre, with its conscious development of an unrealistic and stylized art form. For two centuries after his death, his preeminence remained unchallenged, but the realistic canons of criticism that came to the fore toward the end of the 19th century produced a reaction in favour of the more "lifelike" drama of Lope de Vega. Calderón appeared mannered and conventional: the structure of his plots artificially contrived, his characters stiff and unconvincing, his verse often affected and rhetorical. Although he used technical devices and stylistic mannerisms that by constant repetition became conventional, Calderón remained sufficiently detached to make his characters, on occasion, poke fun at his own conventions. This detachment indicates a conception of art as a formal medium that employs its artistic devices so as to compress and abstract the externals of human life, the better to express its essentials.

In this direction Calderón developed the dramatic form and conventions established by Lope de Vega, based on primacy of action over characterization, with unity in the theme rather than in the plot. He created a tightly knit structure of his own, while leaving intact the formal framework of Lope's drama. From the start he manifested his technical skill by utilizing the characters and incidents of his plots in the development of a dominant idea. As his art matured his plots became more complex and the action more constricted and compact. The creation of complex dramatic patterns in which the artistic effect arises from perception of the totality of the design through the inseparability of the parts is Calderón's greatest achievement as a craftsman. *El pintor de su deshonra* (c. 1645; *The Painter of His Own Dishonor*) and *La cisma de Ingalaterra* (c. 1627; "The Schism of England") are masterly examples of this technique, in which poetic imagery, characters, and action are subtly interconnected by dominant symbols that elucidate the significance of the theme. Although rhetorical devices typical of the Spanish Baroque style remained a feature of his diction, his verse developed away from excessive ornamentation toward a taut style compressed and controlled by a penetrating mind.

Secular Plays

The difficulties that Calderón's art presents to the modern reader have tended to obscure the originality of his themes. Accepting the conventions of the comedy of intrigue, a favourite form on the Spanish stage, he used them for a fundamentally serious purpose: *La dama duende* (1629; *The Phantom Lady*) is a neat and lively example. In *Casa con dos puertas, mala es de guardar* (1629; "A House with Two Doors Is Difficult to Guard"), the intrigues of secret courtship and the disguises that it necessitates are so presented that the traditional seclusion of women on which these intrigues are based is shown to create social disorder by breeding enmity and endangering love and friendship. *No siempre lo peor es cierto* (*c.* 1640; "The Worst Is Not Always True") and *No hay cosa como callar* (1639; "Silence Is Golden") mark the peak of this development: although the conventions of comedy remain, the overtones are tragic. Both plays also implicitly criticize the accepted code of honour. Calderón's rejection of the rigid assumptions of the code of honour is evident also in his tragedies. In the famous *El alcalde de Zalamea*, the secrecy and the vengeance demanded by the code are rejected. This play also presents a powerful contrast between the aristocracy and the people: the degeneration of the aristocratic ideal is exposed, wealth is associated with manual labour, and honour is shown to be the consequence and prerogative of moral integrity regardless of class. Yet Calderón's humanity has been questioned in connection with *El médico de su honra*. The critics who allege that he approves of the murder of an innocent wife because honour demands it overlook the fact that the horror one feels at this deed is precisely what he intended.

A keynote of Calderon's tragic view of life is his deep-seated realization that a man can be responsible through his own wrongdoing for the wrongdoing of another. This realization probably derives from Calderón's own family experience. In *La devoción de la cruz* (*c.* 1625; *Devotion to the Cross*) and *Las tres justicias en una* (*c.* 1637; *Three Judgments at a Blow*), the heart of the tragedy lies in the fact that the greatest sinner is also the most sinned against—in that others, before he was born, had begun to dig his grave. *El pintor de su deshonra* is built on a similar plot.

The fully developed court plays are best represented by *La hija del aire*. This play in two parts dramatizes the legend of Semiramis (the warrior queen of Babylon whose greed for political power led her to conceal and imperonate her son on his accession). It is often considered Calderón's masterpiece. Highly stylized, it conveys a strong impression of violence. It presents, with considerable complexity, the contrast between passion and reason. Passion, in its self-seeking, in its grasping for power and devouring of everything in the urge to domination, breeds disorder and leads to destruction; reason, in its sacrificing of self-interest to justice and loyalty, produces order. This basic contrast underlies the themes of Calderón's last period, its various aspects being expanded in a number of interesting variations, many directly concerned with the positive values of civilization. Though none has the intensity of *La hija del aire*, most exemplify a thoughtful, dignified, and restrained art. Mythological themes predominate, with a more or less allegorical treatment, as in *Eco y Narciso* (1661; "Echo and Narcissus"), *La estatua de Prometeo* (1669; "The Statue of Prometheus"), and *Fieras afemina amor* (1669; "Wild Beasts Are Tamed by Love").

Religious Plays

Calderón's vision of the human world in his secular plays is one of confusion and discord arising out of the inevitable clash of values in the natural order. His religious plays round off his view of life by confronting natural values with supernatural ones. The most characteristic of these religious plays, following the tradition established outside

Spain by the Jesuit drama, are based on stories of conversion and martyrdom, usually of the saints of the early church. One of the most beautiful is *El príncipe constante* (1629; *The Constant Prince*), which dramatizes the martyrdom of Prince Ferdinand of Portugal. *El mágico prodigioso* (1637; *The Wonder-Working Magician*) is a more complex religious play; *Los dos amantes del cielo* (*The Two Lovers of Heaven*) and *El Joséf de las mujeres* (*c.* 1640; "The Joseph of Womankind") are the most subtle and difficult. The basic human experience upon which Calderón relies for rational support of religious faith is decay and death and the consequent incapacity of the world to fulfill its promise of happiness. This promise is centred in such natural values as beauty, love, wealth, and power that, although true values if pursued with prudence, cannot satisfy the mind's aspiration for truth or the heart's longing for happiness. Only the apprehension of an "infinite Good" can assuage the restlessness of men.

This religious philosophy is given its most moving expression, in terms of Christian dogma, in the *autos sacramentales* ("sacramental acts," a Spanish dramatic genre popularized by Calderón). Seventy-six of these allegorical plays, written for open-air performance on the Feast of Corpus Christi, are extant. In them Calderón brought the tradition of the medieval morality play to a high degree of artistic perfection. The range of his scriptural, patristic, and scholastic learning, together with the assurance of his structural technique and poetic diction, enable him to endow the abstract concepts of dogmatic and moral theology with convincing dramatic life. At their weakest the *autos* tend to depend for their effect upon the ingenuity of their allegories, but at their best they are imbued with profound moral and spiritual insight and with a poetic feeling varying from tenderness to forcefulness. His highest achievement in this type of drama is to be found among those *autos* of his old age that dramatize the dogmas of the Fall and the redemption, such as *La viña del Señor* (1674; "The Lord's Vineyard"), *La nave del mercader* (1674; "The Merchant's Ship"), and *El pastor fido* (1678; "The Faithful Shepherd"). Here is found Calderón's most moving expression of his compassionate understanding of human waywardness.

PIERRE CORNEILLE

(b. June 6, 1606, Rouen, France—d. October 1, 1684, Paris)

The French poet and dramatist Pierre Corneille is considered the creator of French classical tragedy.

Early Life and Career

Pierre Corneille was born into a well-to-do, middle-class Norman family. His grandfather, father, and an uncle were all lawyers; another uncle and a brother entered the church; his younger brother, Thomas, became a well-known poet and popular playwright. Pierre was educated at the Jesuit school in his hometown, won two prizes for Latin verse composition, and was educated to become a lawyer. From 1628 to 1650 he held the position of king's counselor in the local office of the department of waterways and forests.

Corneille's first play, written before he was 20 and apparently drawing upon a personal love experience, was an elegant and witty comedy, *Mélite*, first performed in Rouen in 1629. When it was repeated in Paris the following year, it built into a steady (and, according to Corneille, surprising) success. His next plays were the tragicomedy *Clitandre* (performed 1631) and a series of comedies including *La Veuve* (performed 1632; *The Widow*), *La Galerie du palais* (performed 1633; *The Palace Corridor*), and *L'Illusion comique* (performed 1636). His talent, meanwhile, had come to the attention of the Cardinal de Richelieu, France's great statesman, who included the playwright among a group known as *les cinq auteurs* ("society of the five authors"), which the cardinal had formed to have plays written, the inspiration and outline of which were provided by himself. Corneille was temperamentally unsuited to this collective endeavour and irritated Richelieu by departing from his part (Act III) of the outline for *La Comédie des Tuileries* (1635). In the event, Corneille's contribution was artistically outstanding.

During these years, support had been growing for a new approach to tragedy that aimed at "regularity" through observance of what were called the "classical" unities. Deriving from Italy, this doctrine of the unities demanded that there be unity of time (strictly, the play's events were to be limited to "the period between sunrise and sunset"), of place (the entire action was to take place in one location), and of action (subplots and the dramatic treatment of more than one situation were to be avoided). All this was based on a misunderstanding of Aristotle's *Poetics*, in which the philosopher attempted to give a critical definition of the nature of tragedy. The new theory was first put into dramatic practice in Jean Mairet's *Sophonisbe* (1634), a tragedy that enjoyed considerable success. Corneille, not directly involved in the call for regular tragedy of this kind, nevertheless responded to *Sophonisbe* by experimenting in the tragic form with *Médée* (1635). He then wrote *Le Cid* (performed early 1637), first issued as a tragicomedy, later as a tragedy.

Le Cid, now commonly regarded as the most significant play in the history of French drama, proved an immense popular success. It sparked off a literary controversy, however, which was chiefly conducted by Corneille's rival dramatists, Mairet and Georges de Scudéry, and which resulted in a bitter pamphlet war. Richelieu, whose motives are not entirely clear, instructed the then recently instituted Académie Française to make a judgment on the play: the resulting document (*Les Sentiments de l'Académie française sur la tragi-comédie du Cid*, 1637), drafted in the main by Jean Chapelain, a critic who advocated "regular" tragedy, was worded tactfully and admitted the play's beauties but criticized *Le Cid* as dramatically implausible and morally defective. Richelieu used the judgment of the Académie as an excuse for suppressing public performances of the play.

Corneille, indeed, had not observed the dramatic unities in *Le Cid*. The play has nevertheless been generally regarded as the first flowering of French "classical" tragedy. For the best French drama of the "classical" period in the 17th century is properly characterized, not so much by rules—which are no more than a structural convention—as by emotional concentration on a moral dilemma and on a supreme moment of truth, when leading characters recognize the depth of their involvement in this dilemma. In *Le Cid*, Corneille rejected the discursive treatment of the subject given in his Spanish source (a long, florid, and violent play by Guillén de Castro y Bellvis, a 17th-century dramatist), concentrating instead on a conflict between passionate love and family loyalty, or honour. Thus *Le Cid* anticipated the "pure" tragedy of Racine, in whose work the "classical" concept of tragic intensity at the moment of self-realization found its most mature and perfect expression.

Major Tragedies

Corneille seems to have taken to heart the criticisms levelled at *Le Cid*, and he wrote nothing for three years (though this time was also taken up with a lawsuit to prevent the creation of a legal office in Rouen on a par with his own). In 1640, however, appeared the Roman tragedy *Horace*; another, *Cinna*, appeared in 1641. In 1641 also Corneille married Marie de Lampérière, the daughter of a local magistrate, who was to bear him seven children to whom he was a devoted father. Corneille's brother Thomas married Marie's sister, and the two couples lived in extraordinary harmony, their households hardly separated; the brothers enjoyed literary amity and mutual assistance.

Le Cid, *Horace*, *Cinna*, and *Polyeucte*, which appeared in 1643, are together known as Corneille's "classical tetralogy" and together represent perhaps his finest body of work for the theatre. *Horace* was based on an account by the Roman historian Livy of a legendary combat between members of the Horatii and Curiatii families, representing Rome and Alba; Corneille, however, concentrated on the murder by one of the patriots of his pacifist sister, the whole case afterward being argued before the king (a "duplicity" of action admitted by Corneille himself, who otherwise seems by now to have decided to follow the classical rules). *Cinna* was about a conspiracy against the first Roman emperor, Augustus, who checkmates his adversaries by granting them a political pardon instead of dealing them the expected violent fate, boasting that he has strength enough to be merciful. The hero of *Polyeucte* (which many critics have considered to be Corneille's finest work), on adopting Christianity seeks a martyr's death with almost militaristic fervour, choosing this as the path to *la gloire* ("glory") in another world, whereas his wife insists that the claims of marriage are as important as those of religion.

These four plays are charged with an energy peculiar to Corneille. Their arguments, presented elegantly, rhetorically, in the grand style, remain firm and sonorous.

The alexandrine verse that he employed (though not exclusively) was used with astonishing flexibility as an instrument to convey all shades of meaning and expression: irony, anger, soliloquy, repartee, epigram. Corneille used language not so much to illumine character as to heighten the clash between concepts, hence the "sentences" in his poetry which are memorable even outside their dramatic context. Action here is reaction. These plays concern not so much what is done as what is resolved, felt, suffered. Their formal principle is symmetry: presentation, by a poet who was also a lawyer, of one side of the case, then of the other, of one position followed by its opposite.

Contribution to Comedy

The fame of his "classical tetralogy" has tended to obscure the enormous variety of Corneille's other drama, and his contribution to the development of French comedy has not always received its proper due. The Roman plays were followed by more tragedies: *La Mort de Pompée* (performed 1644; *The Death of Pompey*), *Rodogune* (performed 1645), which was one of his greatest successes, *Théodore* (performed 1646), which was his first taste of failure, and *Héraclius* (performed 1647). But in 1643 Corneille had successfully turned to comedy with *Le Menteur* (*The Liar*), following it with the less successful *La Suite du Menteur* (performed 1645; *Sequel to the Liar*). Both were lively comedies of intrigue, adapted from Spanish models; and *Le Menteur* is the one outstanding French comedy before the plays of Molière, Corneille's young contemporary, who acknowledged its influence on his own work. *Le Menteur*, indeed, stands in relation to French classical comedy much as *Le Cid* does to tragedy.

In 1647 Corneille moved with his family to Paris and was at last admitted to the Académie Française, having twice previously been rejected on the grounds of non-residence in the capital. *Don Sanche d'Aragon* (performed 1650), *Andromède* (performed 1650), a spectacular play in which stage machinery was very important, and *Nicomède* (performed 1651) were all written during the political upheaval and civil war of the period known as the Fronde (1648–53), with *Don Sanche* in particular carrying contemporary political overtones. In 1651 or 1652 his play *Pertharite* seems to have been brutally received, and for the next eight years Corneille wrote nothing for the theatre, concentrating instead on a verse translation of St. Thomas à Kempis' *Imitatio Christi (Imitation of Christ)*, which he completed in 1656, and also working at critical discourses on his plays that were to be included in a 1660 edition of his collected works.

Years of Declining Power

Corneille did not turn again to the theatre until 1659, when, with the encouragement of the statesman and patron of the arts Nicolas Fouquet, he presented *Oedipe*. For the next 14 years he wrote almost one play a year, including *Sertorius* (performed 1662) and *Attila* (performed 1667), both of which contain an amount of violent and surprising incident.

Corneille's last plays, indeed, were closer in spirit to his works of the 1640s than to his classical tragedies. Their plots were endlessly complicated, their emotional climate close to that of tragicomedy. In collaboration with Molière and Philippe Quinault he wrote *Psyché* (1671), a play employing music, incorporating ballet sequences, and striking a note of lyrical tenderness. A year earlier, however, he had presented *Tite et Bérénice*, in deliberate contest with a play on the same subject by Racine. Its failure indicated the public's growing preference for the younger playwright.

Corneille's final play was *Suréna* (performed 1674), which showed an uncharacteristic delicacy and sentimental appeal. After this he was silent except for some beautiful verses, which appeared in 1676, thanking King Louis XIV for ordering the revival of his plays. Although not in desperate poverty, Corneille was by no means wealthy; and his situation was further embarrassed by the intermittent stoppage of a state pension that had been granted by Richelieu soon after the appearance of *Horace* in 1640. Corneille died in his house on the rue d'Argenteuil, Paris, and was buried in the church of Saint-Roch. No monument marked his tomb until 1821.

JOHN MILTON

(b. December 9, 1608, London, England—
d. November 8?, 1674, London?)

John Milton was an English poet, pamphleteer, and historian and is considered the most significant English author after William Shakespeare.

Early Life and Education

Milton's paternal grandfather, Richard, was a staunch Roman Catholic who expelled his son John, the poet's father, from the family home in Oxfordshire for reading an English (i.e., Protestant) Bible. Banished and disinherited, Milton's father established in London a business as a scrivener, preparing documents for legal transactions. He was also a moneylender, and he negotiated with creditors to arrange for loans on behalf of his clients. He and his wife, Sara Jeffrey, whose father was a merchant tailor, had three children who survived their early years: Anne, the oldest, followed by John and Christopher. Though Christopher became a lawyer, a Royalist, and perhaps a Roman Catholic, he maintained throughout his life a cordial relationship with his older brother. After the Stuart monarchy was restored in 1660, Christopher, among others, may have interceded to prevent the execution of his brother.

Milton enrolled at Christ's College, Cambridge, in 1625, presumably to be educated for the ministry. In 1629 Milton was awarded a Bachelor of Arts degree, and in 1632 he received a Master of Arts degree. Despite his initial intent to enter the ministry, Milton did not do so, a situation that has not been fully explained. Possible reasons are that Milton lacked respect for his fellow students who were planning to become ministers but whom he considered ill-equipped academically or that his Puritan inclinations, which became more radical as he matured, caused him to dislike the hierarchy of the established church and its insistence on uniformity of worship; perhaps, too, his self-evident disaffection impelled the Church of England to reject him for the ministry.

Overall, Milton was displeased with Cambridge, possibly because study there emphasized Scholasticism, which he found stultifying to the imagination. Nonetheless, Milton excelled academically. At Cambridge he composed several academic exercises called prolusions, which were presented as oratorical performances in the manner of a debate. Milton authorized publication of seven of his prolusions, composed and recited in Latin, in 1674, the year of his death.

In 1632, after seven years at Cambridge, Milton returned to his family home, now in Hammersmith, on the outskirts of London. Three years later, perhaps because of an outbreak of the plague, the family relocated to a more pastoral setting, Horton, in Buckinghamshire.

John Milton, chromolithograph after a pastel by William Faithorne.
Photos.com/Thinkstock

In these two locations, Milton spent approximately six years in studious retirement, during which he read Greek and Latin authors chiefly. Without gainful employment, Milton was supported by his father during this period.

Early Translations and Poems

In 1638, accompanied by a manservant, Milton undertook a tour of the Continent for about 15 months, most of which he spent in Italy, primarily Rome and Florence, where he met with Galileo. (Galileo would become the only contemporary whom Milton mentioned by name in *Paradise Lost*.) By the time he returned to England in 1639, Milton had manifested remarkable talent as a linguist and translator and extraordinary versatility as a poet. While at St. Paul's, as a 15-year-old student, Milton had translated Psalm 114 from the original Hebrew, a text that recounts the liberation of the Israelites from Egypt. Beginning such work early in his boyhood, he continued it into adulthood, especially from 1648 to 1653, a period when he was also composing pamphlets against the Church of England and the monarchy. Also in his early youth Milton composed letters in Latin verse. These letters, which range over many topics, are called elegies because they employ elegiac metre—a verse form, Classical in origin, that consists of couplets, the first line dactylic hexameter, the second dactylic pentameter.

In 1628 Milton composed an occasional poem, *On the Death of a Fair Infant Dying of a Cough,* which mourns the loss of his niece Anne, the daughter of his older sister. Milton tenderly commemorates the child, who was two years old. The poem's conceits, Classical allusions, and theological overtones emphasize that the child entered the supernal realm because the human condition, having been enlightened by her brief presence, was ill-suited to bear her any longer.

In this early period, Milton's principal poems included *On the Morning of Christ's Nativity, On Shakespeare,* and the so-called companion poems *L'Allegro* and *Il Penseroso.Comus* and *Lycidas*

Milton's most important early poems, *Comus* and *Lycidas,* are major literary achievements, to the extent that his reputation as an author would have been secure by 1640 even without his later works. *Comus*, a dramatic entertainment, or masque, is also called *A Mask*; it was first published as *A Maske Presented at Ludlow Castle* in 1638, but, since the late 17th century, it has typically been called by the name of its most vivid character, the villainous Comus. Performed in 1634 on the church festival of Michaelmas (September 29) at Ludlow Castle in Shropshire, *Comus* celebrates the installation of John Egerton, earl of Bridgewater and Viscount Brackley and a member of Charles I's Privy Council, as lord president of Wales. In addition to various English and Welsh dignitaries, the installation was attended by Egerton's wife and children; the latter all had parts in the dramatic entertainment.

The masque develops the theme of a journey through the woods by the three Egerton children, in the course of which the daughter, called "the Lady," is separated from her brothers. While alone, she encounters Comus, who is disguised as a villager and who claims that he will lead her to her brothers. Deceived by his amiable countenance, the Lady follows him, only to be victimized by his necromancy. Despite being restrained against her will, she continues to exercise right reason (*recta ratio*) in her disputation with Comus, thereby manifesting her freedom of mind. Whereas the would-be seducer argues that appetites and desires issuing from one's nature are "natural" and therefore licit, the Lady contends that only rational self-control is enlightened and virtuous. To be self-indulgent and intemperate, she adds, is to forfeit one's higher nature and to yield to baser impulses. As she continues to assert her freedom of mind and to exercise her free will by resistance, even defiance, she is rescued by the attendant spirit and her brothers. Ultimately, she and her brothers are reunited with their parents in a triumphal celebration, which signifies the heavenly bliss awaiting the wayfaring soul that prevails over trials and travails, whether these are the threats posed by overt evil or the blandishments of temptation.

Late in 1637 Milton composed a pastoral elegy called *Lycidas,* which commemorates the death of a fellow student at Cambridge, Edward King, who drowned while crossing the Irish Sea. Published in 1638 in *Justa Edouardo King Naufrago* ("Obsequies in Memory of Edward King"), a compilation of elegies by Cambridge students, *Lycidas* is one of several poems in English, whereas most of the others are in Greek and Latin. As a pastoral elegy—often considered the most outstanding example of the genre—Milton's poem is richly allegorical. King is called Lycidas, a shepherd's name that recurs in Classical elegies. By choosing this name, Milton signals his participation in the tradition of memorializing a loved one through pastoral poetry, a practice that may be traced from ancient Greek Sicily through Roman culture and into the Christian Middle Ages and early Renaissance. The poem's speaker, a persona for Milton's own voice, is a fellow shepherd who mourns the loss of a friend with whom he shared duties in tending sheep. In the course of commemorating King, the speaker challenges divine justice obliquely. Through allegory, the speaker accuses God of unjustly punishing the young, selfless King, whose premature death ended a career that would have unfolded in stark contrast to the majority of the ministers and bishops of the Church of England, whom the speaker condemns as depraved, materialistic, and selfish.

Religious, Political, and Societal Tracts

Having returned from abroad in 1639, Milton turned his attention from poetry to prose. In doing so, he entered the controversies surrounding the abolition of the Church of England and of the Royalist government, at times replying to, and often attacking vehemently, English and Continental polemicists who targeted him as the apologist of radical religious and political dissent. In 1641–42 Milton composed five tracts on the reformation of church government. One of these tracts, *Of Reformation*, examines the historical changes in the Church of England since its inception under King Henry VIII and criticizes the continuing resemblances between the Church of England and the Roman Catholic Church, especially the hierarchy in ecclesiastical government.

Soon after these controversies, Milton became embroiled in another conflict, one in his domestic life. Having married Mary Powell in 1642, Milton was a few months afterward deserted by his wife, who returned to her family's residence in Oxfordshire. The reason for their separation is unknown, though perhaps Mary adhered to the Royalist inclinations of her family whereas her husband was progressively anti-Royalist. Or perhaps the discrepancy in their ages—he was 34, she was 17—led to a lack of mutual understanding. During her absence of approximately three years, Milton may have been planning marriage to another woman. But after Mary's return, she and Milton evidently overcame the causes of their estrangement. Three daughters (Anne, Mary, and

Deborah) were born, but a son, John, died at age one. Milton's wife died in 1652 after giving birth to Deborah.

During his domestic strife and after his wife's desertion, Milton probably began to frame the arguments of four prose tracts: *The Doctrine and Discipline of Divorce* (1643, enlarged 2nd ed. 1644), *The Judgment of Martin Bucer Concerning Divorce* (1644), *Tetrachordon* (1645), and *Colasterion* (1645). Whether or not his personal experience with Mary affected his views on marriage, Milton mounts a cogent, radical argument for divorce, an argument informed by the concepts of personal liberty and individual volition, the latter being instrumental in maintaining or ending a marriage. For Milton, marriage depends on the compatibility of the partners, and to maintain a marriage that is without mutual love and sympathy violates one's personal liberty.

About the time that the first and second editions of *The Doctrine and Discipline of Divorce* appeared, Milton published *Of Education* (1644). In line with the ideal of the Renaissance gentleman, Milton outlines a curriculum emphasizing the Greek and Latin languages not merely in and of themselves but as the means to learn directly the wisdom of Classical antiquity in literature, philosophy, and politics.

The most renowned tract by Milton is *Areopagitica* (1644), which opposes governmental licensing of publications or procedures of censorship. Milton contends that governments insisting on the expression of uniform beliefs are tyrannical. In his tract, he investigates historical examples of censorship, which, he argues, invariably emanate from repressive governments. The aim of *Areopagitica*, he explains, is to promote knowledge, test experience, and strive for the truth without any hindrances.

Counterbalancing the antiprelatical tracts of 1641–42 are the antimonarchical polemics of 1649–55. Composed after Milton had become allied to those who sought to form an English republic, *The Tenure of Kings and Magistrates* (1649)—probably written before and during the trial of King Charles I though not published until after his death on January 30, 1649—urges the abolition of tyrannical kingship and the execution of tyrants. Thereafter, Milton was appointed secretary for foreign tongues (also called Latin secretary) for the Council of State, the executive body of the Commonwealth under Oliver Cromwell. Milton was entrusted with the duties of translating foreign correspondence, drafting replies, composing papers in which national and international affairs of state were addressed, and serving as an apologist for the Commonwealth against attacks from abroad.

Major Poems

Blind, probably from glaucoma, and once a widower, Milton married Katherine Woodcock in 1656. Their marriage lasted only 15 months: she died within months of the birth of their child. He wedded Elizabeth Minshull in 1663, who, along with the daughters from his first marriage, assisted him with his personal needs, read from books at his request, and took dictation to record verses that he dictated. In the era after the Restoration, Milton published his three major poems, though he had begun work on two of them, *Paradise Lost* and *Samson Agonistes*, many years earlier.

Paradise Lost

Abandoning his earlier plan to compose an epic on Arthur, Milton instead turned to biblical subject matter and to a Christian idea of heroism. In *Paradise Lost*—first published in 10 books in 1667 and then in 12 books in 1674, at a length of almost 11,000 lines—Milton observed but adapted a number of the Classical epic conventions that distinguish works such as Homer's *The Iliad* and *The Odyssey* and Virgil's *The Aeneid*.

Among these conventions is a focus on the elevated subjects of war, love, and heroism. In Book 6 Milton describes the battle between the good and evil angels; the defeat of the latter results in their expulsion from heaven. In the battle, the Son (Jesus Christ) is invincible in his onslaught against Satan and his cohorts. But Milton's emphasis is less on the Son as a warrior and more on his love for humankind; the Father, in his celestial dialogue with the Son, foresces the sinfulness of Adam and Eve, and the Son chooses to become incarnate and to suffer humbly to redeem them. Though his role as saviour of fallen humankind is not enacted in the epic, Adam and Eve before their expulsion from Eden learn of the future redemptive ministry of Jesus, the exemplary gesture of self-sacrificing love. The Son's selfless love contrasts strikingly with the selfish love of the heroes of Classical epics, who are distinguished by their valour on the battlefield, which is usually incited by pride and vainglory. Their strength and skills on the battlefield and their acquisition of the spoils of war also issue from hate, anger, revenge, greed, and covetousness. If Classical epics deem their protagonists heroic for their extreme passions, even vices, the Son in *Paradise Lost* exemplifies Christian heroism both through his meekness and magnanimity and through his patience and fortitude.

Paradise Lost also directly invokes Classical epics by beginning its action in medias res (a Latin term meaning "in the midst of things"). Book 1 recounts the aftermath of the war in heaven, which is described only later, in Book 6. At the outset of the epic, the consequences of the loss of the war include the expulsion of the fallen angcls from heaven and their descent into hell, a place of infernal torment. With the punishment of the fallen angels having been described early in the epic, Milton in later books recounts how and why their disobedience occurred. Disobedience and its consequences, therefore, come to the fore in Raphael's instruction of Adam and Eve, who (especially in Books 6 and 8) are admonished to remain obedient. By examining the sinfulness of Satan in thought and in deed, Milton positions this part of his narrative close to the temptation of Eve. This arrangement enables Milton to highlight how and why Satan, who inhabits a serpent to seduce Eve in Book 9, induces in her the inordinate pride that brought about his own downfall. Satan arouses in Eve a comparable state of mind, which is enacted in her partaking of the forbidden fruit, an act of disobedience.

Paradise Lost is ultimately not only about the downfall of Adam and Eve but also about the clash between Satan and the Son. Many readers have admired Satan's splendid recklessness, if not heroism, in confronting the Godhead. Satan's defiance, anger, willfulness, and resourcefulness define a character who strives never to yield. In many ways Satan is heroic when compared to such Classical prototypes as Achilles, Odysseus, and Aeneas and to similar protagonists in medieval and Renaissance epics. In sum, his traits reflect theirs.

But Milton composed a biblical epic in order to debunk Classical heroism and to extol Christian heroism, exemplified by the Son. Notwithstanding his victory in the battle against the fallen angels, the Son is more heroic because he is willing to undergo voluntary humiliation, a sign of his consummate love for humankind. He foreknows that he will become incarnate in order to suffer death, a selfless act whereby humankind will be redeemed. By such an act, moreover, the Son fulfills what Milton calls the "great argument" of his poem: to "justify the ways of

God to man," as Milton writes in Book 1. Despite Satan's success against Adam and Eve, the hope of regeneration after sinfulness is provided by the Son's self-sacrifice. Such hope and opportunity enable humankind to cooperate with the Godhead so as to defeat Satan, avoid damnation, overcome death, and ascend heavenward.

Paradise Regained

Milton's last two poems were published in one volume in 1671. *Paradise Regained*, a brief epic in four books, was followed by *Samson Agonistes*, a dramatic poem not intended for the stage.

Paradise Regained hearkens back to the Book of Job, whose principal character is tempted by Satan to forgo his faith in God and to cease exercising patience and fortitude in the midst of ongoing and ever-increasing adversity. By adapting the trials of Job and the role of Satan as tempter and by integrating them with the accounts of Matthew and Luke of Jesus' temptations in the wilderness, Milton dramatizes how Jesus embodies Christian heroism.

In effect, *Paradise Regained* unfolds as a series of debates—an ongoing dialectic—in which Jesus analyzes and refutes Satan's arguments. With clarity and cogency, Jesus rebuts any and all arguments by using right reason (*recta ratio*), always informed by faith in God, his father. Strikingly evident also is Jesus' determination, an overwhelming sense of resolve to endure any and all trials visited upon him. Though *Paradise Regained* lacks the vast scope of *Paradise Lost*, it fulfills its purpose admirably by pursuing the idea of Christian heroism as a state of mind. More so than *Paradise Lost*, it dramatizes the inner workings of the mind of Jesus, his perception, and the interplay of faith and reason in his debates with Satan. When Jesus finally dismisses the tempter at the end of the work, the reader recognizes that the encounters in *Paradise Regained* reflect a high degree of psychological verisimilitude.

Samson Agonistes

Like *Paradise Regained*, *Samson Agonistes* focuses on the inner workings of the mind of the protagonist. This emphasis flies in the face of the biblical characterization of Samson in the Book of Judges, which celebrates his physical strength. Milton's dramatic poem, however, begins the story of Samson after his downfall—after he has yielded his God-entrusted secret to Dalila (Delilah), suffered blindness, and become a captive of the Philistines. Tormented by anguish over his captivity, Samson is depressed by the realization that he, the prospective liberator of the Israelites, is now a prisoner, blind and powerless in the hands of his enemies. Samson vacillates from one extreme to another emotionally and psychologically. He becomes depressed, wallows in self-pity, and contemplates suicide; he becomes outraged at himself for having disclosed the secret of his strength; he questions his own nature, whether it was flawed with excessive strength and too little wisdom so that he was destined at birth to suffer eventual downfall.

Unlike the biblical account in Judges, *Samson Agonistes* focuses only on the last day of Samson's life. Discerning that he was victimized by his own pride, Samson becomes chastened and humbled. He becomes acutely aware of the necessity to atone for his sinfulness. In a series of debates not unlike those in *Paradise Regained* between the Son and Satan, Samson engages Manoa, his father; Dalila, his temptress; and Harapha, a stalwart Philistine warrior. In each of these encounters, Samson's discourse manifests an upward trajectory, through atonement and toward regeneration, which culminates in the climactic action at the temple of Dagon where Samson, again chosen by God, vindicates himself. Echoing *Paradise Lost*, which dramatizes the self-sacrifice of the Son, *Samson Agonistes* creates in its hero a Hebrew Bible prefiguration of the very process of regeneration enabled by the Redeemer and afforded to fallen humankind. In this way, moreover, Samson exhibits the traits of Christian heroism that Milton elsewhere emphasized.

But where the Son of *Paradise Regained* maintains steadfastly his resistance to temptation, Samson typifies human vulnerability to downfall. Accordingly, where in *Paradise Regained* the Son never loses God's favour, *Samson Agonistes* charts how a victim of temptation can reacquire it. Despite the superficial resemblance between his muscular, warlike acts of destruction and those of Classical heroes, Samson is ultimately a Christian hero.

Milton's Later Years and Death

After the Restoration and despite jeopardy to himself, Milton continued to advocate freedom of worship and republicanism for England while he supervised the publication of his major poems and other works. For a time soon after the succession of Charles II, Milton was under arrest and menaced by possible execution for involvement in the regicide and in Cromwell's government. Although the circumstances of clemency toward Milton are not fully known, it is likely that certain figures influential with the regime of Charles II—such as Christopher Milton, Andrew Marvell, and William Davenant—interceded on his behalf. The exact date and location of Milton's death remain unknown; he likely died in London on November 8, 1674, from complications of the gout (possibly renal failure). He was buried inside St. Giles Cripplegate Church in London.

SIR JOHN SUCKLING

(b. February 1609, Whitton, Middlesex, England—d. 1642, Paris,
France)

The English Cavalier poet, dramatist, and courtier Sir John Suckling is best known for his lyrics.

He was educated at Cambridge and inherited his father's considerable estates at the age of 18. He entered Gray's Inn in 1627 and was knighted in 1630. He became a prominent figure at court with a reputation for being "the greatest gallant of his time, and the greatest gamester both for bowling and cards"; and he is credited with having invented the game of cribbage. He was a gentleman of the privy chamber to Charles I and a friend of the poets Thomas Carew, Richard Lovelace, and Sir William Davenant. When the war with the Scots broke out in 1639, Suckling raised a troop of soldiers, supplying them with horses at his own expense, and accompanied Charles I on his ill-fated expedition. The costumes of Suckling's gaudy warriors and the troop's poor performance in the field were the subjects of much ridicule.

In 1641 Suckling took an active part in the plot to rescue the Earl of Strafford from the Tower. When the plot was discovered, Suckling fled to France and is believed to have committed suicide.

Suckling was the author of four plays, the most ambitious of which is the tragedy *Aglaura*, magnificently staged in 1637 and handsomely printed at the author's expense (1638); the best is the lively comedy *The Goblins* (1638). They all contain echoes of Shakespeare and Beaumont and Fletcher.

His reputation as a poet rests on his lyrics, the best of which justifies the description of him as "natural, easy

Suckling." He inherited from Donne the tradition of the "anti-platonic" deflation of high-flown love sentiment and uses it with insouciance.

Out upon it I have loved
Three whole days together;
And am like to love three more,
If it prove fair weather.

He can even be cynically chiding in such songs as this:

Why so pale and wan, fond lover?
Prithee, why so pale?
Will, when looking well can't move her,
Looking ill prevail?
Prithee, why so pale?

A Session of the Poets (1637; published 1646) is an amusing skit for which he probably took a hint from an Italian work by Traiano Boccalini; it is the prototype of a long line of similar works in the 17th and 18th centuries. His masterpiece is undoubtedly "A Ballad Upon a Wedding," in the style and metre of the contemporary street ballad. Suckling's extant letters are in lively, colloquial prose that anticipates that of the Restoration wits.

ANNE BRADSTREET

(b. *c.* 1612, Northampton, Northamptonshire?, England—d. September 16, 1672, Andover, Massachusetts Bay Colony [U.S.])

A nne Bradstreet was one of the first poets to write English verse in the American colonies. Long considered primarily of historical interest, she won critical

ANNE BRADSTREET

acceptance in the 20th century as a writer of enduring verse, particularly for her sequence of religious poems, "Contemplations," written for her family and not published until the mid-19th century.

Anne Dudley was the daughter of Thomas Dudley, chief steward to Theophilus Clinton, the Puritan Earl of Lincoln. She married Simon Bradstreet, another protégé of the earl's, when she was 16, and two years later she, her husband, and her parents sailed with other Puritans to settle on Massachusetts Bay.

She wrote her poems while rearing eight children, functioning as a hostess, and performing other domestic duties. The Bradstreets moved frequently in the Massachusetts colony, first to Cambridge, then to Ipswich, and then to Andover, which became their permanent home. Bradstreet's brother-in-law, without her

A stained glass portrait of Anne Bradstreet is in St. Botolph's Church in Boston, Lincolnshire, England. Eileen Tweedy/The Art Archive at Art Resource, NY

knowledge, took her poems to England, where they were published as *The Tenth Muse Lately Sprung Up in America* (1650). The first American edition of *The Tenth Muse* was published in revised and expanded form as *Several Poems Compiled with Great Variety of Wit and Learning* (1678).

Most of the poems in the first edition are long and rather dully imitative works based on the standard poetic conventions of the time, but the last two poems— "Of the Vanity of All Worldly Creatures" and "David's Lamentation for Saul and Jonathan"—are individual and genuine in their recapitulation of her own feelings.

Her later poems, written for her family, show her spiritual growth as she came fully to accept the Puritan creed. She also wrote more personal poems of considerable beauty, treating in them such subjects as her thoughts before childbirth and her response to the death of a grandchild. These shorter poems benefit from their lack of imitation and didacticism. Her prose works include "Meditations," a collection of succinct and pithy aphorisms. A scholarly edition of her work was edited by John Harvard Ellis in 1867. In 1956 the poet John Berryman paid tribute to her in *Homage to Mistress Bradstreet,* a long poem that incorporates many phrases from her writings.

SAVINIEN CYRANO DE BERGERAC

(b. March 6, 1619, Paris—d. July 28, 1655, Paris)

Savinien Cyrano de Bergerac was a French satirist and dramatist whose works combining political satire and science-fantasy inspired a number of later writers. He has been the basis of many romantic but unhistorical legends, of which the best known is Edmond Rostand's play *Cyrano de Bergerac* (1897), in which he is portrayed as a gallant and brilliant but shy and ugly lover, possessed (as in fact he was) of a remarkably large nose.

As a young man, Cyrano joined the company of guards and was wounded at the Siege of Arras in 1640. But he gave up his military career in the following year to study under the philosopher and mathematician Pierre Gassendi. Under the influence of Gassendi's scientific theories and libertine philosophy, Cyrano wrote his two best known works, *Histoire comique des états et empires de la lune* and *Histoire comique des états et empires du soleil* (*A Voyage to the moon: with some account of the Solar World*, 1754). These stories of imaginary journeys to the Moon and Sun, published posthumously in 1656 and 1662, satirize 17th-century religious and astronomical beliefs, which saw man and the world as the centre of creation.

Cyrano's use of science helped to popularize new theories; but his principal aim was to ridicule authority, particularly in religion, and to encourage freethinking materialism. He "predicted" a number of later discoveries such as the phonograph and the atomic structure of matter; but they were merely offshoots from an inquiring and poetic mind, not attempts to demonstrate theories in practical terms.

Cyrano's plays include a tragedy, *La Mort d'Agrippine* (published 1654, "The Death of Agrippine"), which was suspected of blasphemy, and a comedy, *Le Pédant joué* (published 1654; "The Pedant Imitated"). As long as classicism was the established taste, *Le Pédant joué*, a colossal piece of fooling, was despised; but its liveliness appeals to modern readers as it did to Molière, who based two scenes of *Les Fourberies de Scapin* on it. *La Mort d'Agrippine* is intellectually impressive because of its daring ideas, and the

Savinien Cyrano de Bergerac.
Hulton Archive/Getty Images

direct and impassioned character of the tragic dialogue makes it interesting theatrically.

As a political writer, Cyrano was the author of a violent pamphlet against the men of the Fronde, in which he defended French cardinal and statesman Jules Mazarin in the name of political realism as exemplified in the tradition of Machiavelli. Cyrano's *Lettres* show him as a master of baroque prose, marked by bold and original metaphors. His contemporaries regarded them as absurdly farfetched, but they came to be esteemed in the 20th century as examples of the baroque style.

GLOSSARY

abbot In Benedictine monastic communities the abbot is an ordained priest elected by secret ballot to lead the community in both spiritual and secular concerns.

adder Any of several groups of venomous snakes in the viper family.

Aldgate One of the gates of London Wall. Apartments, including those occupied by Chaucer in the 14th century, were located above the gate.

alexandrine Twelve-syllable line of French verse.

aphorism Expression of some generally accepted truth in a memorable, short statement.

Berber Member of any of various pre-Arab peoples living in North Africa.

caliphate Political-religious Muslim state formed to head off a leadership crisis brought on by the death in 632 of Muhammad.

canto Derived from *cantus*, the Latin word for song, one of the major divisions of a long poem.

Carthusian Ascetic contemplative religious order founded by St. Bruno of Cologne in 1084.

chancery In public administration, an office of public records or a public archives—so called because from medieval times the chancellor, the principal advisor to the sovereign, was the caretaker of public deeds, contracts, and other documents relating to the crown and realm.

chapbook Small book containing ballads, poems, tales, or tracts that were popular between the 15th and 19th centuries.

colophon Inscription placed at the end of a book or manuscript usually with facts relative to its production.

conclave In the Roman Catholic Church, the assembly of cardinals gathered to elect a new pope and the system of strict seclusion to which they submit. No more than 120 cardinals may vote, all of whom must be under age 80.

concordance Alphabetical index of the principal words in a book or the works of an author with their immediate contexts.

corpus The complete works of an author.

courtier One in attendance at a royal court.

cuckold Man whose wife is unfaithful.

dauphin Title of the eldest son of a king of France from 1350 to 1830.

dialectic Discussion and reasoning by dialogue as a method of intellectual investigation.

didactic That designed or intended to teach.

eclogue Short pastoral poem, usually in which shepherds converse.

Eddic Of or relating to the Old Norse Edda, which is a 13th-century collection of mythological, heroic, and gnomic poems, many of which were composed at a much earlier date.

elegy Song or poem expressing sorrow or lamentation especially for one who is dead.

encomiast One who praises.

encomium Glowing and warmly enthusiastic praise.

epigram Concise poem dealing pointedly and often satirically with a single thought or event and often ending with an ingenious turn of thought.

epistle Composition in prose or poetry written in the form of a letter to a particular person or group.

epitaph Inscription in verse or prose upon a tomb; and, by extension, anything written as if to be inscribed on a tomb.

esquire Originally, a knight's shield bearer, who would probably himself in due course be dubbed a knight.

euphuism Elegant Elizabethan literary style marked by excessive use of balance, antithesis, and alliteration and by frequent use of similes drawn from mythology and nature.

extant Currently existing.

Extremadura Region of western Spain.

fabliau Short, usually comic, frankly coarse, and often cynical tale in verse popular especially in the 12th and 13th centuries.

fortnight Two-week period.

frontispiece Illustration preceding and usually facing the title page of a book or magazine.

grandee Spanish or Portuguese nobleman of the first rank.

hegemony Preponderant influence or authority.

hendecasyllabic Consisting of 11 syllables or composed of verses of 11 syllables.

hermetic Relating to or characterized by occultism, alchemy, magic, or whatever is obscure and mysterious.

hexameter Poetry written in lines of six feet, usually in dactyls. (A dactyl is a metrical foot consisting of one long and two short syllables or of one stressed and two unstressed syllables [as in *tenderly*]).

holy order In Christian churches, a rite for the dedication and commissioning of ministers. (Also known as ordination.)

humanism Philosophy that usually emphasizes the secular and rejects supernaturalism as it stresses an individual's dignity and worth and capacity for self-realization through reason.

in toto Latin for totally, entirely.

irrational number Any real number that cannot be expressed as the quotient of two integers. For example, there is no number among integers and fractions that equals the square root of two.

jurisprudence The science or philosophy of law.

lampoon Harsh satire usually directed against an individual.

League of Cambrai Alliance (1508) against Venice formed by Pope Julius II, Louis XII of France, Ferdinand II of Aragon (and united Spain), and the Holy Roman emperor Maximilian I.

Marprelate controversy Brief but well-known pamphlet war (1588–89) carried on by English Puritans using secret presses to attack the episcopacy. The tracts never had the support of Puritan leaders and ceased when the presses were discovered by government agents.

masque Short allegorical dramatic entertainment of the 16th and 17th centuries performed by masked actors.

minbar In Islam, the pulpit from which the sermon is delivered.

minnesinger One of a class of aristocratic German lyric poets and musicians of the 12th to the 14th centuries inspired by the French troubadors and characterized by having love and beauty as the subject of their songs.

Mishna The first part of the Talmud (the authoritative body of Jewish tradition), which states the oral laws.

mitre Headdress worn by Roman Catholic bishops and abbots and some Anglican and Lutheran bishops.

necromancy Conjuration of the spirits of the dead for purposes of magically revealing the future or influencing the course of events.

novice One admitted to probationary membership in a religious community.

obscurantism Opposition to the spread of knowledge.

oeuvre French word meaning a substantial body of work constituting the lifework of a writer, an artist, or a composer.

ottava rima Italian stanza form composed of eight 11-syllable lines, rhyming abababcc. It originated in the late 13th and early 14th centuries and was developed by Tuscan poets for religious verse and drama and in troubadour songs.

palatine High officer of an imperial palace.

panegyrist One who writes eulogies (a commendatory oration or writing especially in honor of one deceased).

paradigm Example, pattern.

pedagogy The art, science, or profession of teaching.

Peripatetic Follower of Aristotle or adherent of Aristotelianism.

picaresque Type of fiction dealing with the episodic adventures of a usually roguish hero.

Platonism Any philosophy that derives its ultimate inspiration from Plato, stressing especially that actual things are copies of transcendent ideas and that these ideas are the objects of true knowledge apprehended by reminiscence.

polemic An aggressive attack on or refutation of the opinions or principles of another.

prebendary Clergyman receiving a prebend (stipend) for serving in the church.

preferment Advancement or promotion in dignity, office, or station.

prelate Ecclesiastic (as a bishop or abbot) of superior rank.

Privy Council Body of officials and dignitaries chosen by the British monarch as an advisory council to the Crown usually functioning through its committees.

prosody The study of all the elements of language that contribute toward acoustic and rhythmic effects, chiefly in poetry but also in prose.

protagonist The principal character in a literary work (as a drama or story).

provost Chief dignitary of a collegiate or cathedral chapter.

quatrain Four-line verse.

rondeau One of several fixed forms that originated in French lyric poetry and song of the 14th and 15th centuries. It has only two rhymes (allowing no repetition of rhyme words) and consists of 13 or 15 lines of 8 or 10 syllables divided into three stanzas.

scrivener Professional or public copyist or writer.

see The jurisdiction (as a diocese or province) of a bishop.

seneschal Agent or steward in charge of a lord's estate in feudal times.

sexton Church custodian charged with keeping the church and parish buildings prepared for meetings, caring for church equipment, and performing related minor duties such as ringing the bell and digging graves.

simoniacal The practice of simony, that is, the buying or selling of a church office or ecclesiastical preferment.

sinecure Office or position that requires little or no work and that usually provides an income.

skald One of the ancient Scandinavian poets and historiographers; a Norse reciter and singer especially of heroic poems and eulogies.

sophistry Subtly deceptive reasoning or argumentation.

Talmudist Specialist in Talmudic studies, the Talmud being the authoritative body of Jewish tradition.

tercet Unit or group of three lines of verse, usually containing rhyme.

topology Branch of mathematics, sometimes referred to as "rubber sheet geometry," in which two objects are considered equivalent if they can be continuously deformed into one another through such motions in space as bending, twisting, stretching, and shrinking while disallowing tearing apart or gluing together parts.

treatise Formal work on a subject that includes facts, principles, and conclusions reached.

vassal Person under the protection of a feudal lord to whom he has vowed loyalty.

virelai Old French verse form consisting of three stanzas, each preceded and followed by a refrain.

vizier High executive officer of various Muslim countries and especially of the Ottoman Empire.

Zealander Native or inhabitant of Zealand in Denmark.

BIBLIOGRAPHY

Notable studies of some of the medieval authors covered in this volume include Israel Davidson and Israel Zangwill, *Selected Religious Poems of Solomon ibn Gabirol* (1923); M.T. Clanchy, *Abelard: A Medieval Life* (1997); Franklin D. Lewis, *Rumi: Past and Present, East and West: The Life, Teaching, and Poetry of Jalâl al-Din Rumi*, rev. ed. (2008), which is a wide-ranging survey of Rūmī's life and influence; Cecil Grayson (ed.), *The World of Dante: Essays on Dante and His Times* (1980); Patrick Boyde, *Dante, Philomythes and Philosopher: Man in the Cosmos* (1981); William Anderson, *Dante the Maker* (1980), which is a critical biographical study with the emphasis on Dante's creative processes; E.H. Wilkins, *The Making of the Canzoniere and Other Petrarchan Studies* (1951); Gordon Rutledge Silber, *The Influence of Dante and Petrarch on Certain of Boccaccio's Lyrics* (1940); James R. Hulbert, *Chaucer's Official Life* (1912, reprinted 1970); and D.B. Wyndham Lewis, *François Villon: A Documented Survey* (1928), with preface by Hilaire Belloc, which is an imaginative reconstruction of Villon's life and times.

Select Renaissance authors of this volume are examined in Roberto Ridolfi, *The Life of Niccolò Machiavelli*, trans. from Italian (1963); James D. Tracy, *Erasmus, the Growth of a Mind* (1972); Lewis Hanke, *Bartolomé de Las Casas: An Interpretation of His Life and Writings* (1951); Donald M. Frame, *François Rabelais: A Study* (1977); Mikhail Bakhtin, *Rabelais and His World* (1968, reissued 1984), which makes a connection between Rabelais's imagery and folk humour; Henry Hersch Hart, *Luis de Camoëns and the Epic of the Lusiads* (1962); Donald M. Frame, *Montaigne* (1965, reprinted 1984), which is a detailed biography by an authority in the field; C.P. Brand, *Torquato Tasso: A Study of the Poet and of His Contribution to English Literature* (1965); Alban K. Forcione, *Cervantes, Aristotle, and the Persiles* (1970), which is a major work on Cervantes and Renaissance literary theory; José Ortega y Gasset, *Meditations on Quixote* (1961, reissued 2000; trans. from Spanish by Evelyn Rugg and Diego Martin), which is an insightful and influential interpretation of Cervantes' iconic novel; Frederick S. Boas, *Christopher Marlowe: A Biographical and Critical Study* (1940, reprinted 1966); Park Honan, *Shakespeare: A Life* (1998); J. Frank Kermode (*Frank Kermode*), *Four Centuries of Shakespearian Criticism* (1965); R.C. Bald, *John Donne: A Life*, ed. by W. Milgate (1970, reprinted with corrections 1986); Ian Donaldson, *Ben Jonson: A Life* (2011); Anthony J. Cascardi, *The Limits of Illusion: A Critical Study of Calderón* (1984); Anna Beer, *Milton: Poet, Pamphleteer, and Patriot* (2008), a biography celebrating the 400th anniversary of Milton's birth; and Stanley Fish, *Surprised by Sin: The Reader in Paradise Lost*, 2nd ed. (1997), which practices reader-response criticism by advocating that the language and style of Milton's epic implicate the reader in a series of judgments and choices that are framed as ongoing exercises in learning.

INDEX